THE LANGUAGE OF LITERATURE

# THE *InterActive* READER™

**McDougal Littell**

A HOUGHTON MIFFLIN COMPANY

Evanston, Illinois • Boston • Dallas

## Reading Consultant, *The InterActive Reader*™

**Sharon Sicinski-Skeans, Ph.D.** Assistant Professor of Reading, University of Houston-Clear Lake; former K-12 Language Arts Program Director, Spring Independent School District, Houston, Texas
The reading consultant guided the conceptual development of the *InterActive Reader*™. She participated in the development of prototype materials, the planning and writing of lessons, and the review of completed materials.

## Senior Consultants, *The Language of Literature*

**Arthur N. Applebee** Professor of Education, State University of New York at Albany; Director, National Research Center on English Learning and Achievements; Senior Fellow, Center for Writing and Literacy

**Andrea B. Bermúdez** Professor of Studies in Language and Culture; Director, Research Center for Language and Culture; Chair, Foundations and Professional Studies, University of Houston-Clear Lake

**Sheridan Blau** Senior Lecturer in English and Education and former Director of Composition, University of California at Santa Barbara; Director, South Coast Writing Project; Director, Literature Institute for Teachers; Past President, National Council of Teachers of English

**Rebekah Caplan** Coordinator, English Language Arts K-12, Oakland Unified School District, Oakland, California; Teacher-Consultant, Bay Area Writing Project, University of California at Berkeley; served on the California State English Assessment Development Team for Language Arts

**Peter Elbow** Professor of English, University of Massachusetts at Amherst; Fellow, Bard Center for Writing and Thinking

**Susan Hynds** Professor and Director of English Education, Syracuse University, Syracuse, New York

**Judith A. Langer** Professor of Education, State University of New York at Albany; Director, National Research Center on English Learning and Achievements; Director, Albany Institute for Research on Education

**James Marshall** Professor of English and English Education, University of Iowa, Iowa City

## Acknowledgments

**Susan Bergholz Literary Services:** Excerpt from "A Celebration of Grandfathers" by Rudolfo Anaya. First published in New Mexico Magazine, March 1983. Copyright © 1983 by Rudolfo Anaya. Reprinted by permission of Susan Bergholz Literary Services, New York. All rights reserved.
**Brandt & Brandt:** "By the Waters of Babylon" by Stephen Vincent Benét, from Selected Works of Stephen Vincent Benét, published by Holt, Rinehart & Winston, Inc. Copyright © 1937 by Stephen Vincent Benét. Copyright renewed © 1955 by Rosemary Carr Benét. Reprinted by permission of Brandt & Brandt Literary Agents, Inc.

*(Continued on page 334)*

ISBN 0-618-00789-X

# Contents

# Introducing *The InterActive Reader*™

*The InterActive Reader*™ is a new kind of literature book. As you will see, this book encourages your involvement at every stage of your reading. It's a book to mark on, write on, and make your own.

## An Easy-to-Carry Literature Text

This book won't weigh you down—it can fit comfortably in your backpack. Yet it contains many of the best-known authors and most popular selections in high school classes, such as the following:

- Kurt Vonnegut's student favorite, the short story "Harrison Bergeron"
- Edgar Allan Poe's chilling horror story, "The Pit and the Pendulum
- Maya Angelou's inspiring nonfiction narrative "Getting a Job"
- Robert Frost's classic poem "Birches"

All major types of literature are represented—fiction, nonfiction, poetry, and drama. *The InterActive Reader*™ is your "take home" book, so that you can study these classic works on your own. The book is also ideal for in-class work.

## Help for Reading

Many works of literature are challenging, especially when you're reading them for the first time. *The InterActive Reader*™ gives you the help you need to make sense of these works. Here's just a sampling of what you'll find:

**Reading Tips**  Simple and effective reading strategies are provided for each selection.

**Preview**  A preview is given at the beginning of each selection so that you'll know what to expect.

**Focus**  Each work is divided into sections, with a focus at the beginning of each section. It tells you what to look for as you read.

**Pause and Reflect**  At the end of each section, you'll find questions that will help you check your understanding.

**Read Aloud**  Special passages are marked for oral interpretation. Reading aloud will increase your understanding—and enjoyment.

## A Book to Write In

Finally! Here's a book that you're supposed to write in! You can mark up this book in a number of different ways. By reading with a pen or a pencil in hand, you'll become a more active reader and a better reader. Look for the  **MARK IT UP** symbol in the following places:

**Keep Track**   This feature suggests an easy marking system—a check, question mark, and exclamation mark—to track your understanding. This system is illustrated on pages vi and x.

**Focus**   Here, you will often be asked to underline or circle passages as you read—or to take notes in the margins.

**Pause and Reflect**   At these stopping points, you will often be asked to go back into the text to mark up key passages.

**Challenge**   This feature occurs at the end of each selection. Often, you will be asked to mark up the text as a way of supporting your judgment.

Also, the **Notes** column in the side margin gives you space to write down reactions, make connections, and explore your thoughts.

## Vocabulary Support

**Words to Know**   In most selections, you'll find Words to Know. These words are underlined in the text and defined at the bottom of the page. To practice your knowledge of these words, use the Words to Know SkillBuilder page at the end of the selection.

**Personal Word List**   You'll also have frequent chances to build your own personal vocabulary. You can mark new words as you come across them in the selections, then add them to your Personal Word List, which begins on page 316.

## SkillBuilder Pages

After each selection, you'll usually find these SkillBuilder pages:

**Active Reading SkillBuilder**
**Literary Analysis SkillBuilder**
**Words to Know SkillBuilder (for most selections)**

These pages will help you practice and apply important skills.

## Links to *The Language of Literature*

If you are using McDougal Littell's *The Language of Literature,* you will find *The InterActive Reader*™ to be a perfect companion. The selections in the *Reader* can all be found in that book, which gives you additional background information and a wide range of follow-up activities. *The InterActive Reader*™ gives you an opportunity to read certain core selections from *The Language of Literature* in greater depth.

## *Read on to learn more!*

# User's Guide

*The InterActive Reader™ has an easy-to-follow organization, illustrated by these sample pages from "Harrison Bergeron."*

## Before You Read

**1** If you are using *The Language of Literature*, this section will help you use features from that book.

## Reading Tips

**2** These practical strategies will help you gain more from your reading.

### PREVIEW

**3** This feature tells you what the selection is about, so that you'll know what to expect.

### FOCUS

**4** Every literary work is broken into sections. Each section is introduced by a Focus that tells you what to look for as you read.

### MARK IT UP

**5** This feature often appears in the Focus. It may ask you to underline or circle key passages in the text or to take notes in the margin as you read.

### MARK IT UP  KEEP TRACK

**6** This easy-to-use marking system will help you track your understanding. Turn to page x to see how a model of the system can be used.

---

**SHORT STORY**

**1** **Before You Read**
If you are using **The Language of Literature**...
- Use the information on page 20 of that book to prepare for reading.
- Look at the art on pages 23 and 25. These images can help you picture the story characters.

**2** **Reading Tips**
As you read "Harrison Bergeron," try to imagine living in the world the writer creates.
- Look for **details** that describe each character's handicap and appearance. Try to picture the **characters** in your mind.
- Pay particular attention to the conversations between George and Hazel Bergeron. Their words provide clues to the author's message, or **theme**.

**6** MARK IT UP  KEEP TRACK
As you read, you can use these marks to keep track of your understanding.
✔ ..... I understand.
? ..... I don't understand this.
! ..... Interesting or surprising idea

Kurt Vonnegut, Jr.

**3** PREVIEW "Harrison Bergeron" is set in the year 2081. George and Hazel Bergeron are living in a society in which everyone is equal—by government order. But equality comes at a price. Many people are "handicapped" to bring them down to "average" levels. The Bergeron's genius son, Harrison, challenges the system in a daring move that society will never forget—or will it?

**4** FOCUS
Read to find out how society in the year 2081 differs from society today.

**5** MARK IT UP  As you read, circle details that describe the society and the handicaps of George Bergeron. Examples are highlighted.

**The year was 2081,** and everybody was finally equal. They weren't only equal before God and the law. They were equal every which way. Nobody was smarter than anybody else. Nobody was better looking than anybody else. Nobody was stronger or quicker than anybody else. All this equality was due to the 211th, 212th, and 213th Amendments to the Constitution, and to the unceasing <u>vigilance</u> of agents of the United States Handicapper General.

Some things about living still weren't quite right, though. April, for instance, still drove people crazy by not being springtime. And it was in that clammy month that the H-G men took George and Hazel Bergeron's fourteen-year-old son, Harrison, away.

It was tragic, all right, but George and Hazel couldn't think about it very hard. Hazel had a perfectly average

**7** WORDS TO KNOW
**vigilance** (vĭjʹə-ləns) *n.* alert attention; watchfulness

---

**7** WORDS TO KNOW
Important **Words to Know** are underlined in each selection. Definitions are given at the bottom of the page.

intelligence, which meant she couldn't think about anything except in short bursts. And George, while his intelligence was way above normal, had a little mental handicap radio in his ear. He was required by law to wear it at all times. It was tuned to a government transmitter.[1] Every twenty seconds or so, the transmitter would send out some sharp noise to keep people like George from taking unfair advantage of their brains.

George and Hazel were watching television. There were tears on Hazel's cheeks, but she'd forgotten for the moment what they were about.

On the television screen were ballerinas.

A buzzer sounded in George's head. His thoughts fled in panic, like bandits from a burglar alarm.

"That was a real pretty dance, that dance they just did," said Hazel.

"Huh?" said George.

"That dance—it was nice," said Hazel.

"Yup," said George. He tried to think a little about the ballerinas. They weren't really very good—no better than anybody else would have been, anyway. They were burdened with sashweights[2] and bags of birdshot,[3] and their faces were masked, so that no one, seeing a free and graceful gesture or a pretty face, would feel like something the cat drug in. George was toying with the vague notion that maybe dancers shouldn't be handicapped. But he didn't get very far with it before another noise in his ear radio scattered his thoughts.

George winced. So did two out of the eight ballerinas.

Hazel saw him wince. Having no mental handicap herself, she had to ask George what the latest sound had been.

"Sounded like somebody hitting a milk bottle with a ball peen hammer,[4]" said George.

---

1. **transmitter:** an electronic device for broadcasting radio signals.
2. **sashweights:** lead weights used in the construction of some kinds of windows.
3. **birdshot:** tiny lead pellets made to be loaded in shotgun shells.
4. **ball peen hammer:** a hammer with a head having one flat side and one rounded side.

| WORDS TO KNOW | **vague** (vāg) *adj.* unclear; hazy<br>**wince** (wĭns) *v.* to shrink or flinch involuntarily, especially in pain |
|---|---|

**NOTES**

READ ALOUD Lines 39–44

**8** As you read aloud this boxed description of the ballerinas, try to picture what their dance actually looks like on television.

Harrison Bergeron **3**

---

**READ ALOUD**

**8** From time to time, you'll be asked to read a passage aloud. That's a great way to increase your understanding —and enjoyment.

**9** The footnotes explain unfamiliar words and help you pronounce difficult names or terms.

*And there's more*

## NOTES

**10** Most pages include write-on lines so that you can take your own notes. Here's where you can write down your reactions, make connections, and explore your own thoughts.

---

**MARK IT UP** WORD POWER

**11** This feature will remind you to mark words that you'd like to add to your **Personal Word List**. After reading, you can look up the definitions and record information about each word. The Personal Word List begins on page 316.

---

**10** N·O·T·E·S

Harrison's scrap-iron handicaps crashed to the floor.

Harrison thrust his thumbs under the bar of the padlock that secured his head harness. The bar snapped like celery. Harrison smashed his headphones and spectacles against the wall.

He flung away his rubber-ball nose, revealed a man that would have awed Thor, the god of thunder.

"I shall now select my Empress!" he said, looking down on the cowering people. "Let the first woman who dares rise to her feet claim her mate and her throne!"

A moment passed, and then a ballerina arose, swaying like a willow.

Harrison plucked the mental handicap from her ear, snapped off her physical handicaps with marvelous delicacy. Last of all, he removed her mask.

She was blindingly beautiful.

"Now—" said Harrison, taking her hand, "shall we show the people the meaning of the word dance? Music!" he commanded.

The musicians scrambled back into their chairs, and Harrison stripped them of their handicaps, too. "Play your best," he told them, "and I'll make you barons and dukes and earls."

The music began. It was normal at first—cheap, silly, false. But Harrison snatched two musicians from their chairs, waved them like batons as he sang the music as he wanted it played. He slammed them back into their chairs.

The music began again and was much improved.

Harrison and his Empress merely listened to the music for a while—listened gravely, as though <u>synchronizing</u> their heartbeats with it.

They shifted their weights to their toes.

Harrison placed his big hands on the girl's tiny waist, letting her sense the weightlessness that would soon be hers.

And then, in an explosion of joy and grace, into the air they sprang!

Not only were the laws of the land abandoned, but the law of gravity and the laws of motion as well.

---

**MARK IT UP** WORD POWER

**11** Remember to mark words that you'd like to add to your **Personal Word List**. Later, you can record the words and their meanings beginning on page 316.

---

| WORDS TO KNOW | **synchronizing** (sĭng′krə-nī′zĭng) *adj.* matching the timing of **synchronize** *v.* |

**8** The InterActive Reader

They reeled, whirled, swiveled, flounced, capered, gamboled,[7] and spun.

They leaped like deer on the moon.

The studio ceiling was thirty feet high, but each leap brought the dancers nearer to it.

It became their obvious intention to kiss the ceiling.

They kissed it.

240 And then, neutralizing gravity with love and pure will, they remained suspended in air inches below the ceiling, and they kissed each other for a long, long time.

It was then that Diana Moon Glampers, the Handicapper General, came into the studio with a double-barreled ten-gauge shotgun. She fired twice, and the Emperor and the Empress were dead before they hit the floor.

Diana Moon Glampers loaded the gun again. She aimed it at the musicians and told them they had ten seconds to get their handicaps back on.

250 It was then that the Bergerons' television tube burned out.

Hazel turned to comment about the blackout to George. But George had gone out into the kitchen for a can of beer.

George came back in with the beer, paused while a handicap signal shook him up. And then he sat down again. "You been crying?" he said to Hazel.

"Yup," she said.

"What about?" he said.

"I forget," she said. "Something real sad on television."

"What was it?" he said.

260 "It's all kind of mixed up in my mind," said Hazel.

"Forget sad things," said George.

"I always do," said Hazel.

"That's my girl," said George. He winced. There was the sound of a riveting[8] gun in his head.

"Gee—I could tell that one was a doozy," said Hazel.

"You can say that again," said George.

"Gee—" said Hazel, "I could tell that one was a doozy."

**12 Pause & Reflect**

---

7. **flounced, capered, gamboled** (găm′bəld): bounced, leaped, frolicked.
8. **riveting** (rĭv′ĭ-tĭng) **gun:** a power tool used to hammer the bolts (called rivets) used in construction work to fasten metal beams or plates together.

**13 Pause & Reflect**

1. What is your response to the story's ending? **(Connect)**

_____

_____

_____

_____

**MARK IT UP** 2. Circle the sentence on this page that tells how Diana Moon Glampers stops Harrison. Why does she do this? **(Cause and Effect)**

_____

_____

_____

_____

3. How does Harrison's death affect his parents? **(Infer)**

_____

_____

_____

_____

**14 CHALLENGE**

Review the passages that describe Harrison and his powers. Circle those sentences that strike you as the most exaggerated or unrealistic. What do you think Vonnegut is trying to achieve by making use of such exaggerated description? **(Evaluate)**

**15 Wrapping Up**

If you are using *The Language of Literature,* you can now move ahead to the questions and activities on pages 27–29 of that book.

**Harrison Bergeron 9**

---

**Pause & Reflect**

12 Whenever you see these words in a selection, stop reading. Go to the side column and answer the questions. Then move ahead to the next Focus and continue your reading.

13 These questions appear at the end of every section. They provide a follow-up to the Focus activity that begins each section, and they give you a quick way to check your understanding. As you can see, some questions have a **Read Aloud** or a **Mark It Up**. The Mark It Up will direct you to go back into the selection to find and mark important details.

**CHALLENGE**

14 This question or activity occurs at the end of the selection. It challenges you to think about issues, ideas, or literary techniques that are important to the selection. Usually, you will be asked to go back into the text to mark key details or passages.

**Wrapping Up**

15 This appears at the end of each selection. If you are using *The Language of Literature,* this will direct you to the appropriate follow-up activities in that book.

# Student Model

NOTES

?

**MARK IT UP** WORD POWER

Mark words that you'd like to add to your **Personal Word List.** After reading, you can record the words and their meanings beginning on page 316.

Note how this student used the following symbols:

✓ marks a place where something is made clear or understandable

? marks where something is not understood or is confusing

! marks a surprising or interesting place in the text

Also notice how one word is circled, *impediment.* This word was marked by the student for her Personal Word List.

!

"I'd think it would be real interesting, hearing all the different sounds," said Hazel, a little envious. "All the things they think up."

"Um," said George.

"Only, if I was Handicapper General, you know what I would do?" said Hazel. Hazel, as a matter of fact, bore a strong resemblance to the Handicapper General, a woman named Diana Moon Glampers. "If I was Diana Moon Glampers," said Hazel, "I'd have chimes on Sunday—just chimes. Kind of in honor of religion."

"I could think, if it was just chimes," said George.

"Well—maybe make 'em real loud," said Hazel. "I think I'd make a good Handicapper General."

"Good as anybody else," said George.

"Who knows better'n I do what normal is?" said Hazel.

"Right," said George. He began to think glimmeringly about his abnormal son who was now in jail, about Harrison, but a twenty-one-gun salute in his head stopped that.

"Boy!" said Hazel, "that was a doozy, wasn't it?"

It was such a doozy that George was white and trembling, and tears stood on the rims of his red eyes. Two of the eight ballerinas had collapsed to the studio floor and were holding their temples.

"All of a sudden you look so tired," said Hazel. "Why don't you stretch out on the sofa, so's you can rest your handicap bag on the pillows, honeybunch." She was referring to the forty-seven pounds of birdshot in a canvas bag, which was padlocked around George's neck. "Go on and rest the bag for a little while," she said. "I don't care if you're not equal to me for a while."

George weighed the bag with his hands. "I don't mind it," he said. "I don't notice it any more. It's just a part of me."

"You been so tired lately—kind of wore out," said Hazel. "If there was just some way we could make a little hole in the bottom of the bag, and just take out a few of them lead balls. Just a few."

"Two years in prison and two thousand dollars fine for every ball I took out," said George. "I don't call that a bargain."

"If you could just take a few out when you came home from work," said Hazel. "I mean—you don't compete with anybody around here. You just set around."

"If I tried to get away with it," said George, "then other people'd get away with it—and pretty soon we'd be right back to the dark ages again, with everybody competing against everybody else. You wouldn't like that, would you?"

"I'd hate it," said Hazel.

"There you are," said George. "The minute people start cheating on laws, what do you think happens to society?"

If Hazel hadn't been able to come up with an answer to this question, George couldn't have supplied one. A siren was going off in his head.

"Reckon it'd fall all apart," said Hazel.

"What would?" said George blankly.

"Society," said Hazel uncertainly. "Wasn't that what you just said?"

"Who knows?" said George.

Pause & Reflect

FOCUS

The dance performance is interrupted by a news bulletin. Harrison Bergeron has made a daring escape from jail.

MARK IT UP As you read, underline details that help you to picture Harrison and his acts of rebellion.

**The television program** was suddenly interrupted for a news bulletin. It wasn't clear at first as to what the bulletin was about, since the announcer, like all announcers, had a serious speech impediment.[5] For about half a minute, and in a state of high excitement, the announcer tried to say, "Ladies and gentlemen—"

He finally gave up, handed the bulletin to a ballerina to read.

"That's all right—" Hazel said of the announcer, "he tried. That's the big thing. He tried to do the best he could with what God gave him. He should get a nice raise for trying so hard."

5. **speech impediment** (ĭm-pĕd′ə-mənt): a physical defect that prevents a person from speaking normally.

---

Pause & Reflect

1. Look at the details you circled as you read. How has society changed by 2081? (Compare and Contrast)

   _Everyone is expected to be like everyone else. Nobody can share their true feelings._

2. Why don't George and Hazel think much about their son, Harrison, even though he has been taken away? (Infer)

   _George's handicap makes it hard for him to think. Hazel's mind seems to forget._

3. Look at the boxed passage on this page. **Summarize** George's beliefs about equality and competition.

   _George thinks that everyone should be exactly like everyone else and that competition is bad._

These pages were completed by Elizabeth Albertson, a student from Skokie, Illinois.

## Before You Read

If you are using **The Language of Literature**...

- Use the information on page 20 of that book to prepare for reading.

- Look at the art on pages 23 and 25. These images can help you picture the story characters.

## Reading Tips

As you read "Harrison Bergeron," try to imagine living in the world the writer creates.

- Look for **details** that describe each character's handicap and appearance. Try to picture the **characters** in your mind.

- Pay particular attention to the conversations between George and Hazel Bergeron. Their words provide clues to the author's message, or **theme**.

---

✏️ **MARK IT UP** **KEEP TRACK**

As you read, you can use these marks to keep track of your understanding.

✔ ..... I understand.

? ..... I don't understand this.

! ..... Interesting or surprising idea

---

# Harrison Bergeron

## Kurt Vonnegut, Jr.

**PREVIEW** "Harrison Bergeron" is set in the year 2081. George and Hazel Bergeron are living in a society in which everyone is equal—by government order. But equality comes at a price. Many people are "handicapped" to bring them down to "average" levels. The Bergeron's genius son, Harrison, challenges the system in a daring move that society will never forget—or will it?

---

**FOCUS**

Read to find out how society in the year 2081 differs from society today.

✏️ **MARK IT UP** As you read, circle details that describe the society and the handicaps of George Bergeron. Examples are highlighted.

🔟

**The year was 2081,** and everybody was finally equal. They weren't only equal before God and the law. They were equal every which way. Nobody was smarter than anybody else. Nobody was better looking than anybody else. Nobody was stronger or quicker than anybody else. All this equality was due to the 211th, 212th, and 213th Amendments to the Constitution, and to the unceasing <u>vigilance</u> of agents of the United States Handicapper General.

Some things about living still weren't quite right, though. April, for instance, still drove people crazy by not being springtime. And it was in that clammy month that the H-G men took George and Hazel Bergeron's fourteen-year-old son, Harrison, away.

It was tragic, all right, but George and Hazel couldn't think about it very hard. Hazel had a perfectly average

---

WORDS
TO
KNOW

**vigilance** (vĭj′ə-ləns) *n.* alert attention; watchfulness

intelligence, which meant she couldn't think about anything except in short bursts. And George, while his intelligence was way above normal, had a little mental handicap radio in his ear. He was required by law to wear it at all times. It was tuned to a government transmitter.[1] Every twenty seconds or so, the transmitter would send out some sharp noise to keep people like George from taking unfair advantage of their brains.

George and Hazel were watching television. There were tears on Hazel's cheeks, but she'd forgotten for the moment what they were about.

On the television screen were ballerinas.

A buzzer sounded in George's head. His thoughts fled in panic, like bandits from a burglar alarm.

"That was a real pretty dance, that dance they just did," said Hazel.

"Huh?" said George.

"That dance—it was nice," said Hazel.

"Yup," said George. He tried to think a little about the ballerinas. They weren't really very good—no better than anybody else would have been, anyway. They were burdened with sashweights[2] and bags of birdshot,[3] and their faces were masked, so that no one, seeing a free and graceful gesture or a pretty face, would feel like something the cat drug in. George was toying with the <u>vague</u> notion that maybe dancers shouldn't be handicapped. But he didn't get very far with it before another noise in his ear radio scattered his thoughts.

George <u>winced.</u> So did two out of the eight ballerinas.

Hazel saw him wince. Having no mental handicap herself, she had to ask George what the latest sound had been.

"Sounded like somebody hitting a milk bottle with a ball peen hammer,[4]" said George.

---

1. **transmitter:** an electronic device for broadcasting radio signals.
2. **sashweights:** <u>lead</u> weights used in the construction of some kinds of windows.
3. **birdshot:** tiny lead pellets made to be loaded in shotgun shells.
4. **ball peen hammer:** a hammer with a head having one flat side and one rounded side.

READ ALOUD **Lines 39–44**

As you read aloud this boxed description of the ballerinas, try to picture what their dance actually looks like on television.

WORDS TO KNOW

**vague** (vāg) *adj.* unclear; hazy

**wince** (wĭns) *v.* to shrink or flinch involuntarily, especially in pain

**Harrison Bergeron** 3

---

*[Handwritten notes in margin:]*

In the year 2081, everybody was equal before God and the law. Nobody was smarter than anybody else. Nobody was better looking than anyone else. And nobody was stronger or quicker than anyone else.

not a very intresting dance. People who all looked alike and danced alike.

Every one controlled
by the government
to be the same, such
as ; looks, intelligence,
same strength

Glimmeringly

"I'd think it would be real interesting, hearing all the different sounds," said Hazel, a little envious. "All the things they think up."

"Um," said George.

"Only, if I was Handicapper General, you know what I would do?" said Hazel. Hazel, as a matter of fact, bore a strong resemblance to the Handicapper General, a woman
60 named Diana Moon Glampers. "If I was Diana Moon Glampers," said Hazel, "I'd have chimes on Sunday—just chimes. Kind of in honor of religion."

"I could think, if it was just chimes," said George.

"Well—maybe make 'em real loud," said Hazel. "I think I'd make a good Handicapper General."

"Good as anybody else," said George.

"Who knows better'n I do what normal is?" said Hazel.

"Right," said George. He began to think glimmeringly about his abnormal son who was now in jail, about
70 Harrison, but a twenty-one-gun salute in his head stopped that.

"Boy!" said Hazel, "that was a doozy, wasn't it?"

It was such a doozy that George was white and trembling, and tears stood on the rims of his red eyes. Two of the eight ballerinas had collapsed to the studio floor and were holding their temples.

"All of a sudden you look so tired," said Hazel. "Why don't you stretch out on the sofa, so's you can rest your handicap bag on the pillows, honeybunch." She was referring
80 to the forty-seven pounds of birdshot in a canvas bag, which was padlocked around George's neck. "Go on and rest the bag for a little while," she said. "I don't care if you're not equal to me for a while."

George weighed the bag with his hands. "I don't mind it," he said. "I don't notice it any more. It's just a part of me."

"You been so tired lately—kind of wore out," said Hazel. "If there was just some way we could make a little hole in the bottom of the bag, and just take out a few of them lead balls. Just a few."
90 "Two years in prison and two thousand dollars fine for every ball I took out," said George. "I don't call that a bargain."

"If you could just take a few out when you came home from work," said Hazel. "I mean—you don't compete with anybody around here. You just set around."

"If I tried to get away with it," said George, "then other people'd get away with it—and pretty soon we'd be right back to the dark ages again, with everybody competing against everybody else. You wouldn't like that, would you?"

100 "I'd hate it," said Hazel.

"There you are," said George. "The minute people start cheating on laws, what do you think happens to society?"

If Hazel hadn't been able to come up with an answer to this question, George couldn't have supplied one. A siren was going off in his head.

"Reckon it'd fall all apart," said Hazel.

"What would?" said George blankly.

"Society," said Hazel uncertainly. "Wasn't that what you just said?"

110 "Who knows?" said George.

**Pause & Reflect**

FOCUS

The dance performance is interrupted by a news bulletin. Harrison Bergeron has made a daring escape from jail.

MARK IT UP As you read, underline details that help you to picture Harrison and his acts of rebellion.

**The television program** was suddenly interrupted for a news bulletin. It wasn't clear at first as to what the bulletin was about, since the announcer, like all announcers, had a serious speech impediment.[5] For about half a minute, and in a state of high excitement, the announcer tried to say, "Ladies and gentlemen—"

120 He finally gave up, handed the bulletin to a ballerina to read.

"That's all right—" Hazel said of the announcer, "he tried. That's the big thing. He tried to do the best he could with what God gave him. He should get a nice raise for trying so hard."

---

5. **speech impediment** (ĭm-pĕd′ə-mənt): a physical defect that prevents a person from speaking normally.

1. Look at the details you circled as you read. How has society changed by 2081? **(Compare and Contrast)**

   _The society has changed because their are people smarter than others, better looking than others. We are still all equal._

2. Why don't George and Hazel think much about their son, Harrison, even though he has been taken away? **(Infer)**

   _Hazel couldn't think about anything except in short bursts. And George had a little mental handicap radio in his ear. It was turned to a government transmitter._

3. Look at the boxed passage on this page. **Summarize** George's beliefs about equality and competition.

   _He thinks everyone shouldn't compete against anyone. No one is better than anyone._

Announcer could
not say "Ladies
and gentelmen"
do to a speech
immpediment

"Ladies and gentlemen—" said the ballerina, reading the bulletin. She must have been extraordinarily beautiful, because the mask she wore was hideous. And it was easy to see that she was the strongest and most graceful of all the dancers, for her handicap bags were as big as those worn by two-hundred-pound men.

And she had to apologize at once for her voice, which was a very unfair voice for a woman to use. Her voice was a warm, <u>luminous</u>, timeless melody. "Excuse me—" she said, and she began again, making her voice absolutely uncompetitive.

"Harrison Bergeron, age fourteen," she said in a grackle[6] squawk, "has just escaped from jail, where he was held on suspicion of plotting to overthrow the government. He is a genius and an athlete, is under-handicapped, and should be regarded as extremely dangerous."

A police photograph of Harrison Bergeron was flashed on the screen—upside down, then sideways, upside down again, then right side up. The picture showed the full length of Harrison against a background <u>calibrated</u> in feet and inches. He was exactly seven feet tall.

The rest of Harrison's appearance was Halloween and hardware. Nobody had ever borne heavier handicaps. He had outgrown <u>hindrances</u> faster than the H-G men could think them up. Instead of a little ear radio for a mental handicap, he wore a tremendous pair of earphones, and spectacles with thick wavy lenses. The spectacles were intended to make him not only half blind, but to give him whanging headaches besides.

Scrap metal was hung all over him. Ordinarily, there was a certain <u>symmetry</u>, a military neatness to the handicaps issued to strong people, but Harrison looked like a walking junkyard. In the race of life, Harrison carried three hundred pounds.

And to offset his good looks, the H-G men required that he wear at all times a red rubber ball for a nose,

---

6. **grackle:** a blackbird with a harsh, unpleasant call.

WORDS
TO
KNOW

**luminous** (lōō'mə-nəs) *adj.* bright; brilliant
**calibrated** (kăl'ə-brā'tĭd) *adj.* marked with different measurements **calibrate** *v.*
**hindrance** (hĭn'drəns) *n.* something that interferes with an activity; obstacle
**symmetry** (sĭm'ĭ-trē) *n.* a similarity between the two sides of something; balance

keep his eyebrows shaved off, and cover his even white teeth with black caps at snaggle-tooth random.

"If you see this boy," said the ballerina, "do not—I repeat, do not—try to reason with him."

There was the shriek of a door being torn from its hinges. Screams and barking cries of <u>consternation</u> came from the television set. The photograph of Harrison Bergeron on the screen jumped again and again, as though dancing to the tune

170 of an earthquake.

George Bergeron correctly identified the earthquake, and well he might have—for many was the time his own home had danced to the same crashing tune. . . . "That must be Harrison!" said George.

The realization was blasted from his mind instantly by the sound of an automobile collision in his head.

**Pause & Reflect**

**FOCUS**
Read to find out what Harrison plans to do and whether his plan succeeds.

180 **When George could open** his eyes again, the photograph of Harrison was gone. A living, breathing Harrison filled the screen.

Clanking, clownish, and huge, Harrison stood in the center of the studio. The knob of the uprooted studio door was still in his hand. Ballerinas, technicians, musicians, and announcers <u>cowered</u> on their knees before him, expecting to die.

"I am the Emperor!" cried Harrison. "Do you hear? I am the Emperor! Everybody must do what I say at once!" He stamped his foot and the studio shook.

"Even as I stand here—" he bellowed, "crippled, hobbled,
190 sickened—I am a greater ruler than any man who ever lived! Now watch me become what I *can* become!"

Harrison tore the straps of his handicap harness like wet tissue paper, tore straps guaranteed to support five thousand pounds.

WORDS
TO
KNOW

**consternation** (kŏn′stər-nā′shən) *n.* a confused amazement or fear
**cower** (kou′ər) *v.* to draw back in fear; cringe

**Pause & Reflect**

1. Review the details you underlined as you read. Describe Harrison and his acts of rebellion. **(Visualize/Clarify)**

   _Escaping from jail is act of rebellion that Harrison did._

2. Harrison has now entered the television studio. What do you predict will happen now? **(Predict)**

   _I think Harrison will reck everything in sight. He is very mad._

📖 **READ ALOUD** **Lines 186–191**

Read aloud the boxed speech in a way that expresses Harrison's mental state. What does he plan to do? **(Predict)**

_He plans to become Emperor._

Harrison's scrap-iron handicaps crashed to the floor.

Harrison thrust his thumbs under the bar of the padlock that secured his head harness. The bar snapped like celery. Harrison smashed his headphones and spectacles against the wall.

**200**     He flung away his rubber-ball nose, revealed a man that would have awed Thor, the god of thunder.

"I shall now select my Empress!" he said, looking down on the cowering people. "Let the first woman who dares rise to her feet claim her mate and her throne!"

A moment passed, and then a ballerina arose, swaying like a willow.

Harrison plucked the mental handicap from her ear, snapped off her physical handicaps with marvelous delicacy. Last of all, he removed her mask.

**210**     She was blindingly beautiful.

"Now—" said Harrison, taking her hand, "shall we show the people the meaning of the word dance? Music!" he commanded.

The musicians scrambled back into their chairs, and Harrison stripped them of their handicaps, too. "Play your best," he told them, "and I'll make you barons and dukes and earls."

The music began. It was normal at first—cheap, silly, false. But Harrison snatched two musicians from their chairs, waved

**220** them like batons as he sang the music as he wanted it played. He slammed them back into their chairs.

The music began again and was much improved.

Harrison and his Empress merely listened to the music for a while—listened gravely, as though <u>synchronizing</u> their heartbeats with it.

They shifted their weights to their toes.

Harrison placed his big hands on the girl's tiny waist, letting her sense the weightlessness that would soon be hers.

And then, in an explosion of joy and grace, into the air

**230** they sprang!

Not only were the laws of the land abandoned, but the law of gravity and the laws of motion as well.

WORDS
TO
KNOW    **synchronizing** (sǐng'krə-nī'zǐng) *adj.* matching the timing of **synchronize** *v.*

They reeled, whirled, swiveled, flounced, capered, gamboled,[7] and spun.

They leaped like deer on the moon.

The studio ceiling was thirty feet high, but each leap brought the dancers nearer to it.

It became their obvious intention to kiss the ceiling.

They kissed it.

240 And then, neutralizing gravity with love and pure will, they remained suspended in air inches below the ceiling, and they kissed each other for a long, long time.

It was then that Diana Moon Glampers, the Handicapper General, came into the studio with a double-barreled ten-gauge shotgun. She fired twice, and the Emperor and the Empress were dead before they hit the floor.

Diana Moon Glampers loaded the gun again. She aimed it at the musicians and told them they had ten seconds to get their handicaps back on.

250 It was then that the Bergerons' television tube burned out.

Hazel turned to comment about the blackout to George. But George had gone out into the kitchen for a can of beer.

George came back in with the beer, paused while a handicap signal shook him up. And then he sat down again. "You been crying?" he said to Hazel.

"Yup," she said.

"What about?" he said.

"I forget," she said. "Something real sad on television."

"What was it?" he said.

260 "It's all kind of mixed up in my mind," said Hazel.

"Forget sad things," said George.

"I always do," said Hazel.

"That's my girl," said George. He winced. There was the sound of a riveting[8] gun in his head.

"Gee—I could tell that one was a doozy," said Hazel.

"You can say that again," said George.

"Gee—" said Hazel, "I could tell that one was a doozy."

**Pause & Reflect**

---

7. **flounced, capered, gamboled** (găm′bəld): bounced, leaped, frolicked.

8. **riveting** (rĭv′ĭ-tĭng) **gun**: a power tool used to hammer the bolts (called rivets) used in construction work to fasten metal beams or plates together.

**1.** What is your response to the story's ending? **(Connect)**

*I like that Harrison removed the handicaps and he was free before he died.*

**MARK IT UP** **2.** Circle the sentence on this page that tells how Diana Moon Glampers stops Harrison. Why does she do this? **(Cause and Effect)**

*Diana does this because Harrison took his and the girls handicaps off. It was against the law.*

**3.** How does Harrison's death affect his parents? **(Infer)**

*His mom is sad, but doesn't know why. His dad just hears the gunshot go off in his head. They don't remember*

**CHALLENGE**

Review the passages that describe Harrison and his powers. Circle those sentences that strike you as the most exaggerated or unrealistic. What do you think Vonnegut is trying to achieve by making use of such exaggerated description? **(Evaluate)** *A great story.*

## Wrapping Up

If you are using *The Language of Literature,* you can now move to the questions and activities on pages 27–29 of that book.

# Active Reading SkillBuilder

## Making Inferences

**Inferences** are logical guesses based on clues in the text and on common sense. In this story, Vonnegut provides clues that lead the reader into making many inferences about the characters and the society portrayed in "Harrison Bergeron." For example, in the sentence "April, for instance, still drove people crazy by not being springtime," the reader might infer that people in that society had trouble accepting that all of the seasons, like the people, would not be the same. Read the story and use the diagram below to identify inferences you can make about the main characters and the society in which they live. An example is given.

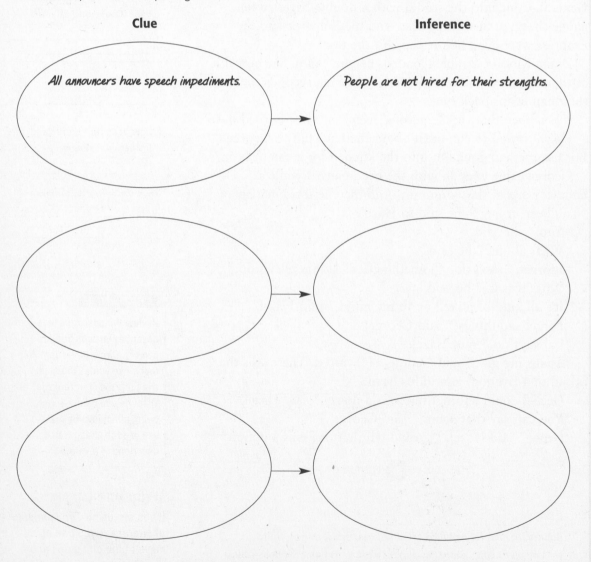

**Clue**

**Inference**

*All announcers have speech impediments.*

*People are not hired for their strengths.*

# Literary Analysis SkillBuilder

### Theme

The **theme** of a story is its central message. The theme expresses an attitude or insight into life or human nature. Readers must infer the theme from clues in the story. One way to uncover the theme is to consider what happens to the main characters. For example, Harrison's death and the subsequent responses of his parents suggest that Vonnegut is criticizing both society and the parents. Uncover the theme of this story by looking back through it to find phrases, sentences, and events that provide clues to the theme. List each clue in one of the spaces of the diagram shown below. Use the clues to infer the theme of the story. Then write a sentence stating that theme. One clue is given.

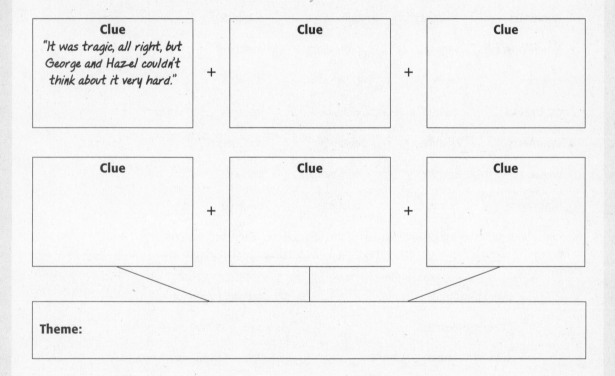

**Clue**
"It was tragic, all right, but George and Hazel couldn't think about it very hard."

+

**Clue**

+

**Clue**

**Clue**

+

**Clue**

+

**Clue**

**Theme:**

# Words to Know SkillBuilder

## Words to Know

| calibrated | cower | luminous | synchronizing | vigilance |
| consternation | hindrance | symmetry | vague | wince |

**A.** Circle the word in each group that is a synonym for the boldfaced word.

1. **vigilance**      carelessness      watchfulness      chaos

2. **wince**      flinch      rejoice      enlarge

3. **consternation**      consolation      delight      fear

4. **luminous**      indistinct      brilliant      complex

5. **synchronizing**      varying      protesting      matching

6. **cower**      frighten      cringe      determine

7. **calibrated**      measured      withstood      insisted

8. **symmetry**      balance      instability      confidence

9. **vague**      specific      common      unclear

10. **hindrance**      comfort      obstacle      privilege

**B.** Think about the meaning of each phrase in the first column. Then find the phrase in the second column that is closest in meaning. Write the letter of that phrase on the blank line.

_____ 1. blurry picture

_____ 2. unending alertness

_____ 3. yelps of confused amazement

_____ 4. obvious obstacle

_____ 5. cringe and conceal

A. unceasing vigilance

B. cower and hide

C. apparent hindrance

D. cries of consternation

E. vague image

**C.** Harrison Bergeron rebelled against the laws of his society that regulated equality. Write a letter that Harrison might have written to his parents explaining his reasons. Use at least **three** Words to Know in your letter.

# BY THE WATERS OF BABYLON

## STEPHEN VINCENT BENÉT

**SHORT STORY**

### Before You Read

If you are using *The Language of Literature*...

- Use the information on page 42 of that book to prepare for reading.

- Look at the art on page 43. What does it tell you about the **setting** of this story— both the time and the place?

### Reading Tips

This story is told by a **narrator** who knows only certain things about the world he describes. The following strategies may help you to understand what is going on, even before the narrator does.

- Look for clues about what is really being described.

- Don't limit yourself to the narrator's perspective. Try to draw your own conclusions about his discoveries.

**PREVIEW** John, the narrator of this story, is one of the Hill People. As the son of a priest, he is taught to read the old writings, which tell about the days when the gods walked the earth. One night, John's dreams reveal that he must make a dangerous journey to the forbidden Place of the Gods.

**FOCUS**

The first pages of the story describe the rules of the narrator's society. **MARK IT UP** As you read, circle the special things that John must know or do as the son of a priest. An example is highlighted on page 14.

**The north and the west** and the south are good hunting ground, but it is forbidden to go east. It is forbidden to go to any of the Dead Places except to search for metal, and then he who touches the metal must be a priest or the son of a priest. Afterwards, both the man and the metal must be purified. These are the rules and the laws; they are well made. It is forbidden to cross the great river and look upon the place that was the Place of the Gods—this is most strictly forbidden. We do not even say its name, though we know its name. It is there that spirits live, and demons—it is there that there are the ashes of the Great Burning. These things are forbidden—they have been forbidden since the beginning of time.

My father is a priest; I am the son of a priest. I have been in the Dead Places near us, with my father—at first, I was

**MARK IT UP** **KEEP TRACK**

As you read, you can use these marks to keep track of your understanding.

✔ ..... I understand.

? ..... I don't understand this.

! ..... Interesting or surprising idea

afraid. When my father went into the house to search for the
**20** metal, I stood by the door, and my heart felt small and weak.
It was a dead man's house, a spirit house. It did not have the
smell of man, though there were old bones in a corner. But it
is not fitting that a priest's son should show fear. I looked at
the bones in the shadow and kept my voice still.

Then my father came out with the metal—a good, strong
piece. He looked at me with both eyes, but I had not run
away. He gave me the metal to hold—I took it and did not
die. So he knew that I was truly his son and would be a priest
in my time. That was when I was very young—nevertheless,
**30** my brothers would not have done it, though they are good
hunters. After that, they gave me the good piece of meat and
the warm corner by the fire. My father watched over me—he
was glad that I should be a priest. But when I boasted or wept
without a reason, he punished me more strictly than my
brothers. That was right.

After a time, I myself was allowed to go into the dead
houses and search for metal. So I learned the ways of those
houses—and if I saw bones, I was no longer afraid. The bones
are light and old—sometimes they will fall into dust if you
**40** touch them. But that is a great sin.

I was taught the chants and the spells—I was taught how to
stop the running of blood from a wound and many secrets. A
priest must know many secrets—that was what my father
said. If the hunters think we do all things by chants and spells,
they may believe so—it does not hurt them. I was taught how
to read in the old books and how to make the old writings—
that was hard and took a long time. My knowledge made me
happy—it was like a fire in my heart. Most of all, I liked to
hear of the Old Days and the stories of the gods. I asked
**50** myself many questions that I could not answer, but it was
good to ask them. At night, I would lie awake and listen to
the wind—it seemed to me that it was the voice of the gods as
they flew through the air.

We are not ignorant like the Forest People—our women
spin wool on the wheel; our priests wear a white robe. We do
not eat grubs from the tree; we have not forgotten the old
writings, although they are hard to understand. Nevertheless,
my knowledge and my lack of knowledge burned in me—I
wished to know more. When I was a man at last, I came to

✏ **MARK IT UP** WORD POWER

Mark words that you'd like to
add to your **Personal Word List**.
After reading, you can record
the words and their meanings
beginning on page 316.

60 my father and said, "It is time for me to go on my journey. Give me your leave."

He looked at me for a long time, stroking his beard; then he said at last, "Yes. It is time." That night, in the house of the priesthood, I asked for and received purification. My body hurt, but my spirit was a cool stone. It was my father himself who questioned me about my dreams.

He bade me look into the smoke of the fire and see—I saw and told what I saw. It was what I have always seen—a river, and, beyond it, a great Dead Place and in it the gods walking. 70 I have always thought about that. His eyes were stern when I told him—he was no longer my father but a priest. He said, "This is a strong dream."

"It is mine," I said, while the smoke waved and my head felt light. They were singing the star song in the outer chamber, and it was like the buzzing of bees in my head.

He asked me how the gods were dressed, and I told him how they were dressed. We know how they were dressed from the book, but I saw them as if they were before me. When I had finished, he threw the sticks three times and studied them 80 as they fell.

"This is a very strong dream," he said. "It may eat you up."

"I am not afraid," I said and looked at him with both eyes. My voice sounded thin in my ears, but that was because of the smoke.

He touched me on the breast and the forehead. He gave me the bow and the three arrows.

"Take them," he said. "It is forbidden to travel east. It is forbidden to cross the river. It is forbidden to go to the Place 90 of the Gods. All these things are forbidden."

"All these things are forbidden," I said, but it was my voice that spoke and not my spirit. He looked at me again.

"My son," he said. "Once I had young dreams. If your dreams do not eat you up, you may be a great priest. If they eat you, you are still my son. Now go on your journey."

I went fasting, as is the law. My body hurt but not my heart. When the dawn came, I was out of sight of the village. I prayed and purified myself, waiting for a sign. The sign was an eagle. It flew east.

Pause & Reflect

NOTES

**Pause & Reflect**

1. List three things that are forbidden in John's society. (Clarify)

_____

_____

_____

_____

2. Review the passages that you circled as you read. Circle the one description below that does *not* describe John. (Infer)

goes into the Dead Places to search for metal

learns chants and spells

afraid to go on his journey

can read the old books

**READ ALOUD** 3. Read aloud the boxed passage on this page. Then write down your prediction of what will happen on John's journey. (Predict)

_____

_____

_____

_____

**100** FOCUS

Now John begins his journey to the Place of the Gods.

✎ MARK IT UP As you read, underline passages that describe dangers or obstacles that John faces on his way.

**Sometimes signs are sent** by bad spirits. I waited again on the flat rock, fasting, taking no food. I was very still—I could feel the sky above me and the earth beneath. I waited till the sun was beginning to sink. Then three deer passed in the valley, going east—they did not wind me or see me. There was a white fawn with them—a very great sign.

**110** I followed them, at a distance, waiting for what would happen. My heart was troubled about going east, yet I knew that I must go. My head hummed with my fasting—I did not even see the panther spring upon the white fawn. But, before I knew it, the bow was in my hand. I shouted, and the panther lifted his head from the fawn. It is not easy to kill a panther with one arrow, but the arrow went through his eye and into his brain. He died as he tried to spring—he rolled over, tearing at the ground. Then I knew I was meant to go east—I knew that was my journey. When the night came, I made my fire **120** and roasted meat.

It is eight suns' journey to the east, and a man passes by many Dead Places. The Forest People are afraid of them, but I am not. Once I made my fire on the edge of a Dead Place at night, and next morning, in the dead house, I found a good knife, little rusted. That was small to what came afterward, but it made my heart feel big. Always when I looked for game, it was in front of my arrow, and twice I passed hunting parties of the Forest People without their knowing. So I knew my magic was strong and my journey clean, in spite of **130** the law.

Toward the setting of the eighth sun, I came to the banks of the great river. It was half a day's journey after I had left the god road—we do not use the god roads now, for they are falling apart into great blocks of stone, and the forest is safer going. A long way off, I had seen the water through trees, but the trees were thick. At last, I came out upon an open place at the top of a cliff. There was the great river below, like a giant in the sun. It is very long, very wide. It could eat all the streams we know and still be thirsty. Its name is Ou-dis-sun, **140** the Sacred, the Long. No man of my tribe had seen it, not even my father, the priest. It was magic, and I prayed.

Then I raised my eyes and looked south. It was there, the Place of the Gods.

How can I tell what it was like—you do not know. It was there, in the red light, and they were too big to be houses. It was there with the red light upon it, mighty and ruined. I knew that in another moment the gods would see me. I covered my eyes with my hands and crept back into the forest.

Surely, that was enough to do, and live. Surely it was enough to spend the night upon the cliff. The Forest People themselves do not come near. Yet, all through the night, I knew that I should have to cross the river and walk in the places of the gods, although the gods ate me up. My magic did not help me at all, and yet there was a fire in my bowels, a fire in my mind. When the sun rose, I thought, "My journey has been clean. Now I will go home from my journey."

But, even as I thought so, I knew I could not. If I went to the Place of the Gods, I would surely die, but, if I did not go, I could never be at peace with my spirit again. It is better to lose one's life than one's spirit, if one is a priest and the son of a priest.

Nevertheless, as I made the raft, the tears ran out of my eyes. The Forest People could have killed me without fight, if they had come upon me then, but they did not come. When the raft was made, I said the sayings for the dead and painted myself for death. My heart was cold as a frog and my knees like water, but the burning in my mind would not let me have peace. As I pushed the raft from the shore, I began my death song—I had the right. It was a fine song.

"I am John, son of John," I sang. "My people are the
   Hill People.
They are the men.
I go into the Dead Places, but I am not slain. I take the
   metal from the Dead Places, but I am not blasted.
I travel upon the god roads and am not afraid. E-yah! I
   have killed the panther; I have killed the fawn!
E-yah! I have come to the great river. No man has come
   there before.
It is forbidden to go east, but I have gone, forbidden to go
   on the great river, but I am there.
Open your hearts, you spirits, and hear my song.
Now I go to the Place of the Gods; I shall not return.

READ ALOUD **Lines 157–161**

Reread the boxed passage. What does the narrator mean when he says, "It is better to die than to lose one's spirit"? (Paraphrase)

_____

_____

_____

_____

*My body is painted for death and my limbs weak, but my
heart is big as I go to the Place of the Gods!"*

All the same, when I came to the Place of the Gods, I was
afraid, afraid. The current of the great river is very strong—it
gripped my raft with its hands. That was magic, for the river
itself is wide and calm. I could feel evil spirits about me, in the
bright morning; I could feel their breath on my neck as I was
190 swept down the stream. Never have I been so much alone—I
tried to think of my knowledge, but it was a squirrel's heap of
winter nuts. There was no strength in my knowledge anymore,
and I felt small and naked as a new-hatched bird—alone upon
the great river, the servant of the gods.

Yet, after a while, my eyes were opened, and I saw. I saw
both banks of the river—I saw that once there had been god
roads across it, though now they were broken and fallen like
broken vines. Very great they were, and wonderful and
broken—broken in the time of the Great Burning when the
200 fire fell out of the sky. And always the current took me nearer
to the Place of the Gods, and the huge ruins rose before
my eyes.

I do not know the customs of rivers—we are the People of
the Hills. I tried to guide my raft with the pole, but it spun
around. I thought the river meant to take me past the Place of
the Gods and out into the Bitter Water of the legends. I grew
angry then—my heart felt strong. I said aloud, "I am a priest
and the son of a priest!" The gods heard me—they showed me
how to paddle with the pole on one side of the raft. The
210 current changed itself—I drew near to the Place of the Gods.

When I was very near, my raft struck and turned over. I can
swim in our lakes—I swam to the shore. There was a great
spike of rusted metal sticking out into the river—I hauled
myself up upon it and sat there, panting. I had saved my bow
and two arrows and the knife I found in the Dead Place, but
that was all. My raft went whirling downstream toward the
Bitter Water. I looked after it, and thought if it had trod me
under, at least I would be safely dead. Nevertheless, when I
had dried my bowstring and restrung it, I walked forward to
220 the Place of the Gods.

**Pause & Reflect**

**Pause & Reflect**

**MARK IT UP** **1.** When John
sees the eagle flying east, he
thinks it's a sign. Circle the
passages on page 16 that
describe other signs that
convince him to go east.
**(Sequence)**

**2.** Imagine how John might
complete this sentence: I have
to go to the forbidden places
because_____

_____

_____

_____.

**(Cause and Effect)**

**3.** Review the passages that you
underlined as you read. In your
judgment, which obstacle
presents the greatest danger?
**(Make Judgments)**

_____

_____

_____

_____

**It felt like ground underfoot;** it did not burn me. It is not true what some of the tales say, that the ground there burns forever, for I have been there. Here and there were the marks and stains of the Great Burning, on the ruins, that is true. But they were old marks and old stains. It is not true either, what some of our priests say,

230 that it is an island covered with fogs and enchantments. It is not. It is a great Dead Place—greater than any Dead Place we know. Everywhere in it there are god roads, though most are cracked and broken. Everywhere there are the ruins of the high towers of the gods.

How shall I tell what I saw? I went carefully, my strung bow in my hand, my skin ready for danger. There should have been the wailings of spirits and the shrieks of demons, but there were not. It was very silent and sunny where I had landed—the wind and the rain and the birds that drop seeds

240 had done their work—the grass grew in the cracks of the broken stone. It is a fair island—no wonder the gods built there. If I had come there, a god, I also would have built.

How shall I tell what I saw? The towers are not all broken—here and there one still stands, like a great tree in a forest, and the birds nest high. But the towers themselves look blind, for the gods are gone. I saw a fish hawk, catching fish in the river. I saw a little dance of white butterflies over a great heap of broken stones and columns. I went there and looked about me—there was a carved stone with cut letters,

250 broken in half. I can read letters, but I could not understand these. They said UBTREAS. There was also the shattered image of a man or a god. It had been made of white stone, and he wore his hair tied back like a woman's. His name was ASHING, as I read on the cracked half of a stone. I thought it wise to pray to ASHING, though I do not know that god.

How shall I tell what I saw? There was no smell of man left, on stone or metal. Nor were there many trees in that wilderness of stone. There are many pigeons, nesting and dropping in the towers—the gods must have loved them, or,

260 perhaps, they used them for sacrifices. There are wild cats that roam the god roads, green-eyed, unafraid of man. At night they wail like demons, but they are not demons. The wild

dogs are more dangerous, for they hunt in a pack, but them I did not meet till later. Everywhere there are the carved stones, carved with magical numbers or words.

I went north—I did not try to hide myself. When a god or a demon saw me, then I would die, but meanwhile I was no longer afraid. My hunger for knowledge burned in me—there was so much that I could not understand. After a while, I 270 knew that my belly was hungry. I could have hunted for my meat, but I did not hunt. It is known that the gods did not hunt as we do—they got their food from enchanted boxes and jars. Sometimes these are still found in the Dead Places—once, when I was a child and foolish, I opened such a jar and tasted it and found the food sweet. But my father found out and punished me for it strictly, for, often, that food is death. Now, though, I had long gone past what was forbidden, and I entered the likeliest towers, looking for the food of the gods.

I found it at last in the ruins of a great temple in the mid-280 city. A mighty temple it must have been, for the roof was painted like the sky at night with its stars—that much I could see, though the colors were faint and dim. It went down into great caves and tunnels—perhaps they kept their slaves there. But when I started to climb down, I heard the squeaking of rats, so I did not go—rats are unclean, and there must have been many tribes of them, from the squeaking. But near there, I found food, in the heart of a ruin, behind a door that still opened. I ate only the fruits from the jars—they had a very sweet taste. There was drink, too, in bottles of glass—the 290 drink of the gods was strong and made my head swim. After I had eaten and drunk, I slept on the top of a stone, my bow at my side.

When I woke, the sun was low. Looking down from where I lay, I saw a dog sitting on his haunches. His tongue was hanging out of his mouth; he looked as if he were laughing. He was a big dog, with a gray-brown coat, as big as a wolf. I sprang up and shouted at him, but he did not move—he just sat there as if he were laughing. I did not like that. When I reached for a stone to throw, he moved swiftly out of the way 300 of the stone. He was not afraid of me; he looked at me as if I were meat. No doubt I could have killed him with an arrow, but I did not know if there were others. Moreover, night was falling.

✎ MARK IT UP WORD POWER

Remember to mark words that you'd like to add to your **Personal Word List**. Later, you can record the words and their meanings beginning on page 316.

I looked about me—not far away there was a great, broken god road, leading north. The towers were high enough, but not so high, and while many of the dead houses were wrecked, there were some that stood. I went toward this god road, keeping to the heights of the ruins, while the dog followed. When I had reached the god road, I saw that there

310  were others behind him. If I had slept later, they would have come upon me asleep and torn out my throat. As it was, they were sure enough of me; they did not hurry. When I went into the dead house, they kept watch at the entrance—doubtless they thought they would have a fine hunt. But a dog cannot open a door, and I knew, from the books, that the gods did not like to live on the ground but on high.

I had just found a door I could open when the dogs decided to rush. Ha! They were surprised when I shut the door in their faces—it was a good door, of strong metal. I

320  could hear their foolish baying beyond it, but I did not stop to answer them. I was in darkness—I found stairs and climbed. There were many stairs, turning around till my head was dizzy. At the top was another door—I found the knob and opened it. I was in a long small chamber—on one side of it was a bronze door that could not be opened, for it had no handle. Perhaps there was a magic word to open it, but I did not have the word. I turned to the door in the opposite side of the wall. The lock of it was broken, and I opened it and went in.

330  Within, there was a place of great riches. The god who lived there must have been a powerful god. The first room was a small anteroom—I waited there for some time, telling the spirits of the place that I came in peace and not as a robber. When it seemed to me that they had had time to hear me, I went on. Ah, what riches! Few, even, of the windows had been broken—it was all as it had been. The great windows that looked over the city had not been broken at all, though they were dusty and streaked with many years. There were coverings on the floors, the colors not greatly faded, and

340  the chairs were soft and deep. There were pictures upon the walls, very strange, very wonderful—I remember one of a bunch of flowers in a jar—if you came close to it, you could see nothing but bits of color, but if you stood away from it, the flowers might have been picked yesterday. It made my

NOTES

READ ALOUD  Lines 304–309

Read this passage aloud in a way that expresses John's sense of wonder. What do you think the "god road" really is? (Infer)

_____

_____

heart feel strange to look at this picture—and to look at the figure of a bird, in some hard clay, on a table and see it so like our birds. Everywhere there were books and writings, many in tongues that I could not read. The god who lived there must have been a wise god and full of knowledge. I felt I had a

350 right there, as I sought knowledge also.

Nevertheless, it was strange. There was a washing place but no water—perhaps the gods washed in air. There was a cooking place but no wood, and though there was a machine to cook food, there was no place to put fire in it. Nor were there candles or lamps—there were things that looked like lamps, but they had neither oil nor wick. All these things were magic, but I touched them and lived—the magic had gone out of them. Let me tell one thing to show. In the washing place, a thing said "Hot," but it was not hot to the touch—another

360 thing said "Cold," but it was not cold. This must have been a strong magic, but the magic was gone. I do not understand— they had ways—I wish that I knew.

It was close and dry and dusty in the house of the gods. I have said the magic was gone, but that is not true—it had gone from the magic things, but it had not gone from the place. I felt the spirits about me, weighing upon me. Nor had I ever slept in a Dead Place before—and yet, tonight, I must sleep there. When I thought of it, my tongue felt dry in my throat, in spite of my wish for knowledge.

370 Almost I would have gone down again and faced the dogs, but I did not.

I had not gone through all the rooms when the darkness fell. When it fell, I went back to the big room looking over the city and made fire. There was a place to make fire and a box with wood in it, though I do not think they cooked there. I wrapped myself in a floor covering and slept in front of the fire—I was very tired.

*Pause* **&** *Reflect*

*Pause* **&** *Reflect*

✎ **MARK IT UP** **1.** Review the notes you made in the margins about what John is actually seeing. Where do you think John is? Star passages in the story that support your opinion. **(Draw Conclusions)**

_____

_____

**2.** How does John escape from the wild dogs? **(Clarify)**

_____

_____

_____

**3.** Reread the boxed passage on this page. What two things does John see in the room? **(Infer)**

_____

_____

_____

_____

**FOCUS**

Read on to learn what John sees in his dream about the Place of the Gods as it once existed.

**MARK IT UP** As you read, circle details that help to explain what happened to "the gods."

**Now I tell** what is very strong magic. I woke in the midst of the night. When I woke, the fire had gone out, and I was cold. It seemed to me that all around me there were whisperings and voices. I closed my eyes to shut them out. Some will say that I slept again, but I do not think that I slept. I could feel the spirits drawing my spirit out of my body as a fish is drawn on a line.

Why should I lie about it? I am a priest and the son of a priest. If there are spirits, as they say, in the small Dead Places near us, what spirits must there not be in that great Place of the Gods? And would not they wish to speak? After such long years? I know that I felt myself drawn as a fish is drawn on a line. I had stepped out of my body—I could see my body asleep in front of the cold fire, but it was not I. I was drawn to look out upon the city of the gods.

It should have been dark, for it was night, but it was not dark. Everywhere there were lights—lines of light—circles and blurs of light—ten thousand torches would not have been the same. The sky itself was alight—you could barely see the stars for the glow in the sky. I thought to myself "This is strong magic" and trembled. There was a roaring in my ears like the rushing of rivers. Then my eyes grew used to the light and my ears to the sound. I knew that I was seeing the city as it had been when the gods were alive.

That was a sight indeed—yes, that was a sight: I could not have seen it in the body—my body would have died. Everywhere went the gods, on foot and in chariots—there were gods beyond number and counting, and their chariots blocked the streets. They had turned night to day for their pleasure—they did not sleep with the sun. The noise of their coming and going was the noise of many waters. It was magic what they could do—it was magic what they did.

I looked out of another window—the great vines of their bridges were mended, and the god roads went east and west. Restless, restless, were the gods and always in motion! They burrowed tunnels under rivers—they flew in the air. With unbelievable tools they did giant works—no part of the earth was safe from them, for, if they wished for a thing, they

**MARK IT UP** KEEP TRACK

Remember to use these marks to keep track of your understanding.

✔ ..... I understand.

? ..... I don't understand this.

! ..... Interesting or surprising idea

summoned it from the other side of the world. And always, as
420 they labored and rested, as they feasted and made love, there
was a drum in their ears—the pulse of the giant city, beating
and beating like a man's heart.

Were they happy? What is happiness to the gods? They
were great; they were mighty; they were wonderful and
terrible. As I looked upon them and their magic, I felt like a
child—but a little more, it seemed to me, and they would pull
down the moon from the sky. I saw them with wisdom
beyond wisdom and knowledge beyond knowledge. And yet
not all they did was well done—even I could see that—and yet
430 their wisdom could not but grow until all was peace.

Then I saw their fate come upon them, and that was
terrible past speech. It came upon them as they walked the
streets of their city. I have been in the fights with the Forest
People—I have seen men die. But this was not like that. When
gods war with gods, they use weapons we do not know. It
was fire falling out of the sky and a mist that poisoned. It was
the time of the Great Burning and the Destruction. They ran
about like ants in the streets of their city—poor gods, poor
gods! Then the towers began to fall. A few escaped—yes, a
440 few. The legends tell it. But, even after the city had become a
Dead Place, for many years the poison was still in the ground.
I saw it happen; I saw the last of them die. It was darkness
over the broken city, and I wept.

**Pause & Reflect**

## Pause & Reflect

1. Look back at the details you circled as you read. In your own words, **summarize** the events that destroyed the Place of the Gods.

_____

_____

_____

_____

2. This story was published in 1937, well before the invention of nuclear bombs. What do you think could have caused the Great Burning and the Destruction? **(Infer)**

_____

_____

_____

_____

**FOCUS**

John now makes a great discovery.

**MARK IT UP** As you read, underline John's discovery about the true nature of "the gods."

450

**All this, I saw.** I saw it as I have told it,
though not in the body. When I woke
in the morning, I was hungry, but I did
not think first of my hunger, for my
heart was perplexed and confused. I
knew the reason for the Dead Places,
but I did not see why it had happened.

It seemed to me it should not have happened, with all the
magic they had. I went through the house looking for an
answer. There was so much in the house I could not

understand—and yet I am a priest and the son of a priest. It was like being on one side of the great river, at night, with no light to show the way.

Then I saw the dead god. He was sitting in his chair, by the window, in a room I had not entered before, and for the first moment, I thought that he was alive. Then I saw the skin on the back of his hand—it was like dry leather. The room was shut, hot and dry—no doubt that had kept him as he was. At first I was afraid to approach him—then the fear left me. He was sitting looking out over the city—he was dressed in the clothes of the gods. His age was neither young nor old—I could not tell his age. But there was wisdom in his face and great sadness. You could see that he would have not run away. He had sat at his window, watching his city die—then he himself had died. But it is better to lose one's life than one's spirit—and you could see from the face that his spirit had not been lost. I knew that, if I touched him, he would fall into dust—and yet, there was something unconquered in the face.

That is all of my story, for then I knew he was a man—I knew then that they had been men, neither gods nor demons. It is a great knowledge, hard to tell and believe. They were men—they went a dark road, but they were men. I had no fear after that—I had no fear going home, though twice I fought off the dogs and once I was hunted for two days by the Forest People. When I saw my father again, I prayed and was purified. He touched my lips and my breast; he said, "You went away a boy. You come back a man and a priest." I said, "Father, they were men! I have been in the Place of the Gods and seen it! Now slay me, if it is the law—but still I know they were men."

He looked at me out of both eyes. He said, "The law is not always the same shape—you have done what you have done. I could not have done it my time, but you come after me. Tell!"

I told, and he listened. After that, I wished to tell all the people, but he showed me otherwise. He said, "Truth is a hard deer to hunt. If you eat too much truth at once, you may die of the truth. It was not idly that our fathers forbade the Dead Places." He was right—it is better the truth should come little by little. I have learned that, being a priest. Perhaps, in the old days, they ate knowledge too fast.

READ ALOUD **Lines 464–472**

Read aloud the boxed passage. What emotions do you think John is experiencing? (Infer)

1. Review what you underlined as you read. What does John discover about the gods who lived in the Dead Places? **(Clarify)**

_____

_____

_____

2. What does John's father mean when he says, "If you eat too much truth at once, you may die of the truth"? **(Paraphrase)**

_____

_____

_____

3. What does John resolve to do after he becomes chief priest? **(Clarify)**

_____

_____

_____

**CHALLENGE**

This story deals with a **paradox:** It is very important to John to search for knowledge, yet too much knowledge is what destroyed a society. Review the story, marking passages that describe the effects of gaining knowledge. How do you think Benét felt about the advances in knowledge brought about by science and technology? **(Author's Perspective)**

## Wrapping Up

If you are using **_The Language of Literature,_** you can now move to the questions and activities on pages 53–55 of that book.

Nevertheless, we make a beginning. It is not for the metal alone we go to the Dead Places now—there are the books and the writings. They are hard to learn. And the magic tools are broken—but we can look at them and wonder. At least, we make a beginning. And, when I am chief priest, we shall go beyond the great river. We shall go to the Place of the Gods—the place newyork—not one man but a company. We shall look for the images of the gods and find the god ASHING and the others—the gods Lincoln and Biltmore[1] and Moses.[2] But they were men who built the city, not gods or demons. They were men. I remember the dead man's face. They were men who were here before us. We must build again.

**Pause** & **Reflect**

---

1. **Biltmore:** the name of a famous hotel in New York City.
2. **Moses:** Robert Moses (1888–1981), a New York City public official whose name appears on many bridges and other structures built during his administration.

# Active Reading SkillBuilder

## Sequence

When reading, it helps to pay close attention to the **sequence** of events. In this story, the main events follow chronological order; that is, the events are arranged in the order that they happen. Read the selection and record important events, in sequence, in the diagram below. Look for signal words and phrases, such as *after a time, then,* and *when,* that mark the order of events. For each event that you list, tell what the narrator learned from it. An example is given.

**Narrator's Journey**

| | |
|---|---|
| **Event:** *Holds piece of metal from Dead Places and does not die*<br>**Narrator learns:** *He has courage and will become a priest like his father.* | **Event:**<br><br>**Narrator learns:** |
| **Event:**<br><br>**Narrator learns:** | **Event:**<br><br>**Narrator learns:** |
| **Event:**<br><br>**Narrator learns:** | **Event:**<br><br>**Narrator learns:** |
| **Event:**<br><br>**Narrator learns:** | **Event:**<br><br>**Narrator learns:** |

# Literary Analysis SkillBuilder

## Plot

The **plot** of a story is the writer's blueprint for what happens, when it happens, and to whom it happens. Most plots include four stages: **Exposition** (when characters are introduced, the setting is described, and conflicts are identified); **Rising Action** (when complications arise causing difficulties for the main characters); **Climax** (the turning point of the story—when an important discovery or decision is made); and **Falling Action** (the events after the climax, when the conflict is often resolved). As you read the selection, classify the events of the story according to these plot stages. Then write them in the appropriate section of the diagram that follows. Two examples are given.

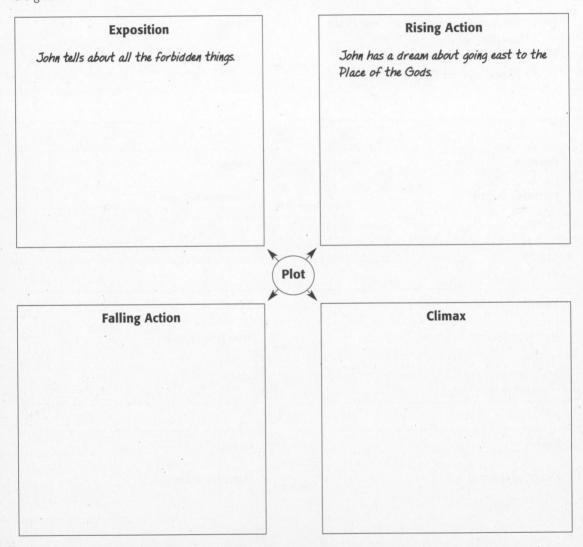

**Exposition**

*John tells about all the forbidden things.*

**Rising Action**

*John has a dream about going east to the Place of the Gods.*

**Plot**

**Falling Action**

**Climax**

# A Sound of Thunder

### RAY BRADBURY

## SHORT STORY

### Before You Read
If you are using *The Language of Literature* . . .

• Use the information on page 71 of that book to prepare for reading.

• Look at the art on pages 76–78 and the two quotes on pages 74 and 79. Predict what might have happened between the first quote and the second.

### Reading Tips
A great deal of information is presented quickly in this story. Don't worry if you don't understand everything at first. Just keep your focus on the **main characters:** the hunter Eckels and the Safari Guide Travis.

• Put an "X" in the margin whenever Travis gives rules or warnings. These warnings might **foreshadow,** or give clues to, future events.

• Pay special attention to Eckels's thoughts, feelings, and actions— especially in relation to Travis's warnings.

**PREVIEW** Ray Bradbury sets this science fiction story in a future where time travel is almost as easy as booking a plane ticket. Eckels, the main character, is going to travel 60 million years back in time to hunt dinosaurs. This "time safari" is dangerous, which makes it important to obey all the rules.

**FOCUS**

In the opening of the story, you will get to know Eckels and Travis as they begin their journey to the past.

**MARK IT UP** As you read, circle details that may hint at events to come. An example is highlighted on page 30.

**The sign on the wall** seemed to quaver under a film of sliding warm water. Eckels felt his eyelids blink over his stare, and the sign burned in this momentary darkness:

TIME SAFARI, INC.

SAFARIS TO ANY YEAR IN THE PAST.

YOU NAME THE ANIMAL.

WE TAKE YOU THERE.

YOU SHOOT IT.

A warm phlegm gathered in Eckels's throat; he swallowed and pushed it down. The muscles around his mouth formed a smile as he put his hand slowly out upon the air, and in that hand waved a check for ten thousand dollars to the man behind the desk.

"Does this safari guarantee I come back alive?"

"We guarantee nothing," said the official, "except the dinosaurs." He turned. "This is Mr. Travis, your Safari Guide in the Past. He'll tell you what and where to shoot.

**MARK IT UP KEEP TRACK**

As you read, you can use these marks to keep track of your understanding.

✔ ..... I understand.

? ..... I don't understand this.

! ..... Interesting or surprising idea

**20** If he says no shooting, no shooting. If you disobey instructions, there's a stiff penalty of another ten thousand dollars,
plus possible government action, on your return."

Eckels glanced across the vast office at a mass and tangle, a
snaking and humming of wires and steel boxes, at an aurora[1]
that flickered now orange, now silver, now blue. There was a
sound like a gigantic bonfire burning all of Time, all the years
and all the parchment calendars, all the hours piled high and
set aflame.

A touch of the hand and this burning would, on the instant,
**30** beautifully reverse itself. Eckels remembered the wording in
the advertisements to the letter. Out of chars and ashes, out of
dust and coals, like golden salamanders, the old years, the
green years, might leap; roses sweeten the air, white hair turn
Irish-black, wrinkles vanish; all, everything fly back to seed,
flee death, rush down to their beginnings, suns rise in western
skies and set in glorious easts, moons eat themselves opposite
to the custom, all and everything cupping one in another like
Chinese boxes,[2] rabbits into hats, all and everything returning
to the fresh death, the seed death, the green death, to the time
**40** before the beginning. A touch of a hand might do it, the
merest touch of a hand.

"Unbelievable." Eckels breathed, the light of the Machine
on his thin face. "A real Time Machine." He shook his head.
"Makes you think. If the election had gone badly yesterday, I
might be here now running away from the results. Thank God
Keith won. He'll make a fine President of the United States."

"Yes," said the man behind the desk. "We're lucky. If
Deutscher had gotten in, we'd have the worst kind of
dictatorship. There's an anti-everything man for you, a
**50** militarist, anti-Christ, anti-human, anti-intellectual. People
called us up, you know, joking but not joking. Said if
Deutscher became President they wanted to go live in 1492.
Of course it's not our business to conduct Escapes, but to
form Safaris. Anyway, Keith's President now. All you got to
worry about is—"

"Shooting my dinosaur," Eckels finished it for him.

"A *Tyrannosaurus rex*. The Tyrant Lizard, the most
incredible monster in history. Sign this release. Anything

---

1. **aurora:** a light that changes colors.

2. **Chinese boxes:** a series of boxes, each of which fits neatly inside the next
larger one.

happens to you, we're not responsible. Those dinosaurs
60 are hungry."

Eckels flushed angrily. "Trying to scare me!"

"Frankly, yes. We don't want anyone going who'll panic at
the first shot. Six Safari leaders were killed last year, and a
dozen hunters. We're here to give you the severest thrill a *real*
hunter ever asked for. Traveling you back sixty million years
to bag the biggest game in all of Time. Your personal check's
still there. Tear it up."

Mr. Eckels looked at the check. His fingers twitched.

"Good luck," said the man behind the desk. "Mr. Travis,
70 he's all yours."

They moved silently across the room, taking their guns with
them, toward the Machine, toward the silver metal and the
roaring light.

First a day and then a night and then a day and then a
night, then it was day-night-day-night-day. A week, a month,
a year, a decade! a.d. 2055. a.d. 2019. 1999! 1957! Gone!
The Machine roared.

They put on their oxygen helmets and tested the intercoms.

Eckels swayed on the padded seat, his face pale, his jaw
80 stiff. He felt the trembling in his arms, and he looked down
and found his hands tight on the new rifle. There were four
other men in the Machine. Travis, the Safari Leader; his
assistant, Lesperance; and two other hunters, Billings and
Kramer. They sat looking at each other, and the years blazed
around them.

"Can these guns get a dinosaur cold?" Eckels felt his
mouth saying.

"If you hit them right," said Travis on the helmet radio.
"Some dinosaurs have two brains, one in the head, another
90 far down the spinal column. We stay away from those. That's
stretching luck. Put your first two shots into the eyes, if you
can, blind them, and go back into the brain."

The Machine howled. Time was a film run backward. Suns
fled, and ten million moons fled after them. "Think," said
Eckels. "Every hunter that ever lived would envy us today.
This makes Africa seem like Illinois."

The Machine slowed; its scream fell to a murmur. The
Machine stopped.

> **MARK IT UP** WORD POWER
>
> Mark words that you'd like to
> add to your **Personal Word List**.
> You can record the words and
> their meanings beginning on
> page 316.

**1.** Now that Eckels has made his voyage to the past, what does he have to be careful about? **(Clarify)**

_____

_____

_____

_____

**2.** Would you like to be going with Eckels and Travis on this safari? Why or why not? **(Connect)**

_____

_____

_____

_____

**3.** Look back at the details you circled as you read. Make a prediction based on at least one of them.

I think that _____

_____

_____

_____ .

**(Predict)**

The sun stopped in the sky.

⟨100⟩ The fog that had enveloped the Machine blew away, and they were in an old time, a very old time indeed, three hunters and two Safari Heads with their blue metal guns across their knees.

"Christ isn't born yet," said Travis. "Moses has not gone to the mountain to talk with God. The Pyramids are still in the earth, waiting to be cut out and put up. *Remember* that. Alexander, Caesar, Napoleon, Hitler—none of them exists."

The man nodded.

"That"—Mr. Travis pointed—"is the jungle of sixty million ⟨110⟩ two thousand and fifty-five years before President Keith."

He indicated a metal path that struck off into green wilderness, over streaming swamp, among giant ferns and palms.

"And that," he said, "is the Path, laid by Time Safari for your use. It floats six inches above the earth. Doesn't touch so much as one grass blade, flower, or tree. It's an antigravity metal. Its purpose is to keep you from touching this world of the past in any way. Stay on the Path. Don't go off it. I repeat. *Don't go off.* For *any* reason! If you fall off, there's a penalty. ⟨120⟩ And don't shoot any animal we don't okay."

"Why?" asked Eckels.

*Pause* **&** **Reflect**

**FOCUS**
Read to learn more about the importance of the Path.
⟨MARK IT UP⟩ As you read, underline passages that explain why everyone has to stay on the Path.

**They sat in the ancient wilderness.** Far birds' cries blew on a wind, and the smell of tar and an old salt sea, moist grasses, and flowers the color of blood.

"We don't want to change the Future. We don't belong here in the Past. The government doesn't *like* us here. We have to pay big graft to keep our ⟨130⟩ franchise.[3] A Time Machine is finicky business. Not knowing it, we might kill an important animal, a small bird, a roach, a

_____

3. **graft to keep our franchise:** money paid as a bribe to officials in return for their approval of the business.

flower even, thus destroying an important link in a growing species."

"That's not clear," said Eckels.

"All right," Travis continued, "say we accidentally kill one mouse here. That means all the future families of this one particular mouse are destroyed, right?"

"Right."

"And all the families of the families of the families of that
140 one mouse! With a stamp of your foot, you <u>annihilate</u> first one, then a dozen, then a thousand, a million, a *billion* possible mice!"

"So they're dead," said Eckels. "So what?"

"So what?" Travis snorted quietly. "Well, what about the foxes that'll need those mice to survive? For want of ten mice, a fox dies. For want of ten foxes, a lion starves. For want of a lion, all manner of insects, vultures, infinite billions of life forms are thrown into chaos and destruction. Eventually it all boils down to this: fifty-nine million years later, a caveman,
150 one of a dozen on the *entire world,* goes hunting wild boar or saber-toothed tiger for food. But you, friend, have stepped on all the tigers in that region. By stepping on one single mouse. So the caveman starves. And the caveman, please note, is not just *any* expendable man, no! He is an *entire future nation.* From his loins would have sprung ten sons. From *their* loins one hundred sons, and thus onward to a civilization. Destroy this one man, and you destroy a race, a people, an entire history of life. It is comparable to slaying some of Adam's grandchildren. The stomp of your foot, on one mouse, could
160 start an earthquake, the effects of which could shake our earth and destinies down through Time, to their very foundations. With the death of that one caveman, a billion others yet unborn are throttled in the womb. Perhaps Rome never rises on its seven hills. Perhaps Europe is forever a dark forest, and only Asia waxes healthy and teeming. Step on a mouse, and you crush the Pyramids. Step on a mouse, and you leave your print, like a Grand Canyon, across Eternity. Queen Elizabeth might never be born; Washington might not cross the Delaware; there might never be a United States at
170 all. So be careful. Stay on the Path. *Never* step off!"

| WORDS<br>TO<br>KNOW | **annihilate** (ə-nī′ə-lāt′) *v.* to destroy completely; wipe out<br>**expendable** (ĭk-spĕn′də-bel) *adj.* dispensable; unnecessary |

"I see," said Eckels. "Then it wouldn't pay for us even to touch the *grass?*"

"Correct. Crushing certain plants could add up <u>infinitesimally.</u> A little error here would multiply in sixty million years, all out of proportion. Of course maybe our theory is wrong. Maybe Time can't be changed by us. Or maybe it can be changed only in little subtle ways. A dead mouse here makes an insect imbalance there, a population disproportion later, a bad harvest further on, a depression, 180 mass starvation, and, finally, a change in *social* temperament in far-flung countries. Something much more subtle, like that. Perhaps only a soft breath, a whisper, a hair, pollen on the air, such a slight, slight change that unless you looked close you wouldn't see it. Who knows? Who really can say he knows? We don't know. We're guessing. But until we do know for certain whether our messing around in Time *can* make a big roar or a little rustle in history, we're being careful. This Machine, this Path, your clothing and bodies, were sterilized, as you know, before the journey. We wear these oxygen 190 helmets so we can't introduce our bacteria into an ancient atmosphere."

"How do we know which animals to shoot?"

"They're marked with red paint," said Travis. "Today, before our journey, we sent Lesperance here back with the Machine. He came to this particular era and followed certain animals."

"Studying them?"

"Right," said Lesperance. "I track them through their entire existence, noting which of them lives longest. Very few. How 200 many times they mate. Not often. Life's short. When I find one that's going to die when a tree falls on him, or one that drowns in a tar pit, I note the exact hour, minute, and second. I shoot a paint bomb. It leaves a red patch on his side. We can't miss it. Then I correlate our arrival in the Past so that we meet the Monster not more than two minutes before he would have died anyway. This way, we kill only animals with no future, that are never going to mate again. You see how *careful* we are?"

"But if you came back this morning in Time," said Eckels

WORDS TO KNOW

**infinitesimally** (ĭn'fĭn-ĭ-tĕs'ə-mə-lē) *adv.* in steps so small as to be immeasurable or incalculable

210 eagerly, "you must've bumped into *us*, our Safari! How did it turn out? Was it successful? Did all of us get through—alive?"

Travis and Lesperance gave each other a look.

"That'd be a paradox," said the latter. "Time doesn't permit that sort of mess—a man meeting himself. When such occasions threaten, Time steps aside. Like an airplane hitting an air pocket. You felt the Machine jump just before we stopped? That was us passing ourselves on the way back to the Future. We saw nothing. There's no way of telling *if* this expedition was a success, *if we* got our monster, or whether
220 all of us—meaning *you*, Mr. Eckels—got out alive."

Eckels smiled palely.

"Cut that," said Travis sharply. "Everyone on his feet!"

They were ready to leave the Machine.

**Pause & Reflect**

FOCUS

Now the men enter the jungle of 60 million years ago. The hunt begins. As you read, pay close attention to the reactions of Eckels and Travis.

**The jungle was high** and the jungle was broad and the jungle was the entire world forever and forever. Sounds like music and sounds like flying tents filled the sky, and those were pterodactyls[4] soaring with cavernous gray wings, gigantic bats of delirium and night
230 fever.[5] Eckels, balanced on the narrow Path, aimed his rifle playfully.

"Stop that!" said Travis. "Don't even aim for fun, blast you! If your guns should go off—"

Eckels flushed. "Where's our *Tyrannosaurus?*"

Lesperance checked his wristwatch. "Up ahead. We'll bisect his trail in sixty seconds. Look for the red paint! Don't shoot till we give the word. Stay on the Path. *Stay on the Path!*"

They moved forward in the wind of morning.

240 "Strange," murmured Eckels. "Up ahead, sixty million years, Election Day over. Keith made President. Everyone celebrating. And here we are, a million years lost, and they

---

4. **pterodactyls** (tĕr′ə-dăk′təlz): extinct flying reptiles having a wingspan of up to 40 feet.

5. **bats . . . fever**: the sort of bats that appear in nightmares and visions caused by drugs or illness.

**Pause & Reflect**

1. Look back at the passages you underlined as you read. Why is it important to stay on the path? Put a check next to the main reason below. **(Main Idea)**

A mouse might be killed.

The future might be changed for the worse.

A caveman might be hurt.

**MARK IT UP** 2. Why are safari members permitted to kill the dinosaur marked with red paint? Circle the passages on page 34 that explain this. **(Clarify)**

3. If you were on the safari, what would you be most concerned about? **(Connect)**

_____

_____

_____

_____

don't exist. The things we worried about for months, a lifetime, not even born or thought of yet."

"Safety catches off, everyone!" ordered Travis. "You, first shot, Eckels. Second, Billings. Third, Kramer."

"I've hunted tiger, wild boar, buffalo, elephant, but now, this is *it*," said Eckels. "I'm shaking like a kid."

"Ah," said Travis.

250 Everyone stopped.

Travis raised his hand. "Ahead," he whispered. "In the mist. There he is. There's His Royal Majesty now."

The jungle was wide and full of twitterings, rustlings, murmurs, and sighs.

Suddenly it all ceased, as if someone had shut a door.

Silence.

A sound of thunder.

Out of the mist, one hundred yards away, came *Tyrannosaurus rex*.

260 "It," whispered Eckels. "It . . ."

"Sh!"

It came on great oiled, <u>resilient</u>, striding legs. It towered thirty feet above half of the trees, a great evil god, folding its delicate watchmaker's claws close to its oily reptilian chest. Each lower leg was a piston, a thousand pounds of white bone, sunk in thick ropes of muscle, <u>sheathed</u> over in a gleam of pebbled skin like the mail of a terrible warrior. Each thigh was a ton of meat, ivory, and steel mesh. And from the great breathing cage of the upper body those two delicate arms 270 dangled out front, arms with hands which might pick up and examine men like toys, while the snake neck coiled. And the head itself, a ton of sculptured stone, lifted easily upon the sky. Its mouth gaped, exposing a fence of teeth like daggers. Its eyes rolled, ostrich eggs, empty of all expression save hunger. It closed its mouth in a death grin. It ran, its pelvic bones crushing aside trees and bushes, its taloned feet clawing damp earth, leaving prints six inches deep wherever it settled its weight. It ran with a gliding ballet step, far too poised and balanced for its ten tons. It moved into a sunlit arena warily, 280 its beautifully reptilian hands feeling the air.

WORDS TO KNOW

**resilient** (rĭ-zĭl′yənt) *adj.* capable of bouncing or springing back to an original shape after being stretched, bent or compressed

**sheathed** (shēth̄d) *adj.* enclosed in a protective covering **sheathe** *v.*

"Why, why," Eckels twitched his mouth. "It could reach up and grab the moon."

"Sh!" Travis jerked angrily. "He hasn't seen us yet."

"It can't be killed." Eckels pronounced this verdict quietly, as if there could be no argument. He had weighed the evidence, and this was his considered opinion. The rifle in his hands seemed a cap gun. "We were fools to come. This is impossible."

"Shut up!" hissed Travis.

290 "Nightmare."

"Turn around," commanded Travis. "Walk quietly to the Machine. We'll remit one-half your fee."

"I didn't realize it would be this *big*," said Eckels. "I miscalculated, that's all. And now I want out."

"It *sees* us!"

"There's the red paint on its chest!"

The Tyrant Lizard raised itself. Its armored flesh glittered like a thousand green coins. The coins, crusted with slime, steamed. In the slime, tiny insects wriggled, so that the entire 300 body seemed to twitch and <u>undulate</u>, even while the monster itself did not move. It exhaled. The stink of raw flesh blew down the wilderness.

"Get me out of here," said Eckels. "It was never like this before. I was always sure I'd come through alive. I had good guides, good safaris, and safety. This time, I figured wrong. I've met my match and admit it. This is too much for me to get hold of."

"Don't run," said Lesperance. "Turn around. Hide in the Machine."

310 "Yes." Eckels seemed to be numb. He looked at his feet as if trying to make them move. He gave a grunt of helplessness.

"Eckels!"

He took a few steps, blinking, shuffling.

"Not *that* way!"

**Pause & Reflect**

**undulate** (ŭn′jə-lāt′) *v.* to move in waves or in a smooth, wavelike motion

**Pause & Reflect**

1. In your own words, describe how Eckels and Travis respond to the challenge of the hunt. **(Clarify)**

Travis:_____

_____

_____

Eckels:_____

_____

_____

2. What happens after Travis tells Eckels to take the first shot? **(Summarize)**

_____

_____

_____

_____

MARK IT UP   3. Reread the boxed description of the *Tyrannosaurus rex* on page 36. Circle the words and phrases that you think best convey its terrifying power. **(Evaluate)**

FOCUS

Read on to learn what happens when the men shoot the dinosaur.

**MARK IT UP** Underline an important event that occurs between the first and second rounds of gunshots.

**The Monster, at the first motion,** lunged forward with a terrible scream. It covered one hundred yards in six seconds. The rifles jerked up and blazed fire. A windstorm from the beast's mouth engulfed them in the stench of slime and old blood. The Monster roared, teeth glittering with sun.

Eckels, not looking back, walked blindly to the edge of the Path, his gun limp in his arms, stepped off the Path, and walked, not knowing it, in the jungle. His feet sank into green moss. His legs moved him, and he felt alone and remote from the events behind.

The rifles cracked again. Their sound was lost in shriek and lizard thunder. The great level of the reptile's tail swung up, lashed sideways. Trees exploded in clouds of leaf and branch. The Monster twitched its jeweler's hands down to fondle at the men, to twist them in half, to crush them like berries, to cram them into its teeth and its screaming throat. Its boulder-stone eyes leveled with the men. They saw themselves mirrored. They fired at the metallic eyelids and the blazing black iris.

Like a stone idol, like a mountain avalanche, *Tyrannosaurus* fell. Thundering, it clutched trees, pulled them with it. It wrenched and tore the metal Path. The men flung themselves back and away. The body hit, ten tons of cold flesh and stone. The guns fired. The Monster lashed its armored tail, twitched its snake jaws, and lay still. A fount of blood spurted from its throat. Somewhere inside, a sac of fluids burst. Sickening gushes drenched the hunters. They stood, red and glistening.

The thunder faded.

The jungle was silent. After the avalanche, a green peace. After the nightmare, morning.

Billings and Kramer sat on the pathway and threw up. Travis and Lesperance stood with smoking rifles, cursing steadily.

In the Time Machine, on his face, Eckels lay shivering. He had found his way back to the Path, climbed into the Machine.

Travis came walking, glanced at Eckels, took cotton gauze from a metal box, and returned to the others, who were sitting on the Path.

"Clean up."

360  They wiped the blood from their helmets. They began to curse too. The Monster lay, a hill of solid flesh. Within, you could hear the sighs and murmurs as the furthest chambers of it died, the organs malfunctioning, liquids running a final instant from pocket to sac to spleen, everything shutting off, closing up forever. It was like standing by a wrecked locomotive or a steam shovel at quitting time, all valves being released or levered tight. Bones cracked; the tonnage of its own flesh, off balance, dead weight, snapped the delicate forearms, caught underneath. The meat settled, quivering.

370  Another cracking sound. Overhead, a gigantic tree branch broke from its heavy mooring, fell. It crashed upon the dead beast with finality.

"There." Lesperance checked his watch. "Right on time. That's the giant tree that was scheduled to fall and kill this animal originally." He glanced at the two hunters. "You want the trophy picture?"

"What?"

"We can't take a trophy back to the Future. The body has to stay right here where it would have died originally, so the 380  insects, birds, and bacteria can get at it, as they were intended to. Everything in balance. The body stays. But we *can* take a picture of you standing near it."

The two men tried to think, but gave up, shaking their heads.

They let themselves be led along the metal Path. They sank wearily into the Machine cushions. They gazed back at the ruined Monster, the stagnating mound, where already strange reptilian birds and golden insects were busy at the steaming armor.

**Pause & Reflect**

**390** FOCUS
Read on to find out what happens when Travis learns that Eckels left the Path.

**A sound on the floor** of the Time Machine stiffened them. Eckels sat there, shivering.

"I'm sorry," he said at last.

"Get up!" cried Travis.

Eckels got up.

"Go out on that Path alone," said Travis. He had his rifle pointed. "You're not coming back in the Machine. We're leaving you here!"

Lesperance seized Travis's arm. "Wait—"

**400** "Stay out of this!" Travis shook his hand away. "This fool nearly killed us. But it isn't *that* so much, no. It's his *shoes!* Look at them! He ran off the Path. That *ruins* us! We'll forfeit! Thousands of dollars of insurance! We guarantee no one leaves the Path. He left it. Oh, the fool! I'll have to report to the government. They might <u>revoke</u> our license to travel. Who knows *what* he's done to Time, to History!"

"Take it easy; all he did was kick up some dirt."

"How do we *know?*" cried Travis. "We don't know anything! It's all a mystery! Get out there, Eckels!"

**410** Eckels fumbled his shirt. "I'll pay anything. A hundred thousand dollars!"

Travis glared at Eckels's checkbook and spat. "Go out there. The Monster's next to the Path. Stick your arms up to your elbows in his mouth. Then you can come back with us."

"That's unreasonable!"

"The Monster's dead, you idiot. The bullets! The bullets can't be left behind. They don't belong in the Past; they might change anything. Here's my knife. Dig them out!"

The jungle was alive again, full of the old tremorings and **420** bird cries. Eckels turned slowly to regard the <u>primeval</u> garbage dump, that hill of nightmares and terror. After a long time, like a sleepwalker he shuffled out along the Path.

He returned, shuddering, five minutes later, his arms soaked and red to the elbows. He held out his hands. Each held a number of steel bullets. Then he fell. He lay where he fell, not moving.

"You didn't have to make him do that," said Lesperance.

"Didn't I? It's too early to tell." Travis nudged the still

WORDS TO KNOW
**revoke** (rĭ-vōk′) *v.* to cancel or withdraw
**primeval** (prī-mē′vəl) *adj.* belonging to the earliest times or ages

body. "He'll live. Next time he won't go hunting game like this. Okay." He jerked his thumb wearily at Lesperance. "Switch on. Let's go home."

1492. 1776. 1812.

They cleaned their hands and faces. They changed their caking shirts and pants. Eckels was up and around again, not speaking. Travis glared at him for a full ten minutes.

"Don't look at me," cried Eckels. "I haven't done anything."

"Who can tell?"

"Just ran off the Path, that's all, a little mud on my shoes— what do you want me to do—get down and pray?"

"We might need it. I'm warning you, Eckels, I might kill you yet. I've got my gun ready."

"I'm innocent. I've done nothing!"

1999. 2000. 2055.

The Machine stopped.

"Get out," said Travis.

*Pause* **&** *Reflect*

FOCUS
The safari group travels forward to the year 2055.
MARK IT UP Circle details that tell what has changed in the world of 2055.

**The room was there** as they had left it. But not the same as they had left it. The same man sat behind the same desk. But the same man did not quite sit behind the same desk.

Travis looked around swiftly.

"Everything okay here?" he snapped.

"Fine. Welcome home!"

Travis did not relax. He seemed to be looking at the very atoms of the air itself, at the way the sun poured through the one high window.

"Okay, Eckels, get out. Don't ever come back."

Eckels could not move.

"You heard me," said Travis. "What're you *staring* at?"

Eckels stood smelling of the air, and there was a thing

*Pause* **&** **Reflect**

1. Reread the boxed passage on page 40. **Summarize** the reasons Travis gives for leaving Eckels behind.

_____

_____

_____

MARK IT UP 2. Circle the passage on page 40 that explains why Travis made Eckels return to the dinosaur. **(Clarify)**

3. Do you think Travis made the right decision in allowing Eckels to return with the group, even though he stepped off the Path? *Yes/No*, because _____

_____

_____

_____

**(Make Judgments)**

to the air, a chemical <u>taint</u> so subtle, so slight, that only a faint cry of his <u>subliminal</u> senses warned him it was there. The colors, white, gray, blue, orange, in the wall, in the furniture, in the sky beyond the window, were . . . were . . . And there was a *feel*. His flesh twitched. His hands twitched. He stood drinking the oddness with the pores of his body. Somewhere, someone must have been screaming one of those whistles that only a dog can hear. His body screamed
**470** silence in return. Beyond this room, beyond this wall, beyond this man who was not quite the same man seated at this desk that was not quite the same desk . . . lay an entire world of streets and people. What sort of world it was now, there was no telling. He could feel them moving there, beyond the walls, almost, like so many chess pieces blown in a dry wind. . . .

But the immediate thing was the sign painted on the office wall, the same sign he had read earlier today on first entering. Somehow, the sign had changed:
**480** TYME SEFARI INC.

SEFARIS TU ANY YEER EN THE PAST.

YU NAIM THE ANIMALL.

WEE TAEKYUTHAIR.

YU SHOOT ITT.

Eckels felt himself fall into a chair. He fumbled crazily at the thick slime on his boots. He held up a clod of dirt, trembling, "No, it *can't* be. Not a *little* thing like that. No!"

Embedded in the mud, glistening green and gold and black, was a butterfly, very beautiful and very dead.
**490** "Not a little thing like *that!* Not a butterfly!" cried Eckels.

It fell to the floor, an exquisite thing, a small thing that could upset balances and knock down a line of small dominoes and then big dominoes and then gigantic dominoes, all down the years across Time. Eckels's mind whirled. It *couldn't* change things. Killing one butterfly couldn't be *that* important! Could it?

His face was cold. His mouth trembled, asking: "Who— who won the presidential election yesterday?"

The man behind the desk laughed. "You joking? You know
**500** very well. Deutscher, of course! Who else? Not that fool

---

✎ **MARK IT UP** WORD POWER

Remember to mark words that you'd like to add to your **Personal Word List.** Later, you can record the words and their meanings beginning on page 316.

---

WORDS TO KNOW

**taint** (tānt) *n.* a trace of something that harms, spoils or corrupts

**subliminal** (sŭb-lĭm′ə-nəl) *adj.* below the level of awareness; subconscious

weakling Keith. We got an iron man now, a man with guts!"
The official stopped. "What's wrong?"

Eckels moaned. He dropped to his knees. He scrabbled at the golden butterfly with shaking fingers. "Can't we," he pleaded to the world, to himself, to the officials, to the Machine, "can't we take it *back*; can't we *make* it alive again? Can't we start over? Can't we—"

He did not move. Eyes shut, he waited, shivering. He heard Travis breathe loud in the room; he heard Travis shift his rifle, 510 click the safety catch, and raise the weapon.

There was a sound of thunder.

Pause & Reflect

**Pause & Reflect**

**MARK IT UP** 1. Look at the details you circled as you read. Star the one detail that seems most important. **(Evaluate)**

2. What caused the world to change? **(Cause and Effect)**

_____

_____

_____

_____

3. What do you think is the main reason Travis shoots Eckels? **(Infer)**

_____

_____

_____

_____

**CHALLENGE**

A work of fiction does not directly express an author's views about a subject. However, fiction may indirectly suggest an **author's attitude.** Based on this story, how does Bradbury view nature? Mark details that suggest Bradbury's attitudes toward nature.

**Wrapping Up**

If you are using *The Language of Literature,* you can now move to the questions and activities on pages 82–83 of that book.

# Active Reading SkillBuilder

## Predicting

**Prediction** involves using text clues to make a reasonable guess about what will happen in a story. Sometimes your predictions will miss the mark. Other times, you'll recognize foreshadowing or other clues in a story and be able to make accurate predictions. As you read this story, use the chart below to record your predictions together with the clues on which you based them. An example is given.

### What Will Happen Next?

| Text Clues | Predictions |
|---|---|
| "We guarantee nothing" (line 17) | Eckels may not come back alive. |
| | |
| | |
| | |

# Literary Analysis SkillBuilder

## Foreshadowing

**Foreshadowing** is a device a writer uses to prepare a reader for an event that happens later in a story. The use of foreshadowing also adds suspense. Foreshadowing takes the form of hints—bits of information that suggest what is coming. Review the story to find examples of foreshadowing. Record your findings in the chart below. An example is given.

| Hint | Outcome |
|---|---|
| *"If you disobey instructions . . ." (lines 20–21)* | *Eckels disobeys instructions.* |
|  |  |
|  |  |
|  |  |

**Follow Up:** Discuss foreshadowing hints with other students to discover ones you may have missed. How does foreshadowing add to the suspense?

# Words to Know SkillBuilder

## Words to Know

| | | | | |
|---|---|---|---|---|
| annihilate | infinitesimally | resilient | sheathed | taint |
| expendable | primeval | revoke | subliminal | undulate |

**A.** On each blank line, write the word from the word list that the rhyme describes.

The sword-fight audience was bored,
For this described each fighter's sword.

_____
(1)

If you tell your boss to go jump in the ocean,
This may be what she'll do to your promotion.

_____
(2)

They say a rotten apple puts the other ones in peril,
So this is what that rotten one does when it's in the barrel.

_____
(3)

If your backpack is too heavy, here's a rule:
Don't take whatever this describes to school.

_____
(4)

This is what exterminators try to do to bugs,
Gardeners to weeds, and the narcotics squad to drugs.

_____
(5)

If you've been ill and this is how much better you have gotten,
You have improved a tiny bit, but you're still feeling rotten.

_____
(6)

Dancers may do this while making movements like the motion
Of the grass upon the prairie or the water in the ocean.

_____
(7)

If this describes your fear, you can't beware,
Since you don't even know your fear is there!

_____
(8)

I wrote about the history of Earth, and now I'm done.
I used this word a *lot* while I was writing Chapter 1.

_____
(9)

Because it's this, a rubber ball,
From any height you let it fall,
Will not give up its shape at all
(Though I'll say voluntarily,
It flattens temporarily).

_____
(10)

**B.** Write several warning signs that you think should have been posted along the
Path described in "A Sound of Thunder." Use at least **four** of the Words to Know.

# DIAL VERSUS DIGITAL

## Isaac Asimov

**Before You Read**

If you are using *The Language of Literature* . . .

- Use the information on page 108 of that book to prepare for reading.

- Look at the art on page 109. What can you predict about the topic of this essay?

**Reading Tips**

As you know, reading **nonfiction** is a different experience than reading fiction. Usually, you have to read slower. You also need to always be on the look out for **main ideas** and **supporting details**.

An **expository essay** is a type of nonfiction that explains a subject. In the following essay, the author examines a simple technological change (a cause) and explains its possible effects. As you read, look for clues that tell how the author feels about the change and its effects.

**PREVIEW** Isaac Asimov wrote thousands of essays and science fiction stories about technological changes large and small, real and imaginary. In this **essay**, Asimov shares his concerns about a technological change that is taking place—the shift from dial clocks to digital clocks.

**FOCUS ON**

Asimov discusses the change from dial clocks to digital clocks.

**MARK IT UP** As you read, circle sentences that reveal how Asimov feels about the change and its possible effects. An example is highlighted.

**MARK IT UP** KEEP TRACK

As you read, you can use these marks to keep track of your understanding.

✔ ..... I understand.

? ..... I don't understand this.

! ..... Interesting or surprising idea

**There seems no question** but that the clock dial, which has existed in its present form since the Seventeenth Century and in earlier forms since ancient times, is on the way out. More common today are digital clocks, which mark off the hours, minutes, and seconds in changing numbers. This certainly seems an advance in

10 technology. People no longer will have to interpret the meaning of "the big hand on the 11 and the little hand on the 5"; digital clocks will indicate at once that it is 4:55.

And yet there will be a loss in the conversion of dial to digital, and few people seem to be worrying about it.

When something turns, it can turn in just one of two ways, either *clockwise* or *counterclockwise*, and we all know which is which. Clockwise is the turning direction of the hands of a clock, and counterclockwise is the opposite of that. Since throughout the day we often stare at clocks
20 (dial clocks that is), we have no trouble in following directions or descriptions that include those words.

But if dial clocks disappear, so will the meaning of those words for anyone who never has stared at anything but digitals. There are no good substitutes for clockwise or counterclockwise. The nearest you can come is by a consideration of your hands. If you clench your fists with your thumbs pointing at your chest and look at your forefingers, you will see that the forefinger of your right hand curves counterclockwise from knuckle to tip, while the
30 forefinger of your left hand curves clockwise. You can then talk about a right-hand twist and a left-hand twist. But people don't stare at their hands the way they stare at clocks, and this will never be an adequate substitute.

Nor is this a minor matter. Astronomers define the north pole and south pole of any rotating body in such terms. If you are hovering above a pole of rotation and the body is rotating counterclockwise, it is the north pole; if it is rotating clockwise, it is the south pole. Astronomers also speak of direct motion and retrograde motion, by which
40 they mean counterclockwise and clockwise, respectively.

Here is another example. Suppose you are looking through a microscope at some object on a slide, or through a telescope at some view in the sky. In either case you may wish to point out something to a colleague. "Notice that object at 11 o'clock," you may say—or 5 o'clock, or 2 o'clock, or whatever.

Everyone knows the location of any number from 1 to 12 on the clock dial and easily can use such a reference to find an object.
50 Once the dial is gone, location by *o'clock* also will be gone, and there is no good substitute. Of course, you can use directions instead: northeast, southwest by south,

MARK IT UP WORD POWER

Mark words that you'd like to add to your **Personal Word List**. After reading, you can record the words and their meanings beginning on page 316.

and so on. However, this would assume you always know which direction is north. Or, if you are arbitrary[1] and decide to let north be straight ahead or straight up regardless of its real location, it still remains true that very few people are as familiar with a compass as they are with a clock face.

**Pause & Reflect**

**FOCUS**

60 Asimov presents one more effect before giving his conclusion.

**Here's still another point.** When children are learning to count, once they master the first few numbers, they quickly get the whole idea. You go from 0 to 9 and 0 to 9 over and over again. In other words, you go from 0 to 9, then from 10 to 19, then from 20 to 29, and so on until you reach 90 to 99, and then you pass on to 100, when the whole thing starts again. It is very systematic, and once you learn it you never forget.

Time is different. Since the early Sumerians[2] couldn't handle fractions very well, they chose 60 as their base
70 because it can be divided evenly in a number of ways. Ever since, we have continued to use 60 in certain applications, the chief of which is in the measurement of time. Thus, there are 60 minutes to an hour.

If you are using a dial, that doesn't matter. You simply note the position of the hands, and they automatically become a measure of time: "half past 5," "a quarter past 3," "a quarter to 10," and so on. You see time as space and not as numbers.

In a digital clock, however, time is measured only as
80 numbers, so you go from 1:01 to 1:59 and then move

---

1. **arbitrary** (är′bĭ-trĕr′ē): making a choice on the basis of what is convenient rather than what is reasonable or natural.

2. **Sumerians** (soo-mîr′ē-ənz): the people of one of the earliest human civilizations, which flourished from 5,000 to 4,000 years ago in the Middle East.

**Pause & Reflect**

1. Asimov identifies two ways in which our language about direction might change. In your own words, state these two effects of the switch from dial to digital. **(Cause and Effect)**

   1._____

   _____

   2._____

   _____

2. Look back at the sentences you circled as you read. How does Asimov feel about the switch from dial to digital? Star the word or phrase below that best describes his feelings.
   **(Author's Perspective)**

   positive

   negative

   both positive and negative

3. Do you agree that "There seems no question but that the clock dial . . . is on the way out"? Support your opinion. **(Evaluate)**

   _____

   _____

   _____

   _____

## Pause & Reflect

1. Circle the sentence below that best summarizes the third effect of digital clocks. **(Main Idea)**

In the future, there will be 100 minutes in an hour.

Digital clocks will change the way children learn and think about time.

2. Do you think that digital clocks cause problems in teaching children to tell time? **(Evaluate)**

_____
_____
_____
_____

✎ **MARK IT UP** 3. Underline the words that Asimov uses to signal the introduction of the third effect. Then go back and underline where Asimov introduces the previous two effects. **(Analyze Text Structure)**

✎ **CHALLENGE**

What is the most accurate way of measuring time? Using reference works, find out about the most scientifically accurate measurement device and how it works. **(Analyze Research)**

## Wrapping Up

If you are using **The Language of Literature,** you can now move to the questions and activities on pages 110–111 of that book.

directly to 2:00. It introduces an irregularity in the number system that is going to insert an unnecessary stumbling block into education. Just think: 5.50 is halfway between 5 and 6 if we measure length or weight or money or anything but time. In time, 5:50 is nearly 6; it is 5:30 that is halfway between 5 and 6.

What shall we do about all this? I can think of nothing. There is an odd conservatism[3] among people that will make them fight to the death against making time decimal and having 100 minutes to the hour.

But even so, what can be done about the lost meaning of clockwise, counterclockwise, and o'clock as points of reference? It will be a pretty problem for our descendants.

**Pause & Reflect**

3. **conservatism** (kən-sûr′və-tĭz′m): unwillingness to change.

# Active Reading SkillBuilder

### Analyzing Text Structure

Writers always choose a **text structure,** or pattern of organization, to present their information. Nonfiction writers can choose from a variety of structures and usually pick one that best fits their purpose for writing. In "Dial Versus Digital," for example, Asimov uses the cause-and-effect structure. He begins by discussing a cause—the loss of the dial clock—and proceeds by examining the effects that are likely to occur. As you read the selection, fill in the diagram below to help you identify each effect that Asimov predicts. An example is given.

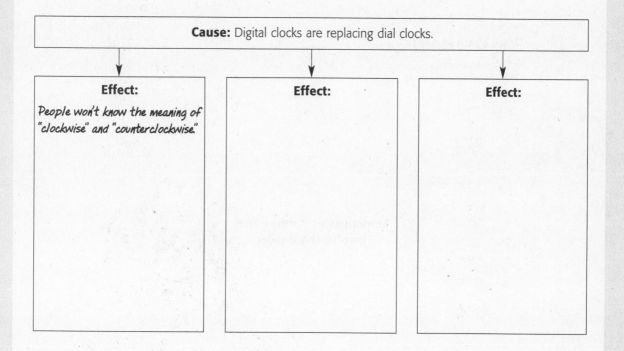

**Cause:** Digital clocks are replacing dial clocks.

**Effect:**
*People won't know the meaning of "clockwise" and "counterclockwise."*

**Effect:**

**Effect:**

# Literary Analysis SkillBuilder

## Expository Essay

An **expository essay** explains a particular subject with the purpose of helping the reader understand the subject more thoroughly. Like other types of essays, it gives information and often reveals the opinions of the writer. In the process of explaining information, authors often involve the reader. When reading this essay, look for ways that Asimov involves the reader—such as his use of the pronoun *you,* as if the reader were actually performing actions. In the chart below, write phrases or sentences that are examples of Asimov's involvement of the reader. An example is given.

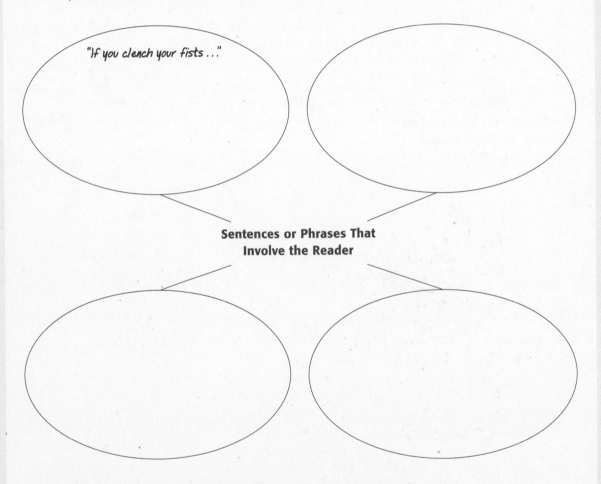

"If you clench your fists . . ."

**Sentences or Phrases That
Involve the Reader**

**Follow Up:** Asimov's expository essay focuses on how the loss of the dial on clocks may affect future society. With a group of classmates, brainstorm a list of other technological changes that Asimov might find worrisome.

# *Once More to the Lake*

## E. B. White

**PREVIEW** In this **personal essay**, E. B. White tells about going to a lake in Maine that he had often gone to as a child. Now, many years later, he is going there again with his son. He wonders how the lake may have changed since he last visited it.

**FOCUS**
White begins by telling us where he is going and why.

**MARK IT UP** As you read, circle details that tell how White feels about this particular lake. An example is highlighted.

*August 1941*

**One summer,** along about 1904, my father rented a camp[1] on a lake in Maine and took us all there for the month of August. We all got ringworm[2] from some kittens and had to rub Pond's Extract on our arms and legs night and morning, and my father rolled over in a canoe with all his clothes on; but outside of that the vacation was a success and from then on none of us ever thought there was any place in the world like that lake in Maine. We returned summer after summer— always on August 1 for one month. I have since become a salt-water man, but sometimes in summer there are days when the restlessness of the tides and the fearful cold of the seawater and the incessant wind that blows across the

10

**MARK IT UP** **KEEP TRACK**

As you read, you can use these marks to keep track of your understanding.

✔ ..... I understand.

? ..... I don't understand this.

! ..... Interesting or surprising idea

---

1. **camp:** a summer cottage.
2. **ringworm:** a contagious skin disease caused by a fungus that produces itchy, ring-shaped patches.

**ESSAY**

### Before You Read
If you are using *The Language of Literature*...

- Use the information on page 112 of that book to prepare for reading.

- Look at the art on pages 113, 115, and 118. What do these paintings tell you about the **setting** of the essay?

### Reading Tips
**Personal essays** reflect the thoughts of the person who wrote them. In this essay, the author's thoughts and memories flow freely between the past and the present.

As you read, don't worry if you find it hard to separate the past and the present. Just watch for **details** that reveal the author's feelings about his experiences—both as a child and as an adult.

afternoon and into the evening make me wish for the placidity of a lake in the woods. A few weeks ago this feeling got so strong I bought myself a couple of bass hooks and a spinner and returned to the lake where we used to go, for a week's
**20** fishing and to revisit old <u>haunts</u>.

I took along my son, who had never had any fresh water up his nose and who had seen lily pads only from train windows. On the journey over to the lake I began to wonder what it would be like. I wondered how time would have marred this unique, this holy spot—the coves and streams, the hills that the sun set behind, the camps and the paths behind the camps. I was sure that the tarred road would have found it out, and I wondered in what other ways it would be desolated. It is strange how much you can remember about places like that
**30** once you allow your mind to return into the grooves that lead back. You remember one thing, and that suddenly reminds you of another thing. I guess I remembered clearest of all the early mornings, when the lake was cool and motionless, remembered how the bedroom smelled of the lumber it was made of and of the wet woods whose scent entered through the screen. The partitions in the camp were thin and did not extend clear to the top of the rooms, and as I was always the first up I would dress softly so as not to wake the others, and sneak out into the sweet outdoors and start out in the canoe, keeping close
**40** along the shore in the long shadows of the pines. I remembered being very careful never to rub my paddle against the gunwale[3] for fear of disturbing the stillness of the cathedral.

The lake had never been what you would call a wild lake. There were cottages sprinkled around the shores, and it was in farming country although the shores of the lake were quite heavily wooded. Some of the cottages were owned by nearby farmers, and you would live at the shore and eat your meals at the farmhouse. That's what our family did. But although it wasn't wild, it was a fairly large and undisturbed lake and
**50** there were places in it that, to a child at least, seemed infinitely remote and primeval.

### Pause & Reflect

---

3. **gunwale** (gŭn′əl): the upper edge of the side of a boat.

WORDS
TO
KNOW    **haunt** (hônt) *n.* a place visited frequently

---

## Pause & Reflect

1. What do you learn about White's childhood visits to the lake? (Summarize)

_____

_____

_____

_____

2. Look back at the details you circled in the essay. Cross out the word below that does *not* describe White's view of the lake. (Infer)

beautiful            unique

dangerous          happy

3. What changes do you think White will find at the lake? (Predict)

_____

_____

_____

_____

FOCUS

White is about to arrive at the lake with his son.

MARK IT UP As you read, underline passages that tell about things that have stayed the same since his last visit.

**I was right about the tar:** it led to within half a mile of the shore. But when I got back there, with my boy, and we settled into a camp near a farmhouse and into the kind of summertime I had known, I could tell that it was going to be pretty much the same as it had been before—I knew it, lying in bed the first morning,

60 smelling the bedroom and hearing the boy sneak quietly out and go off along the shore in a boat. I began to sustain the illusion that he was I, and therefore, by simple transposition, that I was my father. This sensation persisted, kept cropping up all the time we were there. It was not an entirely new feeling, but in this setting it grew much stronger. I seemed to be living a dual existence. I would be in the middle of some simple act, I would be picking up a bait box or laying down a table fork, or I would be saying something, and suddenly it would be not I but my father who was saying the words or

70 making the gesture. It gave me a creepy sensation.

We went fishing the first morning. I felt the same damp moss covering the worms in the bait can, and saw the dragonfly alight on the tip of my rod as it hovered a few inches from the surface of the water. It was the arrival of this fly that convinced me beyond any doubt that everything was as it always had been, that the years were a mirage and that there had been no years. The small waves were the same, chucking the rowboat under the chin as we fished at anchor, and the boat was the same boat, the same color green and the

80 ribs broken in the same places, and under the floorboards the same freshwater leavings and débris—the dead hellgrammite,[4] the wisps of moss, the rusty discarded fishhook, the dried blood from yesterday's catch. We stared silently at the tips of our rods, at the dragonflies that came and went. I lowered the tip of mine into the water, <u>tentatively</u>, pensively dislodging the fly, which darted two feet away, poised, darted two feet back, and came to rest again a little farther up the rod. There had been no years between the ducking of this dragonfly and the other one—the one that was part of memory. I looked at the

READ ALOUD **Lines 61–70**

Reread the boxed passage. Why do you think White says, "I was my father"? **(Analyze)**

_____

_____

_____

_____

MARK IT UP WORD POWER

Mark words that you'd like to add to your **Personal Word List.** After reading, you can record the words and their meanings beginning on page 316.

---

4. **hellgrammite:** the larva of an insect, often used as fish bait.

WORDS
TO
KNOW    **tentatively** (tĕn′tə-tĭv-lē) *adv.* hesitantly; uncertainly

1. Look at the passages you underlined as you read. How does White feel when he finds so many things the same? **(Infer)**

_____

_____

_____

✏️ **MARK IT UP** 2. Writers often use **repetition** to make a point. Go back and star the three times White writes "there had been no years." What point is White making by repeating this phrase? **(Draw Conclusions)**

_____

_____

_____

_____

3. What do White and his son do on their first morning at the lake? **(Summarize)**

_____

_____

⑨⓪ boy, who was silently watching his fly, and it was my hands that held his rod, my eyes watching. I felt dizzy and didn't know which rod I was at the end of.

We caught two bass, hauling them in briskly as though they were mackerel, pulling them over the side of the boat in a businesslike manner without any landing net, and stunning them with a blow on the back of the head. When we got back for a swim before lunch, the lake was exactly where we had left it, the same number of inches from the dock, and there was only the merest suggestion of a breeze. This seemed an ⓵⓪⓪ utterly enchanted sea, this lake you could leave to its own devices for a few hours and come back to, and find that it had not stirred, this constant and trustworthy body of water. In the shallows, the dark, water-soaked sticks and twigs, smooth and old, were undulating in clusters on the bottom against the clean ribbed sand, and the track of the mussel was plain. A school of minnows swam by, each minnow with its small individual shadow, doubling the attendance, so clear and sharp in the sunlight. Some of the other campers were in swimming, along the shore, one of them with a cake of soap, ⓵⓵⓪ and the water felt thin and clear and unsubstantial. Over the years there had been this person with the cake of soap, this cultist, and here he was. There had been no years.

**Pause & Reflect**

**FOCUS**
White continues to remember the past and to note similarities and differences about the lake then and now.
✏️ **MARK IT UP** As you read, underline the differences White notices.

**Up to the farmhouse to dinner** through the teeming, dusty field, the road under our sneakers was only a two-track road. The middle track was missing, the one with the marks of the hooves and the splotches of dried, flaky manure. There had always been three tracks to choose from in choosing which track to walk ⓵②⓪ in; now the choice was narrowed down to two. For a moment I missed terribly the middle alternative. But the way led past the tennis court, and something about the way it lay there in the sun reassured me; the tape had loosened along the back line, the alleys were green with plantains and other weeds, and the net (installed in June and removed in September) sagged in the dry noon, and the whole place steamed with

midday heat and hunger and emptiness. There was a choice of
pie for dessert, and one was blueberry and one was apple, and
130　the waitresses were the same country girls, there having been
no passage of time, only the illusion of it as in a dropped
curtain—the waitresses were still fifteen; their hair had been
washed, that was the only difference—they had been to the
movies and seen the pretty girls with the clean hair.

Summertime, oh, summertime, pattern of life indelible, the
fade-proof lake, the woods unshatterable, the pasture with the
sweet fern and the juniper forever and ever, summer without
end; this was the background, and the life along the shore was
the design, the cottagers with their innocent and tranquil
140　design, their tiny docks with the flagpole and the American
flag floating against the white clouds in the blue sky, the little
paths over the roots of the trees leading from camp to camp
and the paths leading back to the outhouses and the can of
lime for sprinkling, and at the souvenir counters at the store
the miniature birch-bark canoes and the postcards that
showed things looking a little better than they looked.

This was the American family at play, escaping the city heat,
wondering whether the newcomers in the camp at the head of
the cove were "common" or "nice," wondering whether it
150　was true that the people who drove up for Sunday dinner at
the farmhouse were turned away because there wasn't
enough chicken.

It seemed to me, as I kept remembering all this, that those
times and those summers had been infinitely precious and
worth saving. There had been jollity and peace and goodness.
The arriving (at the beginning of August) had been so big a
business in itself, at the railway station the farm wagon drawn
up, the first smell of the pine-laden air, the first glimpse of the
smiling farmer, and the great importance of the trunks and
160　your father's enormous authority in such matters, and the feel
of the wagon under you for the long ten-mile haul, and at the
top of the last long hill catching the first view of the lake after
eleven months of not seeing this cherished body of water. The
shouts and cries of the other campers when they saw you, and
the trunks to be unpacked, to give up their rich burden.
(Arriving was less exciting nowadays, when you sneaked up in
your car and parked it under a tree near the camp and took

> **READ ALOUD** Lines 135–146
>
> Read the boxed passage aloud in
> different ways—fast and slow, or
> soft and loud, or with different
> pauses and emphasis. Which
> reading seems to work best?
> **(Draw Conclusions)**

> **MARK IT UP** **KEEP TRACK**
>
> Remember to use these marks to
> keep track of your understanding.
>
> ✔ ..... I understand.
>
> ? ..... I don't understand this.
>
> ! ..... Interesting or surprising
> idea

WORDS
TO
KNOW
**indelible** (ĭn-děl'ə-bəl) *adj.* impossible to remove or
eliminate; permanent

out the bags and in five minutes it was all over, no fuss, no loud wonderful fuss about trunks.)

170   Peace and goodness and jollity. The only thing that was wrong now, really, was the sound of the place, an unfamiliar nervous sound of the outboard motors. This was the note that jarred, the one thing that would sometimes break the illusion and set the years moving. In those other summertimes all motors were inboard; and when they were at a little distance, the noise they made was a sedative, an ingredient of summer sleep. They were one-cylinder and two-cylinder engines, and some were make-and-break and some were jump-spark, but they all made a sleepy sound across the lake. The one-lungers

180   throbbed and fluttered, and the twin-cylinder ones purred and purred, and that was a quiet sound, too. But now the campers all had outboards. In the daytime, in the hot mornings, these motors made a <u>petulant,</u> irritable sound; at night, in the still evening when the afterglow lit the water, they whined about one's ears like mosquitoes. My boy loved our rented outboard, and his great desire was to achieve single-handed mastery over it, and authority, and he soon learned the trick of choking it a little (but not too much), and the adjustment of the needle valve. Watching him I would remember the

190   things you could do with the old one-cylinder engine with the heavy flywheel, how you could have it eating out of your hand if you got really close to it spiritually. Motorboats in those days didn't have clutches, and you would make a landing by shutting off the motor at the proper time and coasting in with a dead rudder. But there was a way of reversing them, if you learned the trick, by cutting the switch and putting it on again exactly on the final dying revolution of the flywheel, so that it would kick back against compression and begin reversing. Approaching a dock in a

200   strong following breeze, it was difficult to slow up sufficiently by the ordinary coasting method, and if a boy felt he had complete mastery over his motor, he was tempted to keep it running beyond its time and then reverse it a few feet from the dock. It took a cool nerve, because if you threw the switch a twentieth of a second too soon you would catch the flywheel when it still had speed enough to go up past center, and the boat would leap ahead, charging bull fashion at the dock.

> ✎ **MARK IT UP** WORD POWER
>
> Remember to mark words that you'd like to add to your **Personal Word List**. Later, you can record the words and their meanings beginning on page 316.

WORDS TO KNOW

**petulant** (pĕch′ə-lənt) *adj.* showing unreasonable annoyance over little things

We had a good week at the camp. The bass were biting well and the sun shone endlessly, day after day. We would be tired
**210** at night and lie down in the accumulated heat of the little bedrooms after the long hot day and the breeze would stir almost imperceptibly outside and the smell of the swamp drift in through the rusty screens. Sleep would come easily and in the morning the red squirrel would be on the roof, tapping out his gay routine. I kept remembering everything, lying in bed in the mornings—the small steamboat that had a long rounded stern like the lip of a Ubangi,[5] and how quietly she ran on the moonlight sails, when the older boys played their mandolins and the girls sang and we ate doughnuts dipped in
**220** sugar, and how sweet the music was on the water in the shining night, and what it had felt like to think about girls then. After breakfast we would go up to the store and the things were in the same place—the minnows in a bottle, the plugs and spinners disarranged and pawed over by the youngsters from the boys' camp, the Fig Newtons and the Beeman's gum. Outside, the road was tarred and cars stood in front of the store. Inside, all was just as it had always been, except there was more Coca-Cola and not so much Moxie and root beer and birch beer and sarsaparilla. We would walk
**230** out with the bottle of pop apiece and sometimes the pop would backfire up our noses and hurt. We explored the streams, quietly, where the turtles slid off the sunny logs and dug their way into the soft bottom; and we lay on the town wharf and fed worms to the tame bass. Everywhere we went I had trouble making out which was I, the one walking at my side, the one walking in my pants.

### Pause & Reflect

**FOCUS**
A storm suddenly comes up at the lake.
**MARK IT UP** As you
**240** read, underline passages that describe how this storm is the same as ones in White's childhood.

**One afternoon while we were there** at that lake a thunderstorm came up. It was like the revival of an old melodrama that I had seen long ago with childish awe. The second-act climax of the drama of the electrical disturbance over a lake in America had not changed in

### Pause & Reflect

1. Look back at the passages you underlined as you read. List three of the differences between the past and the present. **(Compare and Contrast)**

_____

_____

_____

_____

**MARK IT UP** 2. Which difference between the past and present bothers White the most? Star the passage on page 58 that explains this. **(Evaluate)**

3. Why do you think the summer means so much to White? **(Draw Conclusions)**

_____

_____

_____

_____

---

5. **Ubangi** (yoo-băng′gē): a woman of a people living near the Ubangi River in Africa, with pierced lips enlarged by saucerlike disks.

1. Review the passages you
   underlined. How does White
   seem to feel about this
   thunderstorm? **(Infer)**

   _____

   _____

   _____

2. The children "scream with
   delight" when they go swimming
   in the rain, but White feels "the
   chill of death." What does he
   mean by this? **(Infer)**

   _____

   _____

   _____

3. Would you have liked to have
   gone on this trip to the lake with
   White and his son? **(Connect)**

   _____

   _____

   _____

CHALLENGE

How would you describe
White's **style?** Mark one
passage that seems typical of
White's style, and describe it.
Think about elements of style
such as word choice, sentence
length, tone, and the use of
figurative language.

## Wrapping Up

If you are using **The Language
of Literature**, you can now
move to the questions and
activities on pages 120–123
of that book.

any important respect. This was the big scene, still the big
scene. The whole thing was so familiar, the first feeling of
oppression and heat and a general air around camp of not
wanting to go very far away. In midafternoon (it was all the
same) a curious darkening of the sky, and a lull in everything
that had made life tick; and then the way the boats suddenly
250 swung the other way at their moorings with the coming of a
breeze out of the new quarter, and the premonitory rumble.
Then the kettledrum, then the snare, then the bass drum and
cymbals, then crackling light against the dark, and the gods
grinning and licking their chops in the hills. Afterward the
calm, the rain steadily rustling in the calm lake, the return of
light and hope and spirits, and the campers running out in joy
and relief to go swimming in the rain, their bright cries
perpetuating the deathless joke about how they were getting
simply drenched, and the children screaming with delight at
260 the new sensation of bathing in the rain, and the joke about
getting drenched linking the generations in a strong
indestructible chain. And the comedian who waded in
carrying an umbrella.

When the others went swimming, my son said he was going
in, too. He pulled his dripping trunks from the line where they
had hung all through the shower and wrung them out.
Languidly, and with no thought of going in, I watched him,
his hard little body, skinny and bare, saw him wince slightly
as he pulled up around his vitals the small, soggy, icy garment.
270 As he buckled the swollen belt, suddenly my groin felt the
chill of death.

**Pause** **&** **Reflect**

WORDS
TO
KNOW

**languidly** (lăng′gwĭd-lē) _adv._ without vigor or
energy; listlessly

# Active Reading SkillBuilder

### Identifying Comparison and Contrast

**Comparison and contrast** is a device used by a writer to identify similarities and differences between two things. In this essay, E. B. White compares his childhood vacations in Maine with a vacation in the present with his own son. While reading this essay, find events and experiences from White's childhood at the Maine lake that compare and contrast with his trip to the lake with his son. Look for words or phrases that signal comparison, such as *same, just as, still,* and *always.* Notice also words or phrases that signal contrast, such as *since, difference, now, nowadays, in those days, more,* and *not so much.* Fill in the Venn diagram below to show the differences and similarites between White's childhood and adult experiences on the Maine lake. Examples are given.

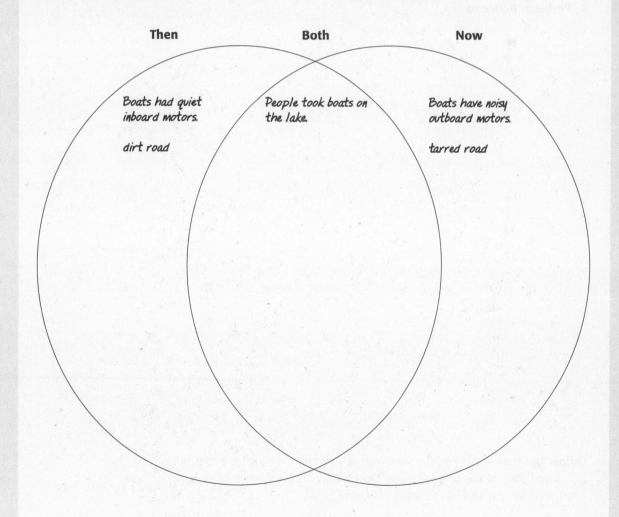

Then        Both        Now

Boats had quiet inboard motors.

dirt road

People took boats on the lake.

Boats have noisy outboard motors.

tarred road

# Literary Analysis SkillBuilder

## Personal Essay

A **personal essay** is a brief nonfiction work that expresses the writer's thoughts, feelings, and opinions on events and issues in his or her own life. Some personal essays focus more on reflections or ideas than on a narrative, or account, of events. Many deal with both. Review this essay and examine how much White uses personal reflection and how much he describes events. Divide the circle shown below into a pie chart that shows the proportion of reflection to narration within the essay. Use the labels that are listed above the circle.

**Actual Events Described**

**Personal Reflection**

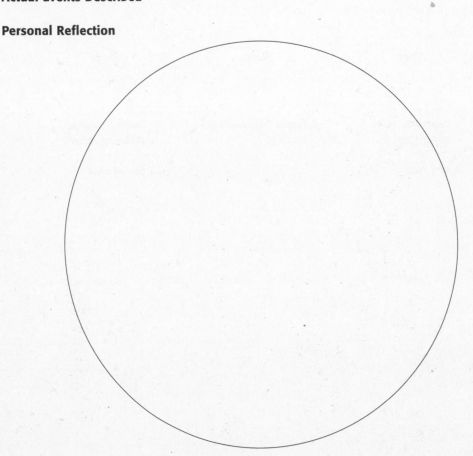

**Follow Up:** Think about how the proportion you showed on your chart contributes to the total effect of this personal essay. Discuss how the piece might have been different if White had used less personal reflection.

# Words to Know SkillBuilder

**Words to Know**

haunt    indelible    languidly    petulant    tentatively

**A.** Fill in each blank with the correct word from the word list.

1. Four kinds of detergent and three kinds of bleach couldn't get the blueberry stains off my shirt. That fruit is one _____ edible!

2. I told Dad about describing a character in English class. "I was trying to say that she was sullen, cross, and irritable, so I said she was petty." "Ah," said Dad. "I'll bet you meant _____."

3. The café on Main Street has many regulars, people who come in every morning for coffee and conversation. I think I'll become a regular, since I, too, want a _____.

4. Bernie has no confidence in his views. Tell him ten-year-olds should be allowed to drive and he'll say, "Well, I'm not sure . . . after all . . . " He drives me nuts; he's so _____ argumentative.

5. Missy was fishing, but not in a lively way. She sat lazily on the bridge, with a pole in her hands and her legs _____ dangling.

**B.** On the blank line next to each group of phrases, write the word from the word list that seems to go with each set of clues.

1. out of steam; loafing around; no get-up-and-go; at a snail's pace; no ball of fire

_____
(1)

2. here to stay; won't wash out; a lasting impression; written in stone

_____
(2)

3. touchy; on edge; out of sorts; with one's teeth on edge; cranky, crabby, and cross

_____
(3)

4. testing the water; hanging back; torn between; sitting on the fence; blowing hot and cold

_____
(4)

5. for die-hard fans, the ballpark; for shopaholics, the mall; for league bowlers, an alley

_____
(5)

**C.** Write a postcard message that White might have sent to a friend during his stay at the lake with his son. Use at least **two** of the Words to Know.

## Before You Read

If you are using *The Language of Literature*, study the information on page 170 of that book to prepare for reading.

## Reading Tips

The authors of the following two **essays** draw upon their experience of living in two worlds. Both authors rely on **comparison and contrast** to organize their materials.

- As you read each essay, look for similarities and differences between the two nations or cultures described.

- Look for **details** that tell you how each author feels about her subject.

---

**MARK IT UP** **KEEP TRACK**

As you read, you can use these marks to keep track of your understanding.

✔ ..... I understand.

? ..... I don't understand this.

! ..... Interesting or surprising idea

---

# THROUGH THE ONE-WAY MIRROR

## Margaret Atwood

**PREVIEW** In this essay, Canadian author Margaret Atwood compares the border between the United States and Canada to a one-way mirror. Canadians are always studying America, but Americans seem unaware of Canadians—or anyone else. Atwood finds this to be an interesting and amusing situation.

**FOCUS**

In the opening paragraphs, Atwood describes some major differences between Canadians and Americans.

**MARK IT UP** As you read, underline at least two statements Atwood makes about Americans. Do the same for the Canadians. An example is highlighted.

**The noses of a great many Canadians** resemble Porky Pig's. This comes from spending so much time pressing them against the longest undefended one-way mirror in the world. The Canadians looking through this mirror behave the way people on the hidden side of such mirrors usually do: they observe, <u>analyze,</u> ponder, snoop and wonder what all the activity on the other side means in decipherable human terms.

The Americans, bless their innocent little hearts, are rarely aware that they are even being watched, much less by the Canadians. They just go on doing body language, playing in the sandbox of the world, bashing one another on the head and planning how to blow things up, same as always. If they

WORDS TO KNOW

**analyze** (ăn′ə-līz′) *v.* to study carefully by separating into parts

think about Canada at all, it's only when things get a bit snowy or the water goes off or the Canadians start fussing over some piddly detail, such as fish.[1] Then they regard them as unpatriotic; for Americans don't really see Canadians as foreigners, not like the Mexicans, unless they do something weird like speak French or beat the New York Yankees at baseball. Really, think the Americans, the Canadians are just like us, or would be if they could.

Or we could switch metaphors and call the border the longest undefended backyard fence in the world. The Canadians are the folks in the neat little bungalow, with the tidy little garden and the duck pond. The Americans are the other folks, the ones in the sprawly mansion with the bad-taste statues on the lawn. There's a perpetual party, or something, going on there—loud music, <u>raucous</u> laughter, smoke billowing from the barbecue. Beer bottles and Coke cans land among the peonies. The Canadians have their own beer bottles and barbecue smoke, but they tend to overlook it. Your own mess is always more forgivable than the mess someone else makes on your patio.

The Canadians can't exactly call the police—they suspect that the Americans are the police—and part of their distress, which seems permanent, comes from their uncertainty as to whether or not they've been invited. Sometimes they do drop by next door, and find it exciting but scary. Sometimes the Americans drop by their house and find it clean. This worries the Canadians. They worry a lot. Maybe those Americans want to buy up their duck pond, with all the money they seem to have, and turn it into a cesspool or a water-skiing emporium.

It also worries them that the Americans don't seem to know who the Canadians are, or even where, exactly, they are. Sometimes the Americans call Canada their backyard, sometimes their front yard, both of which imply ownership. Sometimes they say they are the Mounties and the Canadians

📖 **READ ALOUD** Lines 26–37

Read aloud the boxed passage. With your voice, express the frustration and amusement Atwood feels about the American "neighbors." **(Tone)**

✏️ **MARK IT UP** WORD POWER

Mark words that you'd like to add to your **Personal Word List.** After reading, you can record the words and their meanings beginning on page 316.

---

1. **some piddly . . . fish:** a reference to the occasional clashes between U.S. and Canadian fishers over the boundaries of their fishing territories.

WORDS
TO
KNOW

**raucous** (rô′kəs) *adj.* loud and disorderly; boisterous

**1.** Why does Atwood say that "the noses of a great many Canadians resemble Porky Pig's"? **(Clarify)**

_____

_____

_____

_____

**2.** Review the passages you underlined as you read. Put a *C* next to the phrases below that describe Canadians and an *A* next to those that describe Americans. **(Compare and Contrast)**

loud and messy

clean and tidy

tend to worry

unaware of being watched

are Rose Marie.[2] (All these things have, in fact, been said by American politicians.) Then they accuse the Canadians of being paranoid and having an identity crisis. Heck, there is no call for the Canadians to fret about their identity, because everyone knows they're Americans, really. If the Canadians disagree with that, they're told not to be so insecure.

One of the problems is that Canadians and Americans are
60 educated backward from one another. The Canadians—except for the Québecois,[3] one keeps saying—are taught about the rest of the world first and Canada second. The Americans are taught about the United States first, and maybe later about other places, if they're of strategic importance. The Vietnam War draft dodgers got more culture shock in Canada than they did in Sweden. It's not the clothing that is different, it's those mental noises.

*Pause* **&** *Reflect*

**FOCUS**

70 In the next part of her essay, Atwood turns to larger world issues. Though Canada and the United States are allies, the two countries sometimes disagree.

**Of course, none of this holds true** when you get close enough, where concepts like "Americans" and "Canadians" dissolve and people are just people, or anyway some of them are, the ones you happen to approve of. I, for instance, have never met any Americans I didn't like, but I only get to meet the nice ones. That's what the businessmen think too, though they have other individuals in mind. But big-scale national mythologies have a way of showing up in things like foreign policy, and at events like international writers' congresses,
80 where the Canadians often find they have more to talk about with the Australians, the West Indians, the New Zealanders[4] and even the once-loathed snooty Brits, now declining into

---

2. **Mounties . . . Rose Marie:** a reference to the 1926 operetta *Rose Marie* (later the basis of a popular film starring Nelson Eddy and Jeanette MacDonald), in which the main characters are a Royal Canadian Mounted Policeman and the woman he loves.

3. **Québecois** (kā′bĕ-kwä′): the French-speaking residents of the Canadian province of Quebec.

4. **Australians . . . New Zealanders:** peoples whose countries were, like Canada, once part of the British Empire.

humanity with the dissolution of empire, than they do with the <u>impenetrable</u> and mysterious Yanks.

But only sometimes. Because surely the Canadians understand the Yanks. Shoot, don't they see Yank movies, read Yank mags, bobble around to Yank music and watch Yank telly, as well as their own, when there is any?

Sometimes the Canadians think it's their job to interpret the
90 Yanks to the rest of the world; explain them, sort of. This is an illusion: they don't understand the Yanks as much as they think they do, and it isn't their job.

But, as we say up here among God's frozen people, when Washington catches a cold, Ottawa sneezes. Some Canadians even refer to their capital city as Washington North and wonder why we're paying those guys in Ottawa when a telephone order service would be cheaper. Canadians make jokes about the relationship with Washington which the Americans, in their thin-skinned, bunion-toed way, <u>construe</u> as
100 anti-American (they tend to see any nonworshipful comment coming from that gray, protoplasmic fuzz outside their borders as anti-American). They are no more anti-American than the jokes Canadians make about the weather: it's there, it's big, it's hard to influence, and it affects your life.

Of course, in any conflict with the Dreaded Menace, whatever it might be, the Canadians would line up with the Yanks, probably, if they thought it was a real menace, or if the Yanks twisted their arms or other bodily parts enough or threatened a "scorched-earth policy" (another real quote).
110 Note the qualifiers. The Canadian idea of a menace is not the same as the U.S. one. Canada, for instance, never broke off diplomatic relations with Cuba, and it was quick to recognize China. Contemplating the U.S.-Soviet growling match, Canadians are apt to recall a line from Blake[5]: "They became what they beheld." Certainly both superpowers suffer from the imperial diseases once so noteworthy among the Romans, the British and the French: arrogance and <u>myopia.</u> But the

5. **Blake:** the British poet and artist William Blake.

WORDS TO KNOW

**impenetrable** (ĭm-pĕn′ĭ-trə-bəl) *adj.* impossible to understand; incapable of being pierced
**construe** (kən-strōō′) *v.* to interpret
**myopia** (mī-ō′pē-ə) *n.* nearsightedness

**MARK IT UP**

**1.** Atwood says that "concepts like 'Americans' and 'Canadians' dissolve" when people get close enough. Circle a passage on page 66 that supports her opinion. **(Logical Argument)**

**2.** Check the sentence below that best reflects Atwood's views. **(Make Generalizations)**

Canadians and Americans often don't understand one another.

Canadians always understand Americans.

The two countries have an equal relationship.

**3.** What is Atwood really saying when she says Americans have Mr. Magoo eyes? **(Paraphrase)**

_____

_____

_____

_____

bodily-parts threat is real enough, and accounts for the observable wimpiness and flunkiness of some Ottawa
120 politicians. Nobody, except at welcoming-committee time, pretends this is an equal relationship.

Americans don't have Porky Pig noses. Instead they have Mr. Magoo eyes, with which they see the rest of the world. That would not be a problem if the United States were not so powerful. But it is, so it is.

*Pause* & Reflect

# The Border
## A Glare of Truth

### Pat Mora

**PREVIEW** The author of this essay is a Mexican American who has lived most of her life in the border town of El Paso, Texas. When she wrote this essay, she had recently moved to Ohio. The move caused her to explore her feelings about the two places.

**FOCUS**
Mora begins by describing how she felt about moving away from El Paso.
**MARK IT UP** As you read, circle details about the things that Mora misses. An example is highlighted.

**I moved away** for the first time from the U.S.-Mexican border in the fall of 1989. Friends were sure I'd miss the visible evidence of Mexico's <u>proximity</u> found in cities such as my native El Paso. Friends smiled that I'd soon be back for good Mexican food, for the delicate taste and smell of cilantro,[1] for soft tortillas freshly made. There were jokes about care packages flying to the Midwest.

Although most of my adult home and work life had been spent speaking English, I was prepared to miss the sound of Spanish weaving in and out of my days like the warm aroma from a familiar bakery. I knew I'd miss the pleasure of moving back and forth between two languages—a pleasure that can

**MARK IT UP** **KEEP TRACK**
As you read, you can use these marks to keep track of your understanding.
✔ ..... I understand.
? ..... I don't understand this.
! ..... Interesting or surprising idea

---

1. **cilantro** (sē-län'trô) *Spanish:* coriander—an herb whose leaves are used as a seasoning.

WORDS
TO
KNOW     **proximity** (prŏk-sĭm'ĭ-tē) *n.* closeness

deepen human understanding and increase our <u>versatility</u> conceptually as well as linguistically.

And indeed, when I hear a phrase in Spanish in a Cincinnati restaurant, my head turns quickly. I listen, silently
20 wishing to be part of that other conversation, if only for a few moments, to feel Spanish in my mouth. I'm reading more poetry in Spanish, sometimes reading the lines aloud to myself, enjoying sounds I don't otherwise hear. Recently I heard a voice on National Public Radio say that learning another language is renaming the world. What an interesting perception. Because language shapes as well as reflects our reality, exploring it allows us to see and to explore our world anew, much as experiencing the world with a young child causes us to pause, savor.

30 I smile when my children, who were too busy when they were younger, now inform me that when they visit they hope we'll be speaking Spanish. They have discovered as I did that languages are channels, sometimes to other people, sometimes to other views of the world, sometimes to other aspects of ourselves. So we struggle with irregular verbs, laughing together.

Is it my family—children, parents, siblings, niece, nephews—that I miss in this land of leaves so unlike my bare desert? Of course, but my family, although miles away, is with
40 me daily. The huge telephone bills and the steady stream of letters and cards are a long-distance version of the web of caring we once created around kitchen tables. Our family web just happens to stretch across these United States, a sturdy, elastic web steadily maintained by each in his or her own way.

Oh, I miss the meals seasoned with that family phrase, "Remember the time when . . . ?" But I've learned through the years to cherish our gatherings when I'm in the thick of them, to sink into the faces and voices, to store the memories and stories like the industrious Ohio squirrel outside my window
50 stores her treasures.

*Pause* **&** **Reflect**

*Pause* **&** **Reflect**

**1.** What did Mora's friends tell her she would miss when she moved away from El Paso? **(Clarify)**

_____

_____

_____

**2.** Review the passages that you circled as you read. What does Mora miss about living near the border? **(Summarize)**

_____

_____

_____

_____

**MARK IT UP** **3.** Mora thinks that having two languages is better than having only one. Put a star next to the passages that tell her reasons for feeling this way. **(Analyze)**

WORDS
TO
KNOW

**versatility** (vûr′sə-tĭl′ĭ-tē) *n.* an ability to do many things well

**FOCUS**

In this section, Mora further explains what she misses about living on the border.

**MARK IT UP** As you read, underline any details that help you to understand what Mora values about her heritage.

**I've enjoyed this furry,** scurrying companion as I've enjoyed the silence of bare tree limbs against an evening sky, updrafts of snow outside our third-floor window, the ivory light of cherry blossoms. I feel fortunate to be experiencing the geographical center of this country, which <u>astutely</u> calls itself the Heartland. If I'm hearing the "heart," its steady, predictable rhythms, what am I

60 missing from this country's southern border, its margin?

Is it other rhythms? I remember my mixed feelings as a young girl whenever my father selected a Mexican station on the radio, feelings my children now experience about me. I wanted so to *be an American,* which in my mind, and perhaps in the minds of many on the border, meant (and means) shunning anything from Mexico.

But as I grew I learned to like dancing to those rhythms. I learned to value not only the rhythms but all that they

70 symbolized. As an adult, such music became associated with celebrations and friends, with warmth and the sharing of emotions. I revel in a certain Mexican passion not for life or about life, but *in* life—a certain intensity in the daily living of it, a certain abandon in such music, in the hugs, sometimes in the anger. I miss the *chispas,* "sparks," that spring from the willingness, the habit, of allowing the inner self to burst through polite restraints. Sparks can be dangerous but, like risks, are necessary.

I brought cassettes of Mexican and Latin American music

80 with us when we drove to Ohio. I'd roll the car window down and turn the volume up, taking a certain delight in sending such sounds like mischievous imps across fields and into trees. Broadcasting my culture, if you will.

**Foreign Spooks**
*Released full blast into the autumn air*
*from trumpets, drums, flutes,*
*the sounds burst from my car like confetti*
*riding the first strong current.*
*The invisible imps from Peru, Spain,*

**MARK IT UP** WORD POWER

Remember to mark words that you'd like to add to your **Personal Word List.** Later, you can record the words and their meanings beginning on page 316.

WORDS
TO
KNOW
**astutely** (ə-stoōt'lē) *adv.* with keen perceptiveness; wisely

The Border: A Glare of Truth **71**

1. Look over the passages that you underlined as you read. What parts of her Mexican heritage does Mora value? **(Infer)**

_____

_____

_____

_____

2. What kind of music makes you feel the way Mora felt when she heard the mariachi music? **(Connect)**

_____

_____

_____

▸ MARK IT UP  **3.** Circle words and phrases on page 71 that describe what Mora appreciates about living in Ohio. **(Analyze)**

90 *Mexico grin as they spring from guitars,*
*harps, hand claps, and violins,*
*they stream across the flat fields of Ohio,*
*hide in the drafts of abandoned gray barns,*
*and the shutters of stern, white houses,*
*burrow into cold cow's ears and the crackle*
*of dry corn, in squirrel fur, pond ripple,*
*   tree gnarl,*
*owl hollow, until the wind sighs*
*and they open their wide, <u>impudent</u>*
100 *mouths, and together con gusto[2]*
*startle sleeping farm wives,*
*sashaying raccoons, and even*
*the old harvest moon.*

On my first return visit to Texas, I stopped to hear a group of *mariachis* playing their instruments with proud gusto. I was surprised and probably embarrassed when my eyes filled with tears not only at the music, but at the sight of wonderful Mexican faces. The musicians were playing for some senior citizens. The sight of brown, knowing eyes that quickly 110 accepted me with a  smile, the stories in those eyes and in the wrinkled faces were more delicious than any *fajitas* or *flan.*[3]

**Pause ❷ Reflect**

**FOCUS**
Now Mora comes to her most important point.
▸ MARK IT UP As you read, underline passages that tell how her life has been shaped by living on the border.

**When I lived on the border,** I had the privilege accorded to a small percentage of our citizens: I daily saw the native land of my grandparents. I grew up in the Chihuahua desert, as did they, only we grew up on different sides of the Rio Grande. That desert— its firmness, resilience, and fierceness,

---

2. **con gusto** (kôn gōͦs′tô): *Spanish:* with pleasure.
3. **fajitas** (fä-hē′täs) . . . **flan** (flän) *Spanish:* two popular Mexican foods—the first a dish of grilled meat wrapped in tortillas, the second a custard dessert.

WORDS
TO    **impudent** (ĭm′pyə-dənt) *adj.* bold and shameless
KNOW

**120** its whispered chants and tempestuous dance, its wisdom and majesty—shaped us as geography always shapes its inhabitants. The desert persists in me, both inspiring and compelling me to sing about her and her people, their roots and blooms and thorns.

The desert is harsh, hard as life, no carpet of leaves cushions a walk, no forest conceals the shacks on the other side of the sad river. Although a Midwest winter is hard, it ends, melts into rich soil yielding the yellow trumpeting of daffodils. But the desert in any season can be relentless as **130** poverty and hunger, realities <u>prevalent</u> as scorpions in that stark terrain. Anthropologist Renato Rosaldo, in his provocative challenge to his colleagues, *Culture and Truth,* states that we live in a world "saturated with inequality, power, and domination."

The culture of the border illustrates this truth daily, glaringly. Children go to sleep hungry and stare at stores filled with toys they'll never touch, with books they'll never read. Oddly, I miss that clear view of the difference between my comfortable life and the lives of so many who also speak **140** Spanish, value family, music, celebration. In a broader sense, I miss the visible reminder of the difference between my insulated, economically privileged life and the life of most of my fellow humans. What I miss about the sights and sounds of the border is, I've finally concluded, its stern honesty. The fierce light of that grand, wide Southwest sky not only filled me with energy, it revealed the glare of truth.

### Pause & Reflect

---

### Pause & Reflect

1. Which of the following statements is *not* true about Mora's perspective? Cross it out. **(Infer)**

   The desert seems to live within her.

   The desert landscape highlights the contrast between rich and poor.

   She fears the truth revealed by the desert.

**MARK IT UP**  2. Look at the passages you underlined as you read. Star the one that most clearly states the importance of living near the border. **(Make Judgments)**

**CHALLENGE**

Review the two essays to determine each **author's purpose** for writing. Then **compare and contrast** the two authors' purposes for writing.

## Wrapping Up

If you are using **The Language of Literature**, you can now move to the questions and activities on pages 179–180 of that book.

---

# Active Reading SkillBuilder

## Comparison and Contrast

Writers often rely on **comparison and contrast** to organize their material and
create a text structure. In a comparison, the similarities of two or more things are
examined. When two or more things are contrasted, however, it is the differences that
are explored. In these essays, each writer compares and contrasts life in two places.
In the chart on the left, record the similarities and differences that Margaret Atwood
uses to develop and organize her essay. In the chart on the right, record the similarities
and differences that Pat Mora uses to develop her essay. Examples are given.

**Atwood Essay**

| Life in U. S. | Life in Canada |
|---|---|
| sprawling / loud | neat / quiet |

**Mora Essay**

| Life in El Paso | Life in Ohio |
|---|---|
| Spanish around her every day | rarely hears Spanish |

# Literary Analysis SkillBuilder

## Theme in Nonfiction

Sometimes the **theme,** or message, of a nonfiction selection is directly stated. Other times it is implied, or stated indirectly. Readers of nonfiction can gain insight into the theme of a work by looking for passages that reveal or hint at the writer's opinion. Review Atwood's essay, then list on the chart below clues that suggest her perceptions of Canadian and American cultural differences. Using the information on this list, write a sentence stating Atwood's theme. Next, review Mora's essay. List examples of what she misses from her border culture; using this information, write a sentence stating Mora's theme. Two examples are given.

| Atwood's Perceptions | What Mora Misses |
|---|---|
| • Canadians are in "the neat little bungalow"; Americans are in "the sprawly mansion." | • Speaking and hearing Spanish |
| **Theme:** | **Theme:** |

# Words to Know SkillBuilder

## Words to Know

| | | | | |
|---|---|---|---|---|
| analyze | construe | impudent | prevalent | raucous |
| astutely | impenetrable | myopia | proximity | versatility |

**A.** Circle the word that is the antonym, or means the opposite of, the boldfaced word.

| | | | | |
|---|---|---|---|---|
| 1. **prevalent** | increase | uncommon | necessary | certain |
| 2. **impudence** | courtesy | flattery | rudeness | imagination |
| 3. **astutely** | cautiously | rapidly | unwisely | preferably |
| 4. **proximity** | distance | desire | location | annoyance |
| 5. **versatility** | adaptability | understanding | single-mindedness | unity |
| 6. **myopia** | knack | farsightedness | comprehension | vision |
| 7. **raucous** | noisy | remarkable | dignified | melodious |
| 8. **impenetrable** | impassable | clear | threatening | delightful |
| 9. **construe** | mislead | create | misinterpret | understand |

**B.** Fill in each blank with the correct Word to Know.

1. Our quiet community is definitely not a _____, lively, or noisy place.

2. Its _____ to the surrounding farms and orchards gives it a wholesome atmosphere.

3. We have to drive an hour or more to get to see a movie, since theaters are not _____ in our area.

4. Many experts have tried to _____ the reasons behind the exodus of young people from the area.

5. Some young people have complained about the lack of career _____; everyone seems to be involved in the same type of work.

6. Others, however, have _____ considered the beauty and value of the land and then made a decision to remain in the area.

**C.** An anecdote is a short, amusing, interesting account of an incident. Write an anecdote about a neighborhood or community that borders your own. Use at least **four** Words to Know in your anecdote.

# Piano

## D. H. LAWRENCE

**PREVIEW** When the speaker of this poem listens to a woman singing, his memories carry him back to childhood. He remembers how his mother played and sang on Sunday evenings at home. So strong are his memories that he is overcome by emotion.

**FOCUS**
As you read, try to imagine the scene from the speaker's childhood.
**MARK IT UP** Underline details in the poem that help you to picture the scene. An example is highlighted.

Softly, in the dusk, a woman is singing to me;
    Taking me back down the vista[1] of years, till I see
A child sitting under the piano, in the boom of the
    tingling strings
And pressing the small, poised feet of a mother who
    smiles as she sings.

In spite of myself, the insidious[2] mastery of song
Betrays me back, till the heart of me weeps to belong
To the old Sunday evenings at home, with winter outside
And hymns in the cozy parlour, the tinkling piano
    our guide.

1. **vista** (vĭs′tə): a distant view.
2. **insidious** (ĭn-sĭd′ē-əs): attractive but harmful.

## Before You Read

If you are using *The Language of Literature,* study the information on page 228 of that book to prepare for reading.

## Reading Tips

These two poems are about memories of childhood.

• As you read each poem, form your own impressions of the **speaker**. What was the speaker like as a child? What is the speaker like as an adult?

• It will help if you try to **visualize** the scene being described in each poem. Look for **imagery** that will help you do this.

**MARK IT UP** **KEEP TRACK**

As you read, you can use these marks to keep track of your understanding.

✔ ..... I understand.

? ..... I don't understand this.

! ..... Interesting or surprising idea

So now it is vain[3] for the singer to burst into clamour[4]
With the great black piano appassionato.[5] The glamour
Of childish days is upon me, my manhood is cast
Down in the flood of remembrance, I weep like a child
    for the past.

**Pause & Reflect**

## Pause & Reflect

1. Who is the child in line 3?
   **(Clarify)**

   _____

2. Circle any of the words below
   that apply:
   The old Sunday evenings were
   times of _____ .

   happiness          work

   singing            weeping

   **(Draw Conclusions)**

3. Review the details you underlined
   as you read. Why do you think
   the childhood scene made such
   a strong impression on the
   speaker? **(Cause and Effect)**

   _____

   _____

   _____

   _____

**MARK IT UP** WORD POWER

Mark words that you'd like to add
to your **Personal Word List**. After
reading, you can record the
words and their meanings
beginning on page 316.

---

3. **vain:** useless.

4. **clamour** (klăm′ ər): a loud, insistent noise.

5. **appassionato** (ə-pä′sē-ə-nä′tō): an Italian word meaning "with deep
   emotion." Used as a direction in a musical composition.

# Those Winter Sundays

## ROBERT HAYDEN

**PREVIEW** The speaker in this poem recalls his father rising early in the bitter cold—even on Sundays—to start a fire and warm the house. Now the speaker has a different understanding of his father's actions.

**FOCUS**

The speaker here remembers both positive and negative things about his life as a child.

MARK IT UP As you read, underline details that seem important.

Sundays too my father got up early
and put his clothes on in the blueblack cold,
then with cracked hands that ached
from labor in the weekday weather made
banked fires[1] blaze. No one ever thanked him.

I'd wake and hear the cold splintering, breaking.
When the rooms were warm, he'd call,
and slowly I would rise and dress,
fearing the chronic[2] angers of that house,

Speaking indifferently to him,
who had driven out the cold
and polished my good shoes as well.
What did I know, what did I know
of love's austere[3] and lonely offices?[4]

### Pause & Reflect

---

1. **banked fires:** fires covered with ashes overnight to keep them burning low.
2. **chronic** (krŏn´ĭk): lasting or occurring repeatedly for a long time.
3. **austere** (ô-stîr´): stern; severe.
4. **offices:** duties; ceremonies.

---

### Pause & Reflect

**1.** Review what you underlined as you read. Briefly **summarize** what the speaker remembers.

_____
_____
_____
_____

MARK IT UP **2.** How are the speaker's feelings about his father different now from when he was a child? Star any lines in the poem that help you to answer. **(Infer)**

_____
_____
_____
_____

### CHALLENGE

Reread the poems and look for words and phrases that tell you something about the **speakers** themselves. What do the two speakers have in common? What makes them different from each other? **(Compare and Contrast)**

### Wrapping Up

If you are using **The Language of Literature,** you can now move to the questions and activities on pages 231–232 of that book.

# Active Reading SkillBuilder

## Visualizing

**Visualizing** is the act of mentally picturing something you read. Visualizing while reading can help you understand and appreciate the imagery in poetry. After reading these poems, answer the five questions listed on the chart below. These questions will help you visualize what you read. Two examples are given.

| | "Piano" | "Those Winter Sundays" |
|---|---|---|
| **Where does poem take place?** | | |
| **When does poem take place?** | "Sunday evenings" (line 7) | |
| **Who are the people?** | | |
| **What do the people look like?** | | |
| **What details in the setting trigger mental pictures?** | | "blueblack cold" (line 2) |
| **What images can be easily visualized?** | | |

# Literary Analysis SkillBuilder

## Imagery

The use of words and phrases to create sensory experiences for readers is called **imagery.** Images can appeal to one or more of the five senses—sight, hearing, taste, smell, and touch—and can help readers interpret what is going on in a poem. List two more images from "Piano" and three from "Those Winter Sundays." Name the sense or senses to which each image appeals. An example is given.

| Poem | Image | Sense(s) |
|---|---|---|
| "Piano" | *"in the dusk" (line 1)* | *sight* |
| | | |
| | | |
| "Those Winter Sundays" | | |
| | | |
| | | |

## Before You Read

If you are using *The Language of Literature,* study the information on page 303 of that book to prepare for reading.

## Reading Tips

This story begins in a quiet way, with lengthy description of the frontier setting. You may be tempted to skim over the description. If you do, you will miss important details that give insight into the characters and plot.

- As you read, notice how the characters react to their surroundings.

- Pay close attention to the character named Henry. How do his friends react to him and his comments about his wife?

---

**MARK IT UP** **KEEP TRACK**

As you read, you can use these marks to keep track of your understanding.

✔ ..... I understand.

? ..... I don't understand this.

! ..... Interesting or surprising idea

---

# The Californian's Tale

# Mark Twain

PREVIEW This story takes place in California around 1870, some years after the California Gold Rush. The narrator is one of the few miners still searching for gold in the mostly deserted hills. After many weeks alone, he meets an ex-miner, Henry, who lives in a cozy cabin. Henry invites the narrator to stay until his wife returns from visiting her family. As the narrator learns, all is not what it seems.

---

FOCUS

**MARK IT UP** As you read, underline words and phrases that describe the loneliness and beauty of the setting. An example is highlighted.

**Thirty-five years ago** I was out prospecting on the Stanislaus,[1] tramping all day long with pick and pan and horn, and washing a hatful of dirt here and there, always expecting to make a rich strike, and never doing it. It was a lovely region, woodsy, <u>balmy</u>, delicious, and had once been populous, long years before, but now the people had vanished and the charming paradise was a solitude. They went away when the surface diggings gave out. In one place, where a busy little city with banks and newspapers and fire companies and a mayor and aldermen had been, was nothing but a wide expanse of emerald turf, with not even the faintest sign that human life had ever been present there. This was down toward Tuttletown.[2] In the country neighborhood thereabouts, along

---

1. **Stanislaus:** a river in California where gold was mined.
2. **Tuttletown:** a mining town near the Stanislaus river.

WORDS
TO
KNOW

**balmy** (bä′mē) *adj.* soothingly fragrant; mild and pleasant

the dusty roads, one found at intervals the prettiest little cottage homes, snug and cozy, and so cobwebbed with vines snowed thick with roses that the doors and windows were
20 wholly hidden from sight—sign that these were deserted homes, forsaken years ago by defeated and disappointed families who could neither sell them nor give them away. Now and then, half an hour apart, one came across solitary log cabins of the earliest mining days, built by the first gold miners, the <u>predecessors</u> of the cottage builders. In some few cases these cabins were still occupied; and when this was so, you could depend upon it that the occupant was the very pioneer who had built the cabin; and you could depend on another thing, too—that he was there because he had once
30 had his opportunity to go home to the States rich, and had not done it; had rather lost his wealth, and had then in his humiliation resolved to <u>sever</u> all communication with his home relatives and friends, and be to them thenceforth as one dead. Round about California in that day were scattered a host of these living dead men—pride-smitten poor fellows, <u>grizzled</u> and old at forty, whose secret thoughts were made all of regrets and longings—regrets for their wasted lives, and longings to be out of the struggle and done with it all.

It was a lonesome land! Not a sound in all those peaceful
40 expanses of grass and woods but the drowsy hum of insects; no glimpse of man or beast; nothing to keep up your spirits and make you glad to be alive. And so, at last, in the early part of the afternoon, when I caught sight of a human creature, I felt a most grateful uplift. This person was a man about forty-five years old, and he was standing at the gate of one of those cozy little rose-clad cottages of the sort already referred to. However, this one hadn't a deserted look; it had the look of being lived in and petted and cared for and looked after; and so had its front yard, which was a garden of
50 flowers, abundant, gay, and flourishing. I was invited in, of course, and required to make myself at home—it was the custom of the country.

**Pause & Reflect**

**Pause & Reflect**

1. Look at the details that you underlined as you read. How would you describe the setting? **(Visualize)**

_____

_____

_____

_____

2. Why are so many of the log cabins now empty? **(Infer)**

_____

_____

_____

_____

3. Why does the narrator spend so much time alone? **(Analyze Setting and Character)**

_____

_____

_____

_____

WORDS TO KNOW

**predecessor** (prĕd′ĭ-sĕs′ər) *n.* someone who came before and has been succeeded or replaced by another
**sever** (sĕv′ər) *v.* to cut or break off
**grizzled** (grĭz′əld) *adj.* streaked with or partly gray

**FOCUS**

The narrator begins to learn more about the man named Henry and his cottage. Read to find out what makes this cottage so cozy and special.

**It was delightful** to be in such a place, after long weeks of daily and nightly familiarity with miners' cabins—with all which this implies of dirt floor, never-made beds, tin plates and cups, bacon and beans and black coffee, and nothing of ornament but war pictures from the Eastern illustrated papers tacked to the log walls. That was all hard, cheerless, materialistic <u>desolation</u>, but here was a nest which had aspects to rest the tired eye and refresh that something in one's nature which, after long fasting, recognizes, when confronted by the belongings of art, howsoever cheap and modest they may be, that it has unconsciously been famishing and now has found nourishment. I could not have believed that a rag carpet could feast me so, and so content me; or that there could be such solace to the soul in wallpaper and framed lithographs,[3] and bright-colored tidies[4] and lamp mats, and Windsor chairs,[5] and varnished whatnots,[6] with seashells and books and china vases on them, and the score of little unclassifiable tricks and touches that a woman's hand distributes about a home, which one sees without knowing he sees them, yet would miss in a moment if they were taken away. The delight that was in my heart showed in my face, and the man saw it and was pleased; saw it so plainly that he answered it as if it had been spoken.

"All her work," he said, caressingly; "she did it all herself— every bit," and he took the room in with a glance which was full of affectionate worship. One of those soft Japanese fabrics with which women drape with careful negligence the upper part of a picture frame was out of adjustment. He noticed it, and rearranged it with cautious pains, stepping back several times to gauge the effect before he got it to suit him. Then he

---

3. **lithographs:** prints made by a process in which portions of a flat surface are treated either to retain or to repel ink.

4. **tidies:** decorative coverings for the arms or headrest of a chair or sofa.

5. **Windsor chairs:** wooden chairs with high-spoked backs, outward-slanting legs, and saddle seats.

6. **whatnots:** a set of light, open shelves for displaying ornaments.

WORDS TO KNOW    **desolation** (dĕs'ə-lā'shən) *n.* the state of being empty, deserted, or forlorn; barrenness; loneliness

gave it a light finishing pat or two with his hand, and said:
"She always does that. You can't tell just what it lacks, but it
does lack something until you've done that—you can see it
yourself after it's done, but that is all you know; you can't
find out the law of it. It's like the finishing pats a mother gives
the child's hair after she's got it combed and brushed, I
reckon. I've seen her fix all these things so much that I can do
them all just her way, though I don't know the law of any of
them. But she knows the law. She knows the why and the how
both; but I don't know the why; I only know the how."

He took me into a bedroom so that I might wash my
hands; such a bedroom as I had not seen for years: white
counterpane,[7] white pillows, carpeted floor, papered walls,
pictures, dressing table, with mirror and pincushion and
dainty toilet things; and in the corner a washstand, with real
chinaware bowl and pitcher, and with soap in a china dish,
and on a rack more than a dozen towels—towels too clean
and white for one out of practice to use without some vague
sense of profanation.[8] So my face spoke again, and he
answered with gratified words:

"All her work; she did it all herself—every bit. Nothing
here that hasn't felt the touch of her hand. Now you would
think—But I mustn't talk so much."

**Pause & Reflect**

**FOCUS**

As the narrator learns
more about Henry and
his wife, he reveals
aspects of his own
character.

**MARK IT UP** As you
read, underline words
and phrases that
describe how the
narrator feels about
Henry's wife.

**By this time** I was wiping my hands and
glancing from detail to detail of the
room's belongings, as one is apt to do
when he is in a new place, where
everything he sees is a comfort to his
eye and his spirit; and I became
conscious, in one of those
unaccountable ways, you know, that
there was something there somewhere
that the man wanted me to discover for
myself. I knew it perfectly, and I knew he was trying to help

**Pause & Reflect**

**MARK IT UP** **1.** How is
Henry's cabin different from a
typical miner's cabin? Circle at
least four details on page 84 that
describe those differences.
**(Locate Specific Details)**

**2.** Who does Henry say is
responsible for the delightful
comforts of his cottage? **(Clarify)**

**3.** How would you describe the
relationship that Henry has with
his wife? **(Draw Conclusions)**

7. **counterpane:** bedspread.
8. **profanation:** the showing of contempt for something regarded as sacred.

me by <u>furtive</u> indications with his eye, so I tried hard to get on
120 the right track, being eager to gratify him. I failed several
times, as I could see out of the corner of my eye without being
told; but at last I knew I must be looking straight at the
thing—knew it from the pleasure issuing in invisible waves
from him. He broke into a happy laugh, and rubbed his hands
together, and cried out:

"That's it! You've found it. I knew you would. It's her
picture."

I went to the little black-walnut bracket[9] on the farther
wall, and did find there what I had not yet noticed—a
130 daguerreotype case.[10] It contained the sweetest girlish face,
and the most beautiful, as it seemed to me, that I had ever
seen. The man drank the admiration from my face, and was
fully satisfied.

"Nineteen her last birthday," he said, as he put the picture
back; "and that was the day we were married. When you see
her—ah, just wait till you see her!"

"Where is she? When will she be in?"

"Oh, she's away now. She's gone to see her people. They
live forty or fifty miles from here. She's been gone two
140 weeks today."

"When do you expect her back?"

"This is Wednesday. She'll be back Saturday, in the
evening—about nine o'clock, likely."

I felt a sharp sense of disappointment.

"I'm sorry, because I'll be gone then," I said, regretfully.

"Gone? No—why should you go? Don't go. She'll be so
disappointed."

She would be disappointed—that beautiful creature! If she
had said the words herself they could hardly have blessed me
150 more. I was feeling a deep, strong longing to see her—a
longing so <u>supplicating</u>, so insistent, that it made me afraid. I
said to myself: "I will go straight away from this place, for my
peace of mind's sake."

---

9. **bracket:** a small shelf.
10. **daguerreotype** (də-gâr′ə-tīp′) **case:** a frame-like case holding an early type of
    photograph.

WORDS
TO
KNOW
**furtive** (fûr′tĭv) *adj.* shifty; having a hidden motive or
purpose
**supplicating** (sŭp′lĭ-kāt′ĭng) *adj.* humbly or sincerely
asking, begging, or praying **supplicate** *v.*

"You see, she likes to have people come and stop with us—people who know things, and can talk—people like you. She delights in it; for she knows—oh, she knows nearly everything herself, and can talk, oh, like a bird—and the books she reads, why, you would be astonished. Don't go; it's only a little while, you know, and she'll be so disappointed."

I heard the words, but hardly noticed them, I was so deep in my thinkings and strugglings. He left me, but I didn't know. Presently he was back, with the picture case in his hand, and he held it open before me and said:

"There, now, tell her to her face you could have stayed to see her, and you wouldn't."

*Pause* **&** *Reflect*

**FOCUS**

As the narrator waits for Henry's wife to return, several neighbors come to visit Henry.

**MARK IT UP** As you read, circle any details that reveal how the neighbors feel about Henry's wife.

**That second glimpse broke down** my good resolution. I would stay and take the risk. That night we smoked the tranquil pipe, and talked till late about various things, but mainly about her; and certainly I had had no such pleasant and restful time for many a day. The Thursday followed and slipped comfortably away. Toward twilight a big miner from three miles away came—one of the grizzled, stranded pioneers—and gave us warm salutation, clothed in grave and sober speech. Then he said:

"I only just dropped over to ask about the little madam, and when is she coming home. Any news from her?"

"Oh yes, a letter. Would you like to hear it, Tom?"

"Well, I should think I would, if you don't mind, Henry!"

Henry got the letter out of his wallet, and said he would skip some of the private phrases, if we were willing; then he went on and read the bulk of it—a loving, <u>sedate</u>, and altogether charming and gracious piece of handiwork, with a postscript full of affectionate regards and messages to Tom,

**Pause** **&** **Reflect**

1. Look back over the details you underlined as you read. How does the narrator feel about Henry's wife? (Infer)

_____

_____

_____

2. At this point in the story, what is your opinion of Henry? (Evaluate)

_____

_____

_____

_____

**READ ALOUD** 3. Read aloud the boxed passage on page 86. Why does the narrator say, "I will go straight away from this place, for my peace of mind's sake"? Circle the answer below. (Infer)

He is attracted to Henry's wife and doesn't want to upset himself.

He is afraid of Henry's jealousy.

He fears that he won't be welcome.

WORDS
TO
KNOW

**sedate** (sǐ-dāt') *adj.* serenely deliberate, composed, and dignified

1. Why do Henry's neighbors visit him? **(Clarify)**

_____

_____

_____

_____

2. Review what you circled as you read. How do the neighbors feel about Henry's wife? **(Infer)**

_____

_____

_____

_____

3. If you were in Henry's position, how would you feel about your neighbors? **(Connect)**

_____

_____

_____

and Joe, and Charley, and other close friends and neighbors.

As the reader finished, he glanced at Tom, and cried out:

"Oho, you're at it again! Take your hands away, and let me see your eyes. You always do that when I read a letter from her. I will write and tell her."

"Oh no, you mustn't, Henry. I'm getting old, you know, and any little disappointment makes me want to cry. I thought she'd be here herself, and now you've got only a letter."

"Well, now, what put that in your head? I thought everybody knew she wasn't coming till Saturday."

"Saturday! Why, come to think, I did know it. I wonder what's the matter with me lately? Certainly I knew it. Ain't we all getting ready for her? Well, I must be going now. But I'll be on hand when she comes, old man!"

Late Friday afternoon another gray veteran tramped over from his cabin a mile or so away, and said the boys wanted to have a little gaiety and a good time Saturday night, if Henry thought she wouldn't be too tired after her journey to be kept up.

"Tired? She tired! Oh, hear the man! Joe, _you_ know she'd sit up six weeks to please any one of you!"

When Joe heard that there was a letter, he asked to have it read, and the loving messages in it for him broke the old fellow all up; but he said he was such an old wreck that _that_ would happen to him if she only just mentioned his name. "Lord, we miss her so!" he said.

**Pause** **&** **Reflect**

**FOCUS**

Saturday has arrived, the day that Henry's wife is supposed to return. Read on to learn about why Henry is worried.

**Saturday afternoon I found** I was taking out my watch pretty often. Henry noticed it, and said, with a startled look:

"You don't think she ought to be here so soon, do you?"

I felt caught, and a little embarrassed; but I laughed, and said it was a habit of mine when I was in a state of expectancy. But he didn't seem quite satisfied; and from that time on he began to show uneasiness. Four times he walked me up the road to a point whence we could see a long distance; and there he would stand, shading his eyes with his hand, and looking. Several times he said:

"I'm getting worried, I'm getting right down worried. I know she's not due till about nine o'clock, and yet something seems to be trying to warn me that something's happened. 230 You don't think anything has happened, do you?"

I began to get pretty thoroughly ashamed of him for his childishness; and at last, when he repeated that <u>imploring</u> question still another time, I lost my patience for the moment, and spoke pretty brutally to him. It seemed to shrivel him up and cow[11] him; and he looked so wounded and so humble after that, that I detested myself for having done the cruel and unnecessary thing. And so I was glad when Charley, another veteran, arrived toward the edge of the evening, and nestled up to Henry to hear the letter read, and talked over the 240 preparations for the welcome. Charley fetched out one hearty speech after another, and did his best to drive away his friend's <u>bodings</u> and apprehensions.

"Anything *happened* to her? Henry, that's pure nonsense. There isn't anything going to happen to her; just make your mind easy as to that. What did the letter say? Said she was well, didn't it? And said she'd *be* here by nine o'clock, didn't it? Did you ever know her to fail of her word? Why, you know you never did. Well, then, don't you fret; she'll be here, and that's absolutely certain, and as sure as you are born. 250 Come, now, let's get to decorating—not much time left."

Pretty soon Tom and Joe arrived, and then all hands set about adorning the house with flowers. Toward nine the three miners said that as they had brought their instruments they might as well tune up, for the boys and girls would soon be arriving now, and hungry for a good, old-fashioned breakdown.[12] A fiddle, a banjo, and a clarinet—these were the

---

11. **cow:** to intimidate; to frighten with threats or a show of force.
12. **breakdown:** a noisy, energetic American country dance.

WORDS TO KNOW

**imploring** (ĭm-plôr′ĭng) *adj.* begging; making an urgent appeal **implore** *v.*
**boding** (bō′dĭng) *n.* a warning or omen about the future, especially of evil **bode** *v.*

instruments. The trio took their places side by side, and began to play some rattling dance music, and beat time with their big boots.

260 It was getting very close to nine. Henry was standing in the door with his eyes directed up the road, his body swaying to the torture of his mental distress. He had been made to drink his wife's health and safety several times, and now Tom shouted:

"All hands stand by! One more drink, and she's here!"

Joe brought the glasses on a waiter,[13] and served the party. I reached for one of the two remaining glasses, but Joe growled, under his breath:

"Drop that! Take the other."

270 Which I did. Henry was served last. He had hardly swallowed his drink when the clock began to strike. He listened till it finished, his face growing pale and paler; then he said:

"Boys, I'm sick with fear. Help me—I want to lie down!"

They helped him to the sofa. He began to nestle and drowse, but presently spoke like one talking in his sleep, and said: "Did I hear horses' feet? Have they come?"

One of the veterans answered, close to his ear: "It was Jimmy Parrish come to say the party got delayed, but they're 280 right up the road a piece, and coming along. Her horse is lame, but she'll be here in half an hour."

"Oh, I'm *so* thankful nothing has happened!"

He was asleep almost before the words were out of his mouth. In a moment those handy men had his clothes off, and had tucked him into his bed in the chamber where I had washed my hands. They closed the door and came back. Then they seemed preparing to leave; but I said: "Please don't go, gentlemen. She won't know me; I am a stranger."

They glanced at each other. Then Joe said:

290 "She? Poor thing, she's been dead nineteen years!"

"Dead?"

"That or worse. She went to see her folks half a year after she was married, and on her way back, on a Saturday evening, the Indians captured her within five miles of this place, and she's never been heard of since."

"And he lost his mind in consequence?"

13. waiter: a tray.

"Never has been sane an hour since. But he only gets bad when that time of the year comes round. Then we begin to drop in here, three days before she's due, to encourage him up, and ask if he's heard from her, and Saturday we all come and fix up the house with flowers, and get everything ready for a dance. We've done it every year for nineteen years. The first Saturday there was twenty-seven of us, without counting the girls; there's only three of us now, and the girls are all gone. We drug him to sleep, or he would go wild; then he's all right for another year—thinks she's with him till the last three or four days come round; then he begins to look for her, and gets out his poor old letter, and we come and ask him to read it to us. Lord, she was a darling!"

**Pause & Reflect**

**Pause & Reflect**

1. Were you surprised by the outcome of the story? Explain why or why not. (Evaluate)

_____

_____

_____

_____

MARK IT UP   2. What happened to Henry's wife? Circle the sentences on page 90 that answer the question. (Clarify)

READ ALOUD   3. Read aloud the boxed passage on this page. Why do Henry's neighbors gather each year to hold a party? (Draw Conclusions)

_____

_____

_____

_____

CHALLENGE

Review the story and mark passages that strike you as memorable. Based on these passages, what do you think is distinctive about Twain's **style?** How does he achieve his style? Consider elements such as dialogue, sentence structure, length, diction, and tone. (Analyze)

## Wrapping Up

If you are using **The Language of Literature,** you can now move to the questions and activities on pages 311–313 of that book.

# Active Reading SkillBuilder

### Interpreting the Relationship Between Setting and Characters

The **setting** of a story may give the reader insights into the characters. To understand the **characters** in Twain's story, you need to understand how the setting has influenced their lives. As you read "The Californian's Tale," note relevant details about both the frontier surroundings and Henry's cottage. Two examples are shown. Then consider what insight each part of the story's setting gives into the characters and their lives.

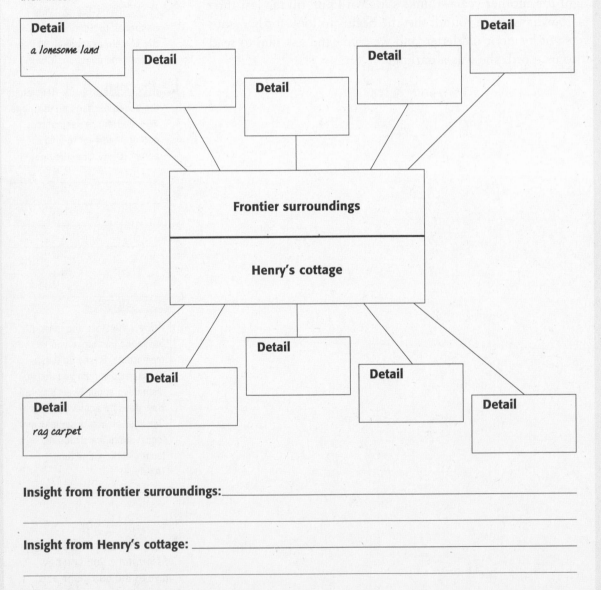

**Detail**
*a lonesome land*

**Detail**

**Detail**

**Detail**

**Detail**

**Frontier surroundings**

**Henry's cottage**

**Detail**

**Detail**

**Detail**

**Detail**
*rag carpet*

**Insight from frontier surroundings:** _____

_____

**Insight from Henry's cottage:** _____

# Literary Analysis SkillBuilder

## Historical Setting

The term **historical setting** is used to describe the time and place of the action of a story that takes place in a particular historical period. The historical setting can contribute to the development of a story's plot and also establish a **mood,** or atmosphere, that enables the reader to understand the characters. Think about other possible historical settings for this story. Use the story map below to help you figure out an alternative setting that still maintains the mood and basic plot structure of Twain's narrative.

| Setting |
| --- |
| **Time:** |
| **Place:** |

| Characters: |
| --- |

| Problem: |
| --- |

| Events: |
| --- |
| 1. |
| 2. |
| 3. |
| 4. |

| Resolution: |
| --- |

# Words to Know SkillBuilder

## Words to Know

| | | | | |
|---|---|---|---|---|
| balmy | desolation | grizzled | predecessor | sever |
| boding | furtive | imploring | sedate | supplicating |

**A.** Decide which word from the word list belongs in each numbered blank.
Then write the word on the blank line on the right.

With these scissors, you can (1)
Any substance whatsoever.

(1) _____

King Charles the Greater, son of Charles the Lesser,
Was quite a bit taller than his (2).

(2) _____

Noises from the children skating
Have become so very grating
That I say, so (3),
"Won't you stop that grating skating?"

(3) _____

On the plains, the lions' roaring
Has become so very boring
That my question is (4),
"Can't you quit that boring roaring?"

(4) _____

The (5) milkman crept inside, as quiet as a mouse.
He'd left the dairy products, now he meant to rob the house.

(5) _____

**B.** Fill in each blank with the correct word from the word list.

1. The _____ breezes of a perfect spring day can blow
   the memory of winter right out of one's mind.

2. The hoot of an owl can seem a _____, especially to
   a mouse.

3. She is much too proper, serious, and _____ to ever
   make a scene.

4. An abandoned house is a scene of _____, even in
   a bustling city.

5. With his wrinkles and _____ hair, he didn't look like
   he was 39, as he claimed to be.

**C.** Imagine you are the director of a movie version of "The Californian's Tale." Write
down the directions you would give the actor playing Henry. Tell him what will be
demanded of him in his role. Use at least **four** of the Words to Know.

# TONIGHT
## *I Can Write . . .*

### PABLO NERUDA

**PREVIEW** The setting of the following poem seems perfect for romantic love. The stars are out, and a soft wind blows. The speaker, however, can think only of his sadness. His romance with the woman he loved is now over. He looks back at the way he used to feel about her, and he tries to explain how he now feels.

**FOCUS**
Read this poem as if you were listening to a friend telling you about the end of a relationship. Does the speaker still love the woman?

**MARK IT UP** Underline any lines that show how the speaker feels now.

Tonight I can write the saddest lines.

Write, for example, 'The night is shattered
and the blue stars shiver in the distance.'

The night wind revolves in the sky and sings.

5  Tonight I can write the saddest lines.
I loved her, and sometimes she loved me too.

Through nights like this one I held her in my arms.
I kissed her again and again under the endless sky.

She loved me, sometimes I loved her too.
10  How could one not have loved her great still eyes.

**Before You Read**
If you are using *The Language of Literature*. . .

• Use the information on page 351 of that book to prepare for reading.

• If you can read any Spanish, look at the original Spanish version of this poem on page 353. Read aloud the first few lines to get a sense of the poem's mood.

**Reading Tips**
The following **poem** is about a romantic relationship that is now over. As you read, look for clues that will help you understand how the **speaker** feels about the woman.

• Pay close attention to the speaker's statements about his feelings. Sometimes he seems to change his mind about his emotions.

• Try putting yourself in the place of the speaker, or imagine you can hear his voice saying the lines.

• Think about the **mood**, or atmosphere, created by the speaker's descriptions, such as "stars that shiver in the distance."

**MARK IT UP** **KEEP TRACK**
As you read, you can use these marks to keep track of your understanding.

✔ ..... I understand.

? ..... I don't understand this.

! ..... Interesting or surprising idea

**1.** What do you learn about the speaker's past relationship with the woman? **(Clarify)**

_____

_____

_____

_____

**2.** Review the lines that you underlined as you read. Do you think the speaker still loves the woman?

He (circle one) *still loves her/no longer loves her/is not sure he loves her* because _____

_____

_____ .

**(Evaluate)**

📖 READ ALOUD  **3.** Read aloud the boxed passage. Do you think the speaker will forget the woman? **(Draw Conclusions)**

_____

_____

_____

_____

✏️ CHALLENGE
Review the lines in the poem that describe nature. How does this nature **imagery** reflect the speaker's feelings?

## Wrapping Up

If you are using **The Language of Literature,** you can now move to the questions and activities on pages 354–355 of that book.

Tonight I can write the saddest lines.
To think that I do not have her. To feel that I have lost
   her.

To hear the immense night, still more immense without
   her.
And the verse falls to the soul like dew to the pasture.

15  What does it matter that my love could not keep her.
The night is shattered and she is not with me.

This is all. In the distance someone is singing. In the
   distance.
My soul is not satisfied that it has lost her.

20  My sight searches for her as though to go to her.
My heart looks for her, and she is not with me.

The same night whitening the same trees.
We, of that time, are no longer the same.

I no longer love her, that's certain, but how I loved her.
My voice tried to find the wind to touch her hearing.

25  Another's. She will be another's. Like my kisses before.
Her voice. Her bright body. Her infinite eyes.

I no longer love her, that's certain, but maybe I love her.
Love is so short, forgetting is so long.

Because through nights like this one I held her in my
   arms
30  my soul is not satisfied that it has lost her.

Though this be the last pain that she makes me suffer
and these the last verses that I write for her.

*Translated by W. S. Merwin*

Pause **&** Reflect

# Active Reading SkillBuilder

## Interpreting Comparisons

Sometimes poets make use of **comparisons** to suggest the speaker's emotions and experiences. In this poem, the speaker says that "blue stars shiver in the distance." This statement reveals more about his own feelings than about the night. As you read the poem, list on the chart below each image from nature that you find. Then describe the human emotions or experiences that are suggested by that image. An example is given.

| Image from Nature | Suggested Human Emotions or Experiences |
|---|---|
| "The night is shattered ..." (line 2) | brokenhearted, upset, hurt |
| | |
| | |
| | |
| | |
| | |

# Literary Analysis SkillBuilder

## Repetition

**Repetition** is a literary technique in which sounds, words, phrases, or lines
are repeated for emphasis or unity. As you read this poem, look for repeated
words, phrases, or lines. Write them in the chart below. Then explain what
each example of repetition helps you understand about the speaker's feelings.
An example has been done for you.

| Repeated Words/Phrases/Lines | Effect on Understanding of Speaker's Feelings |
|---|---|
| *"Tonight I can write the saddest lines" (lines 1, 5, 11)* | *The speaker is overcome with sorrow.* |
| | |
| | |
| | |

**Follow Up:** Why do you think that Neruda sometimes repeats part of a line and
then adds new information?

# ONE THOUSAND DOLLARS

## O. HENRY

PREVIEW "One Thousand Dollars" is set in New York City, early in the 1900s. Bobby Gillian has just inherited one thousand dollars from his very wealthy uncle. His uncle's will states, however, that young Gillian has to explain in writing how the money is spent. So Gillian asks several people for their advice on how best to spend his fortune. What he finally does with his inheritance would surprise them all, if they were ever to learn the truth.

## Before You Read
If you are using *The Language of Literature* . . .

- Use the information on page 386 of that book to prepare for reading.

- For help in visualizing the **characters,** examine the art on pages 388–389, 391, and 393.

## Reading Tips

The author O. Henry is famous for his finely crafted short stories.

- As you read, look closely for details that hint at how the main character, Bobby Gillian, will resolve the **conflict** he faces.

- Notice how the author uses **dialogue** to advance the **plot,** or move it forward. Watch for ways in which the main character's actions are influenced by his conversations with others.

---

**FOCUS**

Read to find out how Bobby Gillian feels about inheriting one thousand dollars from his rich uncle.

**MARK IT UP** As you read, underline words and phrases that describe how young Gillian feels about the inheritance. Some examples are highlighted.

---

**"One thousand dollars,"** repeated Lawyer Tolman, solemnly and severely, "and here is the money."

Young Gillian gave a decidedly amused laugh as he fingered the thin package of new fifty-dollar notes. It's such a confoundedly awkward amount," he explained, genially, to the lawyer. "If it had been ten thousand a fellow might wind up with a lot of fireworks and do himself credit. Even $50 would have been less trouble."

"You heard the reading of your uncle's will," continued Lawyer Tolman, professionally dry in his tones. "I do not know if you paid much attention to its details. I must remind you of one. You are required to render to us an account of the manner of <u>expenditure</u> of this $1,000 as

---

**MARK IT UP KEEP TRACK**

As you read, you can use these marks to keep track of your understanding.

✔ ..... I understand.

? ..... I don't understand this.

! ..... Interesting or surprising idea

---

WORDS TO KNOW

**genially** (jēn′yə-lē) *adv.* in a friendly manner
**expenditure** (ĭk-spĕn′də-chər) *n.* an act of spending

soon as you have disposed of it. The will <u>stipulates</u> that. I trust that you will so far comply with the late Mr. Gillian's wishes."

"You may depend upon it," said the young man, politely, "in spite of the extra expense it will entail. I may have to engage a secretary. I was never good at accounts."

Gillian thrust the package of notes into his coat pocket and went to his club. There he hunted out one whom he called Old Bryson.

Old Bryson was calm and forty and sequestered.[1] He was in a corner reading a book, and when he saw Gillian approaching he sighed, laid down his book and took off his glasses.

"Old Bryson, wake up," said Gillian. "I've a funny story to tell you."

"I wish you would tell it to some one in the billiard-room," said Old Bryson. "You know how I hate your stories."

"This is a better one than usual," said Gillian, rolling a cigarette; "and I'm going to tell it to you. It's too sad and funny to go with the rattling of billiard balls. I've just come from my late uncle's firm of legal corsairs.[2] He leaves me an even thousand dollars. Now, what can a man possibly do with a thousand dollars?"

"I thought," said Old Bryson, showing as much interest as a bee shows in a vinegar cruet, "that the late Septimas Gillian was worth something like half a million."

"He was," assented Gillian, joyously, "and that's where the joke comes in. He's left his whole cargo of doubloons to a microbe. That is, part of it goes to the man who invents a new bacillus and the rest to establish a hospital for doing away with it again.[3] There are one or two trifling bequests on the side. The butler and the housekeeper get a seal ring and $10 each. His nephew gets $1,000."

**READ ALOUD** **Lines 44–45**

Gillian says that the story of his inheritance is both "sad and funny." Read aloud his explanation of his uncle's will in a way that expresses Gillian's feelings.

---

1. **sequestered** (sĭ-kwĕs′tərd): solitary; alone.
2. **corsairs** (kôr′sârz′): pirates.
3. **microbe** (mī′krōb′) . . . **bacillus** (bə-sĭl′əs) . . . **away with it again:** *Microbe* and *bacillus* refer to a bacterium, or germ, that causes disease. The "joke" of Gillian's uncle's will is that he left part of his money (**doubloons**) to any person who could develop a new strain of bacteria. The rest goes to building a hospital for curing the victims of the new disease and finding a way to destroy the bacteria (**doing away with it again**).

WORDS
TO
KNOW      **stipulate** (stĭp′yə-lāt′) *v.* to state as a condition; specify

"You've always had plenty of money to spend," observed Old Bryson.

"Tons," said Gillian. "Uncle was the fairy godmother as far as an allowance was concerned."

"Any other heirs?" asked Old Bryson.

"None." Gillian frowned at his cigarette and kicked the upholstered leather of a divan uneasily. "There is a Miss Hayden, a ward of my uncle, who lived in his house. She's a quiet thing—musical—the daughter of somebody who was unlucky enough to be his friend. I forgot to say that she was in on the seal ring and $10 joke, too. I wish I had been. Then I could have had two bottles of brut,[4] tipped the waiter with the ring and had the whole business off my hands. Don't be superior and insulting, old Bryson—tell me what a fellow can do with a thousand dollars."

Old Bryson rubbed his glasses and smiled. And when Old Bryson smiled Gillian knew that he intended to be more offensive than ever.

"A thousand dollars," he said, "means much or little. One man may buy a happy home with it and laugh at Rockefeller.[5] Another could send his wife South with it and save her life. A thousand dollars would buy pure milk for one hundred babies during June, July, and August and save fifty of their lives. You could count upon a half hour's diversion with it at faro[6] in one of the fortified art galleries. It would furnish an education to an ambitious boy. I am told that a genuine Corot[7] was secured for that amount in an auction room yesterday. You could move to a New Hampshire town and live respectably for two years on it.

"You could rent Madison Square Garden for one evening with it, and lecture your audience, if you should have one, on the <u>precariousness</u> of the profession of heir presumptive."[8]

4. **brut** (brōōt): very dry (that is, not sweet) champagne.
5. **Rockefeller:** John D. Rockefeller, who built a great oil-refining corporation in the late 1800s and became the first American billionaire.
6. **faro** (fâr′ō): a gambling game played with cards.
7. **Corot** (kô-rō′): painting by Jean Baptiste Camille Corot, a 19th-century French artist known for his landscapes.
8. **heir** (âr) **presumptive:** one who is expected to inherit the estate of another.

**MARK IT UP** WORD POWER
Mark words that you'd like to add to your **Personal Word List.** After reading, you can record the words and their meanings beginning on page 316.

WORDS TO KNOW

**precariousness** (prĭ-kâr′ē-əs-nĭs) *n.* insecurity; uncertainty

1. Review the words and phrases you underlined as you read. How would you describe Gillian's feelings about his inheritance? **(Draw Conclusions)**

_____

_____

_____

_____

✏️ **MARK IT UP** 2. Circle the passage on pages 99–100 that explains the rich uncle's will. What requirements must Gillian follow? **(Clarify)**

_____

_____

_____

_____

3. Which of the words below do you think describe Gillian's character? Circle any that apply. **(Infer)**

funny             greedy

spoiled           carefree

friendly          worried

4. How would you spend the money if you were in Gillian's position? **(Connect)**

_____

_____

_____

_____

"People might like you, Old Bryson," said Gillian, always unruffled, "if you wouldn't moralize. I asked you to tell me what I could do with a thousand dollars."

"You?" said Bryson, with a gentle laugh, "Why, Bobby Gillian, there's only one logical thing you could do. You can go buy Miss Lotta Lauriere a diamond <u>pendant</u> with the money, and then take yourself off to Idaho and inflict your
90 presence upon a ranch. I advise a sheep ranch, as I have a particular dislike for sheep."

"Thanks," said Gillian, rising. "I thought I could depend on you, Old Bryson. You've hit on the very scheme. I wanted to chuck the money in a lump, for I've got to turn in an account for it, and I hate itemizing."

Gillian phoned for a cab and said to the driver: "The stage entrance of the Columbine Theatre."

**FOCUS**
Gillian considers different ways of spending his money. Read to learn more about his options.

100

**Miss Lotta Lauriere was assisting** nature with a powder puff, almost ready for her call at a crowded matinee, when her dresser mentioned the name of Mr. Gillian.

"Let it in," said Miss Lauriere. "Now, what is it, Bobby? I'm going on in two minutes."

"Rabbit-foot your right ear a little," suggested Gillian, critically. "That's better. It won't take two minutes for me. What do you say to a little thing in the pendant line. I can stand three ciphers[9] with a figure in front of 'em."

"Oh, just as you say," carolled Miss Lauriere. "My right
110 glove, Adams. Say, Bobby, did you see that necklace Della Stacey had on the other night? Two thousand two hundred dollars it cost at Tiffany's. But, of course—pull my sash a little to the left, Adams."

---

9. **ciphers** (sī′fərz): zeroes.

WORDS
TO
KNOW

**pendant** (pĕn′dənt) _n._ a piece of jewelry made to hang from a necklace or bracelet

"Miss Lauriere for the opening chorus!" cried the call boy without.

Gillian strolled out to where his cab was waiting.

"What would you do with a thousand dollars if you had it?" he asked the driver.

"Open a s'loon," said the cabby promptly and huskily. "I know a place I could take money in with both hands. It's a four-story brick on a corner. I've got it figured out. Second story . . . chop suey; third floor—manicures and foreign missions; fourth floor—pool-room. If you was thinking of putting up the cap"—[10]

"Oh, no," said Gillian, "I merely asked from curiosity. I take you by the hour. Drive till I tell you to stop."

Eight blocks down Broadway Gillian poked up the trap[11] with his cane and got out. A blind man sat upon a stool on the sidewalk selling pencils. Gillian went out and stood before him.

"Excuse me," he said, "but would you mind telling me what you would do if you had a thousand dollars?"

"You got out of that cab that just drove up, didn't you?" asked the blind man.

"I did," said Gillian.

"I guess you are all right," said the pencil dealer, "to ride in a cab by daylight. Take a look at that, if you like."

He drew a small book from his coat pocket and held it out. Gillian opened it and saw that it was a bank deposit book. It showed a balance of $1,785 to the blind man's credit.

Gillian returned the book and got into the cab.

"I forgot something," he said. "You may drive to the law offices of Tolman & Sharp, at ——, Broadway."

Lawyer Tolman looked at him hostilely[12] and inquiringly through his gold-rimmed glasses.

"I beg your pardon," said Gillian cheerfully, "but may I ask you a question? It is not an impertinent[13] one, I am sure. Was Miss Hayden left anything by my uncle's will besides the ring and the $10?"

---

10. **putting up the cap:** supplying the capital (**cap**), or money, to buy the four-story brick building.

11. **poked up the trap:** pushed open the door in the roof of the cab (to tell the driver that he wanted to stop). Cabs at this time were enclosed horse-drawn carriages. The driver sat outside the carriage.

12. **hostilely:** in a way that shows strong dislike.

13. **impertinent:** rude.

**1.** Complete the following summary:

Gillian doesn't give jewelry to Miss Lauriere because _____

_____

_____ .

He rides with a cab driver who

_____

_____ .

He meets a blind man who _____

_____ .

**(Summarize)**

**2.** Why does Gillian return to the lawyers' office? **(Draw Conclusions)**

_____

_____

_____

_____

**3.** Now Gillian is on his way to his late uncle's house. What do you **predict** Gillian will do there?

_____

_____

_____

---

✎ **MARK IT UP** **KEEP TRACK**

Remember to use these marks to keep track of your understanding.

✔ ..... I understand.

? ..... I don't understand this.

! ..... Interesting or surprising idea

---

**150** "Nothing," said Mr. Tolman.

"I thank you very much, sir," said Gillian, and out he went to his cab. He gave the driver the address of his late uncle's home.

**Pause & Reflect**

**FOCUS**
Read to find out what Gillian reveals to Miss Hayden—and what he keeps secret.

**Miss Hayden was writing letters** in the library. She was small and slender and clothed in black. But you would have noticed her eyes. Gillian drifted in with his air of regarding the world as inconsequent.[14]

**160** "I've just come from old Tolman's," he explained. "They've been going over the papers down there. They found a"—Gillian searched his memory for a legal term—"they found an amendment[15] or a postscript or something to the will. It seems that the old boy loosened up a little on second thoughts and willed you a thousand dollars. I was driving up this way and Tolman asked me to bring you the money. Here it is. You'd better count it to see if it's right." Gillian laid the money beside her hand on the desk.

**170** Miss Hayden turned white. "Oh!" she said, and again "Oh!" Gillian half turned and looked out the window.

"I suppose, of course," he said, in a low voice, "that you know I love you."

"I am sorry," said Miss Hayden, taking up her money.

"There is no use?" asked Gillian, almost light-heartedly.

"I am sorry," she said again.

"May I write a note?" asked Gillian, with a smile. He seated himself at the big library table. She supplied him with paper and pen, and then went back to her **180** secretaire.[16]

---

14. **inconsequent:** unimportant.

15. **amendment:** a formal change in a will.

16. **secretaire** (sĕk′rə-târ′): a desk with a small bookcase on top.

Gillian made out his account of his expenditure of the thousand dollars in these words:

"Paid by the black sheep, Robert Gillian, $1,000 on the account of eternal happiness, owed by Heaven to the best and dearest woman on earth."

Gillian slipped his writing into an envelope, bowed and went his way.

His cab stopped again at the office of Tolman & Sharp.

*Pause* & **Reflect**

FOCUS
190
Gillian returns to the lawyer's office to tell how he spent his money. Read the rest of the story to find out what happens.

"**I have expended the thousand dollars,**" he said, cheerily, to Tolman of the gold glasses, "and I have come to render account of it, as I agreed. There is quite a feeling of summer in the air—do you not think so, Mr. Tolman?" He tossed a white envelope on the lawyer's table. "You will find there a memorandum, sir, of the modus operandi[17] of the vanished dollars."

Without touching the envelope, Mr. Tolman went to a door and called his partner, Sharp. Together they explored the caverns of the immense safe. Forth they dragged as trophy of their search a big envelope sealed with wax. This they forcibly invaded, and wagged their <u>venerable</u> heads together over its contents. Then Tolman became spokesman.

"Mr. Gillian," he said, formally, "there was a codicil[18] to your uncle's will. It was intrusted to us privately, with instructions that it be not opened until you furnished us with a full account of your handling of the $1,000

---

17. **modus operandi** (mō′dəs ŏp′ə-răn′dē): method of functioning.

18. **codicil** (kŏd′ə-sĭl): a supplement to a will.

WORDS
TO
KNOW

**venerable** (vĕn′ər-ə-bəl) *adj.* worthy of respect by virtue of age or dignity

---

*Pause* & **Reflect**

1. Gillian gives all his money to Miss Hayden. Why doesn't he tell her that the money was really his inheritance? **(Infer)**

_____

_____

_____

_____

MARK IT UP   2. Circle the passage on this page that describes Gillian's written account of his spending. What do his comments reveal about his feelings for Miss Hayden? **(Draw Conclusions)**

_____

_____

_____

_____

3. What is your reaction to Gillian's good deed? **(Connect)**

_____

_____

_____

_____

MARK IT UP WORD POWER

Remember to mark words that you'd like to add to your **Personal Word List**. Later, you can record the words and their meanings beginning on page 316.

bequest in the will. As you have fulfilled the conditions
210 my partner and I have read the codicil. I do not wish
to <u>encumber</u> your understanding with its legal
phraseology, but I will <u>acquaint</u> you with the spirit
of its contents.

"The codicil promises that in the event that your
disposition[19] of the $1,000 demonstrates that you possess
any of the qualifications that deserve reward, much
benefit will accrue to you. Mr. Sharp and I are named
as the judges, and I assure you that we will do our duty
strictly according to justice—with liberality.[20] We are
220 not at all unfavorably disposed toward you, Mr. Gillian.
But let us return the letter of the codicil. If your disposal
of the money in question has been <u>prudent</u>, wise, or
unselfish, it is in our power to hand you over bonds to
the value of $50,000 which have been placed in our
hands for that purpose. But if—as our client, the late
Mr. Gillian, explicitly[21] provides—you have used this
money as you have used money in the past—I quote the
late Mr. Gillian—in reprehensible dissipation[22] among
<u>disreputable</u> associates—the $50,000 is to be paid to
230 Miriam Hayden, ward of the late Mr. Gillian, without
delay. Now, Mr. Gillian, Mr. Sharp and I will examine
your account in regard to the $1,000. You submit it in
writing, I believe. I hope you will repose[23] confidence in
our decision."

Mr. Tolman reached out for the envelope. Gillian was
a little the quicker in taking it up. He tore the account
and its cover leisurely into strips and dropped them into
his pocket.

---

19. **disposition** (dĭs′pə-zĭsh′ən): handling; use.
20. **liberality** (lĭb′ə-răl′ĭ-tē): generosity.
21. **explicitly** (ĭk-splĭs′ĭt-lē): in a clear, direct way.
22. **reprehensible dissipation** (rĕp′rĭ-hĕn′sə-bəl dĭs′ə-pā′shən): shameful,
    immoral living.
23. **repose** (rĭ-pōz′): place; put.

WORDS
TO
KNOW

**encumber** (ĕn-kŭm′bər) v. to burden
**acquaint** (ə-kwānt′) v. to inform; familiarize
**prudent** (prōōd′nt) adj. characterized by good judgment
**disreputable** (dĭs-rĕp′yə-tə-bəl) adj. having a bad
reputation; not respectable

"It's all right," he said, smiling. "There isn't a bit of need
to bother you with this. I don't suppose you'd understand
these itemized bets, anyway. I lost the thousand dollars on
the races. Good-day to you, gentlemen."

Tolman & Sharp shook their heads mournfully at each
other when Gillian left, for they heard him whistling gayly
in the hallway as he waited for the elevator.

### Pause & Reflect

### Pause & Reflect

1. Were you surprised by the
   ending of the story? *Yes/No,*
   because_____

   _____

   _____.

   **(Connect)**

2. Reread the boxed passage on
   page 106. What new information
   does Gillian learn about the will?
   **(Clarify)**

   _____

   _____

   _____

   _____

3. How does Gillian respond to Mr.
   Tolman's news about the will?
   **(Cause and Effect)**

   _____

   _____

   _____

   _____

**CHALLENGE**

The plot of " One Thousand
Dollars" is constructed in a way
that piques the reader's interest.

Review the story and star at
least three passages that
demonstrate surprising turns in
events. Explain how each of
these plot twists adds to your
enjoyment of the story. **(Plot)**

## Wrapping Up

If you are using *The Language
of Literature,* you can now
move to the questions and
activities on pages 394–396
of that book.

# Active Reading SkillBuilder

## Cause and Effect

Events that make up the plot in a work of fiction are often related by **cause and effect.** One event in a story can cause another, which is the effect. The effect may in turn cause another event, and so on. The events in "One Thousand Dollars" unfold through a series of conversations, each one leading to the next. As you read the story, use the graphic below to record a summary of each conversation and to show how these conversations are related. Examples are shown.

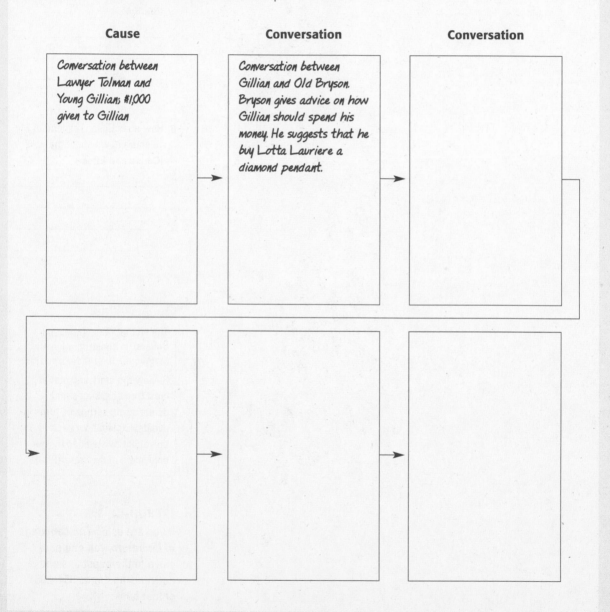

| Cause | Conversation | Conversation |
|---|---|---|
| Conversation between Lawyer Tolman and Young Gillian; $1,000 given to Gillian | Conversation between Gillian and Old Bryson. Bryson gives advice on how Gillian should spend his money. He suggests that he buy Lotta Lauriere a diamond pendant. | |

# Literary Analysis SkillBuilder

### Plot

**Plot** refers to the chain of related events that take place in a story. Most plots include these stages: the **exposition,** in which important background information is given; the **rising action,** in which the conflict becomes more complicated and difficult; the **climax,** or turning point, of the story, usually an important event, decision, or discovery; and the **falling action,** in which the conflict is worked out. Using the plot diagram below, list each conversation in this story next to the plot stage in which it falls. Two examples have been given.

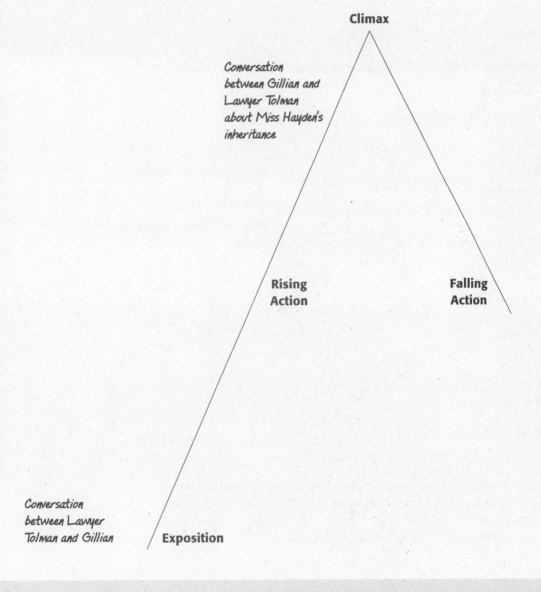

**Climax**

*Conversation between Gillian and Lawyer Tolman about Miss Hayden's inheritance*

**Rising Action**

**Falling Action**

*Conversation between Lawyer Tolman and Gillian*

**Exposition**

# Words to Know SkillBuilder

## Words to Know

| | | | | |
|---|---|---|---|---|
| acquaint | encumber | genially | precariousness | stipulate |
| disreputable | expenditure | pendant | prudent | venerable |

**A.** Complete each sentence with the correct Word to Know.

1. Someone who is _____ with money is not likely
   to spend it all on lottery tickets.

2. People who keep track of an _____ can tell you
   exactly how much money they have spent.

3. Friends who are celebrating a happy occasion are likely to greet each other
   _____ .

4. A man with only a few dollars feels the uncertainty and
   _____ of his position.

5. The diamond _____ in the jewelry store window
   is magnificent.

6. Did the contract _____ when and where the
   project will take place, as well as when it is to be completed?

7. The _____ physician received several awards at
   his retirement dinner.

8. Did you _____ yourself with the rules and
   regulations of the contest?

9. A _____ person is not likely to be trustworthy
   or respected.

10. While a lack of money would _____ most people,
    others might feel oppressed by their wealth.

**B.** Before directors cast the parts in a play, they often provide actors with a
description of each character. Write a description of Mr. Gillian that might be useful
to an actor playing the role of Mr. Gillian in a production of "One Thousand Dollars."
Use at least **four** Words to Know in your description.

# Getting a Job

## Maya Angelou

PREVIEW  Maya Angelou was born Marguerite Johnson. This excerpt from her autobiography, *I Know Why the Caged Bird Sings,* tells how she got her first job. Because many men were overseas fighting during World War II, new jobs opened to women. African-American women, however, faced racial prejudice that limited their opportunities. As you will see, the 15-year-old Marguerite refuses to back down from her dream of becoming a streetcar conductor.

**AUTOBIOGRAPHY**

### Before You Read

If you are using *The Language of Literature . . .*

- Use the information on page 411 of that book to prepare for reading.

- Look at the newspaper clippings on page 412 and the photograph on pages 414–415. What can you learn about the selection from these pictures?

### Reading Tips

This excerpt from the author's **autobiography** is an example of **narrative nonfiction**. It is a true story that contains many of the same elements as a work of fiction.

- As you read, look for evidence of the author's **character traits.** What type of person is she?

- Note the steps that the author takes to resolve the **conflict** and get what she wants.

- Pay attention to the role the **setting** plays in the conflict. How might the experience be different if the author were looking for a job today?

**FOCUS**

Read to find out why Marguerite decides to get a job.

**MARK IT UP** As you read, underline the difficulties she faces in looking for work. An example is highlighted.

**My room had all the cheeriness** of a dungeon and the appeal of a tomb. It was going to be impossible to stay there, but leaving held no attraction for me, either. . . . The answer came to me with the suddenness of a collision. I would go to work. Mother wouldn't be difficult to convince; after all, in school I was a year ahead of my grade and Mother was a firm believer in self-sufficiency. In fact, she'd be pleased to think that I had that much gumption,[1] that much of her in my character. (She liked to speak of herself as the original "do-it-yourself girl.")

Once I had settled on getting a job, all that remained was to decide which kind of job I was most fitted for. My intellectual pride had kept me from selecting typing, shorthand or filing as subjects in school, so office work was ruled out. War plants and shipyards demanded birth certificates, and mine would reveal me to be fifteen, and ineligible for work. So the well-paying defense jobs were also

**MARK IT UP** KEEP TRACK

As you read, you can use these marks to keep track of your understanding.

✔ ..... I understand.

? ..... I don't understand this.

! ..... Interesting or surprising idea

---

1. **gumption:** initiative; boldness.

_____

_____

_____

_____

_____

_____

_____

*Pause* **&** *Reflect*

**1.** Review what you underlined as you read. What might make it difficult for Marguerite to find a job? Circle three items below. **(Clarify)**

lack of office skills

her age

no college degree

her race

women not hired

**2.** Why does Marguerite want the job of streetcar conductor? **(Cause and Effect)**

_____

_____

_____

_____

**MARK IT UP** **3.** How would you describe Marguerite's personality? Write your answer below. Then circle passages on pages 111–112 that support your opinion. **(Infer)**

_____

_____

_____

_____

out. Women had replaced men on the streetcars as conductors and motormen, and the thought of sailing up and down the hills of San Francisco in a dark-blue uniform, with a money changer at my belt, caught my fancy.

Mother was as easy as I had anticipated. The world was moving so fast, so much money was being made, so many people were dying in Guam,[2] and Germany, that hordes of strangers became good friends overnight. Life was cheap and death entirely free. How could she have the time to think
30 about my academic career?

To her question of what I planned to do, I replied that I would get a job on the streetcars. She rejected the proposal with: "They don't accept colored people on the streetcars."

I would like to claim an immediate fury which was followed by the noble determination to break the restricting tradition. But the truth is, my first reaction was one of disappointment. I'd pictured myself, dressed in a neat blue serge suit, my money changer swinging jauntily at my waist, and a cheery smile for the passengers which would make their
40 own work day brighter.

From disappointment, I gradually <u>ascended</u> the emotional ladder to <u>haughty</u> indignation, and finally to that state of stubbornness where the mind is locked like the jaws of an enraged bulldog.

I would go to work on the streetcars and wear a blue serge suit. Mother gave me her support with one of her usual <u>terse</u> asides, "That's what you want to do? Then nothing beats a trial but a failure. Give it everything you've got. I've told you many times, 'Can't do is like Don't Care.' Neither of them
50 have a home."

Translated, that meant there was nothing a person can't do, and there should be nothing a human being didn't care about. It was the most positive encouragement I could have hoped for.

*Pause* **&** *Reflect*

_____

2. **Guam:** a U.S. island territory that was a scene of fierce fighting during World War II.

| WORDS | **ascend** (ə-sĕnd´) *v.* to rise; climb |
| TO | **haughty** (hô´tē) *adj.* proud; arrogant |
| KNOW | **terse** (tûrs) *adj.* brief; concise |

**FOCUS**
Read to find out what happens when Marguerite applies for the job of conductorette.

**In the offices** of the Market Street Railway Company, the receptionist seemed as surprised to see me there as I was surprised to find the interior dingy and the décor drab. Somehow I had expected waxed surfaces and carpeted floors. If I had met no resistance, I might have decided against working for such a poor-mouth-looking concern. As it was, I explained that I had come to see about a job. She asked, was I sent by an agency, and when I replied that I was not, she told me they were only accepting applicants from agencies.

The classified pages of the morning papers had listed advertisements for motorettes[3] and conductorettes and I reminded her of that. She gave me a face full of astonishment that my suspicious nature would not accept.

"I am applying for the job listed in this morning's *Chronicle* and I'd like to be presented to your personnel manager." While I spoke in supercilious[4] accents, and looked at the room as if I had an oil well in my own backyard, my armpits were being pricked by millions of hot pointed needles. She saw her escape and dived into it.

"He's out. He's out for the day. You might call tomorrow and if he's in, I'm sure you can see him." Then she swiveled her chair around on its rusty screws and with that I was supposed to be dismissed.

"May I ask his name?"

She half turned, acting surprised to find me still there.

"His name? Whose name?"

"Your personnel manager."

We were firmly joined in the <u>hypocrisy</u> to play out the scene.

"The personnel manager? Oh, he's Mr. Cooper, but I'm not sure you'll find him here tomorrow. He's . . . Oh, but you can try."

"Thank you."

"You're welcome."

And I was out of the musty room and into the even mustier lobby. In the street I saw the receptionist and myself going faithfully through paces that were stale with familiarity,

▶**MARK IT UP** WORD POWER

Mark words that you'd like to add to your **Personal Word List**. After reading, you can record the words and their meanings beginning on page 316.

---

3. **motorettes:** female streetcar drivers.

4. **supercilious** (sŏō′pər-sĭl′ē-əs): disdainful; haughty.

WORDS
TO
KNOW    **hypocrisy** (hĭ-pŏk′rĭ-sē) *n.* a pretense of being what one is not; falsehood

1. Review the boxed passage on page 113. Why does the receptionist make it so hard for Marguerite to see the personnel manager? **(Evaluate)**

_____

_____

_____

_____

✏️ MARK IT UP   2. When Marguerite first leaves the office, she feels that the secretary is (circle one) *a victim of an old tragedy/an evil person.* Circle passages on this page that show how she later changed her mind. **(Analyze)**

3. How would you feel if you were in Marguerite's place? **(Connect)**

_____

_____

_____

_____

although I had never encountered that kind of situation before and, probably, neither had she. We were like actors who, knowing the play by heart, were still able to cry afresh over the old tragedies and laugh spontaneously at the comic situations.

The miserable little encounter had nothing to do with me, the me of me, any more than it had to do with that silly clerk. The incident was a recurring dream, concocted years before 100 by stupid whites and it eternally came back to haunt us all. The secretary and I were like Hamlet and Laertes[5] in the final scene, where, because of harm done by one ancestor to another, we were bound to duel to the death. Also because the play must end somewhere.

I went further than forgiving the clerk, I accepted her as a fellow victim of the same puppeteer.

On the streetcar, I put my fare into the box and the conductorette looked at me with the usual hard eyes of white contempt. "Move into the car, please move on in the car." She 110 patted her money changer.

Her Southern nasal accent sliced my meditation and I looked deep into my thoughts. All lies, all comfortable lies. The receptionist was not innocent and neither was I. The whole <u>charade</u> we had played out in that crummy waiting room had directly to do with me, Black, and her, white.

I wouldn't move into the streetcar but stood on the ledge over the conductor, glaring. My mind shouted so energetically that the announcement made my veins stand out, and my mouth tighten into a prune.

120 I WOULD HAVE THE JOB. I WOULD BE A CONDUCTORETTE AND SLING A FULL MONEY CHANGER FROM MY BELT. I WOULD.

**FOCUS**
Read to find out whether Marguerite gets the job.

**The next three weeks** were a honeycomb of determination with apertures[6] for the days to go in and out. The Negro

---

5. **Hamlet and Laertes** (lā-ûr′tēz): characters who kill each other in a sword fight in the last scene of Shakespeare's *Hamlet*.

6. **apertures** (ăp′ər-chərz): openings.

WORDS
TO
KNOW

**charade** (shə-rād′) *n.* an ill-disguised pretense

organizations to whom I appealed for support bounced me back and forth like a shuttlecock on a badminton court. Why did I insist on that particular job? Openings were going begging that paid nearly twice the money. The minor officials 130 with whom I was able to win an audience thought me mad. Possibly I was.

Downtown San Francisco became alien and cold, and the streets I had loved in a personal familiarity were unknown lanes that twisted with malicious intent. Old buildings, whose gray rococo façades housed my memories of the Forty-Niners, and Diamond Lil, Robert Service, Sutter and Jack London,[7] were then imposing structures viciously joined to keep me out. My trips to the streetcar office were of the frequency of a person on salary. The struggle expanded. I was no longer in 140 conflict only with the Market Street Railway but with the marble lobby of the building which housed its offices, and elevators and their operators.

During this period of strain Mother and I began our first steps on the long path toward mutual adult admiration. She never asked for reports and I didn't offer any details. But every morning she made breakfast, gave me carfare and lunch money, as if I were going to work. She <u>comprehended</u> the perversity of life, that in the struggle lies the joy. That I was no glory seeker was obvious to her, and that I had to exhaust 150 every possibility before giving in was also clear.

On my way out of the house one morning she said, "Life is going to give you just what you put in it. Put your whole heart in everything you do, and pray, then you can wait." Another time she reminded me that "God helps those who help themselves." She had a store of aphorisms[8] which she dished out as the occasion demanded. Strangely, as bored as I

**READ ALOUD** Lines 151–156

Read these lines in a way that expresses the mother's feelings for Marguerite.

---

7. **Forty-Niners . . . Jack London:** Forty-niners were people who flocked to northern California in the gold rush of 1849; Diamond Lil was a colorful character of the gold-rush era; Robert Service was a Canadian poet who wrote about life in the mining camps of the 1897 Klondike gold rush; John Sutter owned the California ranch where gold was discovered in 1848; Jack London was a writer who grew up in the San Francisco area and joined the Klondike gold rush.

8. **aphorisms** (ăf´ə-rĭz´əmz): proverbs.

WORDS
TO        **comprehend** (kŏm´prĭ-hĕnd´) v. to understand
KNOW

**1.** Why do you think Marguerite is finally hired? **(Cause and Effect)**

_____

_____

_____

_____

**2.** How does Marguerite's mother help her in her struggle to get a job? **(Draw Conclusions)**

_____

_____

_____

_____

**3.** Do you think Marguerite's new job will bring her happiness? _Yes/No,_ because _____

_____

_____

_____ .

**(Predict)**

was with clichés, her inflection gave them something new, and set me thinking for a little while at least. Later when asked how I got my job, I was never able to say exactly. I only knew that one day, which was tiresomely like all the others before it, I sat in the Railway office, <u>ostensibly</u> waiting to be interviewed. The receptionist called me to her desk and shuffled a bundle of papers to me. They were job application forms. She said they had to be filled in triplicate. I had little time to wonder if I had won or not, for the standard questions reminded me of the necessity for <u>dexterous</u> lying. How old was I? List my previous jobs, starting from the last held and go backward to the first. How much money did I earn, and why did I leave the position? Give two references (not relatives).

Sitting at a side table my mind and I wove a cat's ladder of near truths and total lies. I kept my face blank (an old art) and wrote quickly the fable of Marguerite Johnson, aged nineteen, former companion and driver for Mrs. Annie Henderson (a White Lady) in Stamps, Arkansas.

I was given blood tests, aptitude tests, physical coordination tests, and Rorschachs,[9] then on a blissful day I was hired as the first Negro on the San Francisco streetcars.

**Pause & Reflect**

**FOCUS**

Read to find out what Marguerite learns from her experience.

**Mother gave me the money** to have my blue serge suit tailored, and I learned to fill out work cards, operate the money changer and punch transfers. The time crowded together and at an End of Days I was swinging on the back of the rackety trolley, smiling sweetly and persuading my charges to "step forward in the car, please."

For one whole semester the street cars and I shimmied up

---

9. **Rorschachs** (rôr′shäks′): psychological tests in which people are asked to interpret a set of inkblots.

| WORDS TO KNOW | **ostensibly** (ŏ-stĕn′sə-blē) _adv._ apparently; supposedly |
| | **dexterous** (dĕk′stər-əs) _adj._ skillful; clever |

and scooted down the sheer hills of San Francisco. I lost some of my need for the Black ghetto's shielding-sponge quality, as I clanged and cleared my way down Market Street, with its honky-tonk homes for homeless sailors, past the quiet retreat of Golden Gate Park and along closed undwelled-in-looking dwellings of the Sunset District.

My work shifts were split[10] so <u>haphazardly</u> that it was easy to believe that my superiors had chosen them maliciously. Upon mentioning my suspicions to Mother, she said, "Don't worry about it. You ask for what you want, and you pay for what you get. And I'm going to show you that it ain't no trouble when you pack double."

She stayed awake to drive me out to the car barn at four thirty in the mornings, or to pick me up when I was relieved just before dawn. Her awareness of life's perils convinced her that while I would be safe on the public conveyances,[11] she "wasn't about to trust a taxi driver with her baby."

When the spring classes began, I resumed my commitment with formal education. I was so much wiser and older, so much more independent, with a bank account and clothes that I had bought for myself, that I was sure that I had learned and earned the magic formula which would make me a part of the gay life my contemporaries led.

Not a bit of it. Within weeks, I realized that my schoolmates and I were on paths moving <u>diametrically</u> away from each other. They were concerned and excited over the approaching football games, but I had in my immediate past raced a car down a dark and foreign Mexican mountain. They concentrated great interest on who was worthy of being student body president, and when the metal bands would be removed from their teeth, while I remembered sleeping for a month in a wrecked automobile and conducting a streetcar in the uneven hours of the morning.

**Pause & Reflect**

---

10. **shifts were split:** a working shift that requires a worker to work at two different times, separated by a number of hours.

11. **conveyances** (kən-vā′ən-səz): means of transportation.

| WORDS TO KNOW | |
|---|---|
| | **haphazardly** (hăp-hăz′ərd-lē) *adv.* in an aimless or random manner |
| | **diametrically** (dī′ə-mĕt′rĭ-klē) *adv.* in complete opposition |

**Pause & Reflect**

1. How does Marguerite benefit from her work experience? (Evaluate)

_____

_____

_____

2. Do you admire Marguerite as a person? Explain. (Connect)

_____

_____

_____

_____

**CHALLENGE**

Angelou includes many details that help the reader "see" the experience from her point of view. Circle details in the story that helped you to visualize the characters or the setting. Then explain how these details influenced your understanding and appreciation of Angelou's experience. (Narrative Nonfiction)

**Wrapping Up**

If you are using *The Language of Literature,* you can now move to the questions and activities on pages 417–418 of that book.

# Active Reading SkillBuilder

### Identifying Cause and Effect in Nonfiction

Recognizing **cause-and-effect** relationships helps readers better understand the events that a writer relates in a work of nonfiction. A **cause** is an event or action that directly results in another event or action. An **effect** is the direct outcome of an event. When reading this selection, use the diagram below to record two causes that led Marguerite to seek the job of streetcar conductor. An example is given. Then list three effects that this experience had on Marguerite's life.

### Marguerite's desire to be a streetcar conductor

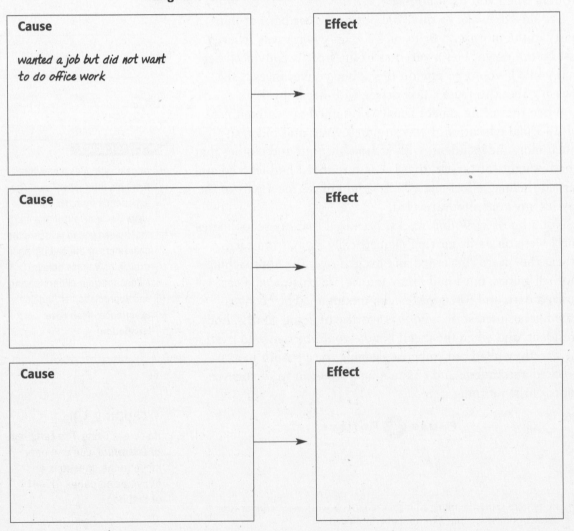

**Cause**

*wanted a job but did not want to do office work*

**Effect**

**Cause**

**Effect**

**Cause**

**Effect**

# Literary Analysis SkillBuilder

### Narrative Nonfiction

A work of **narrative nonfiction** tells a story about real-life people, places, and events. It uses elements typically found in fictional narratives to present factual information and to bring these facts to life for the reader. For instance, the vivid settings that Angelou creates in this piece include the offices of the Market Street Railway Company and the hills of San Francisco. As you read this selection, identify passages in Angelou's text that illustrate the specific elements of fiction listed in the chart below. Record each passage in the appropriate section of the chart.

| Passages from "Getting a Job" |
| --- |
| **Plot:** |
| **Character:** |
| **Setting:** |
| **Theme:** |
| **Point of View:** |

# Words to Know SkillBuilder

## Words to Know

| | | | | |
|---|---|---|---|---|
| ascend | comprehend | diametrically | haughty | ostensibly |
| charade | dexterous | haphazardly | hypocrisy | terse |

**A.** Circle the correct word in each group that is an antonym, or means the opposite, of the boldfaced word.

1. **ascend**        stumble        meander        descend

2. **terse**        withdrawn        rambling        concise

3. **haughty**        humble        smooth        arrogant

4. **dexterous**        reluctant        awkward        agile

5. **haphazardly**        purposefully        randomly        slowly

**B.** Decide which Word to Know is described by each clue. Then write the word in the blank to the right of the sentence.

1. You would show this if you said and did the things you did not really believe in.

_____
(1)

2. This word means what "seems to be."

_____
(2)

3. If you grasp the meaning of this message, then you are doing this.

_____
(3)

4. This word describes ways of thinking that are completely opposite.

_____
(4)

5. This is an act that is really a sham, with no basis in truth.

_____
(5)

# A Celebration of Grandfathers

## Rudolfo A. Anaya

PREVIEW  The author Rudolfo A. Anaya grew up in rural New Mexico. In this memoir, he recalls his grandfather and other old people from his childhood. A simple farmer, Anaya's grandfather shared his wisdom and values with his grandson. Anaya wonders whether such values can be kept alive in the world of today.

**Before You Read**

If you are using *The Language of Literature*. . .

• Use the information on page 455 of that book to prepare for reading.

• Look at the title of this memoir and at the art on page 456. What do you predict this selection will be about?

**Reading Tips**

In this **memoir**, the author strings together various memories of his past. At first, you may not understand how these memories are all related. Be patient and keep reading. Eventually, the **author's purpose** is made clear. As you read, watch for statements that help to explain the author's purpose for writing.

---

**FOCUS**

Anaya begins by remembering old people from his childhood.

MARK IT UP  As you read, circle details that describe what Anaya admires about his grandfather and others like him. An example is highlighted.

**"Buenos días le de Dios, abuelo."** God give you a good day, grandfather. This is how I was taught as a child to greet my grandfather, or any grown person. It was a greeting of respect, a cultural value to be passed on from generation to generation, this respect for the old ones.

The old people I remember from my childhood were strong in their beliefs, and as we lived daily with them, we learned a wise path of life to follow. They had something important to share with the young, and when they spoke, the young listened. These old *abuelos* and *abuelitas*[1] had worked the earth all their lives, and so they knew the value of nurturing, they knew the sensitivity of the earth. . . . They knew the rhythms and cycles of time, from the preparation of the earth in the spring to the digging of the *acequias*[2] that brought the water to the dance of harvest in the

---

MARK IT UP  **KEEP TRACK**

As you read, you can use these marks to keep track of your understanding.

✔ ..... I understand.

? ..... I don't understand this.

! ..... Interesting or surprising idea

---

1. *abuelos* (ä-bwě′lôs) . . . *abuelitas* (ä-bwě-lē′täs) *Spanish:* grandfathers . . . grannies.

2. *acequias* (ä-sě′kyäs) *Spanish:* irrigation ditches.

✏️ **MARK IT UP** **WORD POWER**

Mark words that you'd like to add to your **Personal Word List**. After reading, you can record the words and their meanings beginning on page 316.

📖 **READ ALOUD** **Lines 41–57**

Read aloud the boxed passage. What does this passage reveal about the grandfather's beliefs? **(Infer)**

_____

_____

_____

_____

fall. They shared good times and hard times. They helped each other through the epidemics and the personal tragedies, and they shared what little they had when the hot winds burned the land and no rain came. They learned that to survive one had to share in the process of life. . . .

My grandfather was a plain man, a farmer from the valley called Puerto de Luna on the Pecos River. He was probably a descendant of those people who spilled over the mountain from Taos, following the Pecos River in search of farmland. There in that river valley he settled and raised a large family.

Bearded and walrus-mustached, he stood five feet tall, but to me as a child he was a giant. I remember him most for his silence. In the summers my parents sent me to live with him on his farm, for I was to learn the ways of a farmer. My uncles also lived in that valley, there where only the flow of the river and the whispering of the wind marked time. For me it was a magical place.

I remember once, while out hoeing the fields, I came upon an anthill, and before I knew it I was badly bitten. After he had covered my welts with the cool mud from the irrigation ditch, my grandfather calmly said: "Know where you stand." That is the way he spoke, in short phrases, to the point.

One very dry summer, the river dried to a trickle; there was no water for the fields. The young plants withered and died. In my sadness and with the impulse of youth I said, "I wish it would rain!" My grandfather touched me, looked up into the sky and whispered, "Pray for rain." In his language there was a difference. He felt connected to the cycles that brought the rain or kept it from us. His prayer was a meaningful action, because he was a participant with the forces that filled our world; he was not a bystander.

A young man died at the village one summer. A very tragic death. He was dragged by his horse. When he was found, I cried, for the boy was my friend. I did not understand why death had come to one so young. My grandfather took me aside and said: "Think of the death of the trees and the fields in the fall. The leaves fall, and everything rests, as if dead. But they bloom again in the spring. Death is only this small transformation in life."

These are the things I remember, these fleeting images, few words. I remember him driving his horse-drawn wagon into Santa Rosa in the fall when he brought his harvest produce to sell in the town. What a tower of strength seemed to come in that small man huddled on the seat of the giant wagon. One click of his tongue and the horses obeyed, stopped or turned as he wished. He never raised his whip. How unlike today, when so much teaching is done with loud words and threatening hands.

I would run to greet the wagon, and the wagon would stop. *"Buenos días le de Dios, abuelo,"* I would say. . . . *"Buenos días te de Dios, mi hijo,"*[3] he would answer and smile, and

70 then I could jump up on the wagon and sit at his side. Then I, too, became a king as I rode next to the old man who smelled of earth and sweat and the other deep aromas from the orchards and fields of Puerto de Luna.

## Pause & Reflect

**FOCUS**
Anaya offers his thoughts about the values of his grandfather's generation. Read to learn more about what Anaya learned from his grandfather.

**We were all sons and daughters** to him. But today the sons and daughters are breaking with the past, putting aside *los abuelitos.* The old values are threatened, and threatened most where it comes to these relationships with the old people. If we don't take the time to watch and feel

80 the years of their final transformation, a part of our humanity will be lessened.

I grew up speaking Spanish, and oh! how difficult it was to learn English. Sometimes I would give up and cry out that I couldn't learn. Then he would say, *"Ten paciencia."* Have patience. *Paciencia,* a word with the strength of centuries, a word that said that someday we would overcome. . . . "You have to learn the language of the *Americanos,*" he said. "Me, I will live my last days in my valley. You will live in a new time."

90 A new time did come; a new time is here. How will we form it so it is fruitful? We need to know where we stand. We need to speak softly and respect others, and to share what we have. We need to pray not for material gain, but for rain for the fields, for the sun to nurture growth, for nights in which we can sleep in peace, and for a harvest in which everyone can share. Simple lessons from a simple man. These lessons he

---

3. *mi hijo* (mē ē′hô) *Spanish:* my boy.

## Pause & Reflect

1. Review the details that you circled as you read. What does Anaya admire about his grandfather? **(Author's Perspective)**

_____

_____

_____

_____

2. In the list below, put a check next to words that describe Anaya's grandfather. **(Clarify)**

simple          calm

strong          loud

angry           wise

3. Would you have liked to have known Anaya's grandfather? Why or why not? **(Connect)**

_____

_____

_____

_____

**1.** Reread the boxed passage on page 123. Which of the "simple lessons from a simple man" do you think is most important? Explain. **(Evaluate)**

_____

_____

_____

_____

**2.** What does Anaya remember about his grandfather's last years? **(Summarize)**

_____

_____

_____

_____

**3.** Circle the best ending to the following sentence:
Anaya describes the end of his grandfather's life_____

to show that old people get cranky.

to provide a complete and honest portrait of his grandfather.

to show that he lost respect for his grandfather.

**(Author's Purpose)**

learned from his past, which was as deep and strong as the currents of the river of life.

He was a man; he died. Not in his valley but nevertheless 100 cared for by his sons and daughters and flocks of grandchildren. At the end, I would enter his room, which carried the smell of medications and Vicks. Gone were the aroma of the fields, the strength of his young manhood. Gone also was his patience in the face of crippling old age. Small things bothered him; he shouted or turned sour when his expectations were not met. It was because he could not care for himself, because he was returning to that state of childhood, and all those wishes and desires were now wrapped in a crumbling, old body.

110 *"Ten paciencia,"* I once said to him, and he smiled. "I didn't know I would grow this old," he said. . . .

I would sit and look at him and remember what was said of him when he was a young man. He could mount a wild horse and break it, and he could ride as far as any man. He could dance all night at a dance, then work the *acequia* the following day. He helped the neighbors; they helped him. He married, raised children. Small legends, the kind that make up every man's life.

He was ninety-four when he died. Family, neighbors, and 120 friends gathered; they all agreed he had led a rich life. I remembered the last years, the years he spent in bed. And as I remember now, I am reminded that it is too easy to romanticize[4] old age. Sometimes we forget the pain of the transformation into old age, we forget the natural breaking down of the body. . . . My grandfather pointed to the leaves falling from the tree. So time brings with its transformation the often painful wearing-down process. Vision blurs, health wanes; even the act of walking carries with it the painful reminder of the autumn of life. But this process is something 130 to be faced, not something to be hidden away by false images. Yes, the old can be young at heart, but in their own way, with their own dignity. They do not have to copy the always-young image of the Hollywood star. . . .

Pause **&** Reflect

4. **romanticize:** view in an unrealistic or sentimental way.

FOCUS

Some years after his
grandfather's death,
Anaya returns to the
village where they
lived.

MARK IT UP  As you
read, underline
sentences that
describe Anaya's
concerns and fears.

140

**I returned to Puerto de Luna** last summer
to join the community in a celebration
of the founding of the church. I drove
by my grandfather's home, my uncles'
ranches, the neglected adobe washing
down into the earth from whence it
came. And I wondered, how might the
values of my grandfather's generation
live in our own? What can we retain to
see us through these hard times? I was
to become a farmer, and I became a writer. As I plow and
plant my words, do I nurture as my grandfather did in his
fields and orchards? The answers are not simple.

"They don't make men like that anymore," is a phrase we
hear when one does honor to a man. I am glad I knew my
grandfather. I am glad there are still times when I can see him
150 in my dreams, hear him in my reverie. Sometimes I think I
catch a whiff of that earthy aroma that was his smell. Then I
smile. How strong these people were to leave such a lasting
impression.

So, as I would greet my *abuelo* long ago, it would help us
all to greet the old ones we know with this kind and
respectful greeting: *"Buenos días le de Dios."*

**Pause & Reflect**

**Pause & Reflect**

1. Review the sentences that you
underlined as you read. Which
sentence below describes one
of Anaya's concerns? Circle it.
**(Main Idea)**

His grandfather's values may
be lost.

Anaya's memory of his
grandfather is fading.

READ ALOUD  **2.** Read aloud
the boxed passage on this page.
Why does Anaya compare his
writing to his grandfather's
farming? **(Compare and
Contrast)**

_____

_____

_____

_____

CHALLENGE

What do you learn about
Anaya's Mexican-American
heritage as a result of reading
this memoir? Review the essay
for details that seem specific to
Mexican-American culture.
Mark passages that seem
especially important.
**(Make Generalizations)**

## Wrapping Up

If you are using **The Language
of Literature,** you can now
move to the questions and
activities on pages 460–461
of that book.

# Active Reading SkillBuilder

## Identifying Author's Purpose

**Author's purpose** refers to a writer's reason for writing. Usually a writer has one main purpose and one or more less important ones. The purposes for writing nonfiction include the following: (1) to inform; (2) to express ideas, opinions, and feelings; (3) to analyze; (4) to persuade; (5) to entertain. In the chart below, record statements from Anaya's memoir that show some of the purposes he had for writing it. At the bottom of the page, write what you think is Anaya's main purpose. An example is given.

| Statements | Purpose |
|---|---|
| "It was a greeting of respect, a cultural value to be passed on from generation to generation..." (lines 4–7) | to express his opinion about the values of his grandfather |
| | |
| | |
| | |

**Main Purpose:** _____

_____

# Literary Analysis SkillBuilder

### Author's Perspective and Tone

**Author's perspective** refers to what a writer thinks, values, and believes. An author's **tone** refers to the attitude he or she has toward a subject, or topic. The tone of a piece of writing can reveal the author's perspective. For example, if a journalist's tone is enthusiastic in support of money for better schools, you know he or she values education. Use the diagram below to show the relationship between tone and author's perspective in Anaya's memoir. In the left box, write two more adjectives that describe the tone of the essay. In the right box, identify the perspective you think the tone reveals. An example is given.

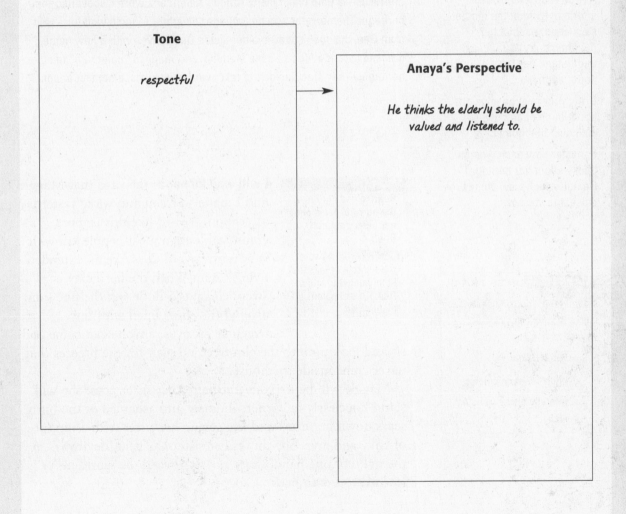

**Tone**

respectful

**Anaya's Perspective**

He thinks the elderly should be valued and listened to.

## Before You Read

If you are using **The Language of Literature,** study the information on page 503 of that book to prepare for reading.

## Reading Tips

The **narrator** of this story is the mother of two daughters who seem to be completely different from one another.

- As you read, pay close attention to what the mother says about each of her daughters. Try to understand her feelings about each one.

- Draw your own conclusions about each character— including the mother.

- Consider how each woman thinks about her heritage. Decide which view comes closest to your own.

# EVERYDAY USE
*Alice Walker*

**MARK IT UP** **KEEP TRACK**

As you read, you can use these marks to keep track of your understanding.

✔ ..... I understand.

? ..... I don't understand this.

! ..... Interesting or surprising idea

**PREVIEW** This story takes place in a poor, rural area of the South during the 1960s—a time when many African Americans were discovering their heritage. The narrator and her younger daughter Maggie wait for a visit from Dee, the sophisticated older sister. Dee arrives with a new name, dressed in fancy African-style clothing, and ready to "celebrate" her heritage. When Dee decides to take two family quilts, a conflict arises.

**FOCUS**
Read to find out how the narrator feels about her older daughter, Dee.

**MARK IT UP** As you read, circle details that help you get to know Dee. An example is highlighted.

**I will wait for her** in the yard that Maggie and I made so clean and wavy yesterday afternoon. A yard like this is more comfortable than most people know. It is not just a yard. It is like an extended living room. When the hard clay is swept clean as a floor and the fine sand around the edges lined with tiny, irregular grooves, anyone can come and

10 sit and look up into the elm tree and wait for the breezes that never come inside the house.

Maggie will be nervous until after her sister goes: she will stand hopelessly in corners, homely and ashamed of the burn scars down her arms and legs, eying her sister with a mixture of envy and awe. She thinks her sister has held life always in the palm of one hand, that "no" is a word the world never learned to say to her.

You've no doubt seen those TV shows where the child who has "made it" is confronted, as a surprise, by her own mother

**20** and father, tottering in weakly from backstage. (A pleasant surprise, of course: What would they do if parent and child came on the show only to curse out and insult each other?) On TV mother and child embrace and smile into each other's faces. Sometimes the mother and father weep, the child wraps them in her arms and leans across the table to tell how she would not have made it without their help. I have seen these programs.

Sometimes I dream a dream in which Dee and I are suddenly brought together on a TV program of this sort. Out **30** of a dark and soft-seated limousine I am ushered into a bright room filled with many people. There I meet a smiling, gray, sporty man like Johnny Carson[1] who shakes my hand and tells me what a fine girl I have. Then we are on the stage and Dee is embracing me with tears in her eyes. She pins on my dress a large orchid, even though she has told me once that she thinks orchids are tacky flowers.

In real life I am a large, big-boned woman with rough, man-working hands. In the winter I wear flannel nightgowns to bed and overalls during the day. I can kill and clean a hog **40** as mercilessly as a man. My fat keeps me hot in zero weather. I can work outside all day, breaking ice to get water for washing; I can eat pork liver cooked over the open fire minutes after it comes steaming from the hog. One winter I knocked a bull calf straight in the brain between the eyes with a sledge hammer and had the meat hung up to chill before nightfall. But of course all this does not show on television. I am the way my daughter would want me to be: a hundred pounds lighter, my skin like an uncooked barley pancake. My hair glistens in the hot bright lights. Johnny Carson has much **50** to do to keep up with my quick and witty tongue.

But that is a mistake. I know even before I wake up. Who ever knew a Johnson with a quick tongue? Who can even imagine me looking a strange white man in the eye? It seems to me I have talked to them always with one foot raised in flight, with my head turned in whichever way is farthest from them. Dee, though. She would always look anyone in the eye. Hesitation was no part of her nature.

*Pause* **&** *Reflect*

1. **Johnny Carson:** famous host of a late-night television show in the 1960s–90s.

Everyday Use   **129**

---

*Pause* **&** *Reflect*

1. Review the details you circled about Dee. What impressions have you formed of her? **(Evaluate)**

_____

_____

_____

_____

2. Which words and phrases below describe the narrator? Circle them. **(Draw Conclusions)**

| | |
|---|---|
| poor | gentle |
| big and strong | direct and plainspoken |
| fearful | a farmer |
| educated | conceited |

3. What questions do you have about the relationship between Dee and her family? Write one down. **(Question)**

_____

_____

_____

4. Do you **predict** that Dee's visit will be pleasant? Why or why not?

_____

_____

_____

_____

✎ MARK IT UP WORD POWER

Mark words that you'd like to add to your **Personal Word List**. After reading, you can record the words and their meanings beginning on page 316.

**FOCUS**
Read to find out how Maggie differs from her older sister, Dee.

MARK IT UP As you read, write notes in the margins to describe the two sisters.

**"How do I look, Mama?"** Maggie says, showing just enough of her thin body enveloped in pink skirt and red blouse for me to know she's there, almost hidden by the door.

"Come out into the yard," I say. Have you ever seen a lame animal, perhaps a dog run over by some careless person rich enough to own a car, <u>sidle</u> up to someone who is ignorant enough to be kind to him? That is the way my Maggie walks. She has been like this, chin on chest, eyes on ground, feet in shuffle, ever since the fire that burned the other house to the ground.

Dee is lighter than Maggie, with nicer hair and a fuller figure. She's a woman now, though sometimes I forget. How long ago was it that the other house burned? Ten, twelve years? Sometimes I can still hear the flames and feel Maggie's arms sticking to me, her hair smoking and her dress falling off her in little black papery flakes. Her eyes seemed stretched open, blazed open by the flames reflected in them. And Dee. I see her standing off under the sweet gum tree she used to dig gum out of; a look of concentration on her face as she watched the last dingy gray board of the house fall in toward the red-hot brick chimney. Why don't you do a dance around the ashes? I'd wanted to ask her. She had hated the house that much.

I used to think she hated Maggie, too. But that was before we raised the money, the church and me, to send her to Augusta[2] to school. She used to read to us without pity; forcing words, lies, other folks' habits, whole lives upon us two, sitting trapped and ignorant underneath her voice. She washed us in a river of make-believe, burned us with a lot of knowledge we didn't necessarily need to know. Pressed us to her with the serious way she read, to shove us away at just the moment, like dimwits, we seemed about to understand.

Dee wanted nice things. A yellow organdy dress to wear to her graduation from high school; black pumps to match a green suit she'd made from an old suit somebody gave me.

📖 READ ALOUD   Lines 86–92

As you read these lines aloud, notice the strength of the verbs. What do they reveal about Dee and her motives for reading to others? (Draw Conclusions)

---

2. **Augusta:** a city in Georgia.

| WORDS TO KNOW | **sidle** (sīd'l) v. to move sideways, especially in a shy or sneaky way |
|---|---|

She was determined to stare down any disaster in her efforts. Her eyelids would not flicker for minutes at a time. Often I fought off the temptation to shake her. At sixteen she had a style of her own: and knew what style was.

100    I never had an education myself. After second grade the school was closed down. Don't ask me why: in 1927 colored asked fewer questions than they do now. Sometimes Maggie reads to me. She stumbles along good-naturedly but can't see well. She knows she is not bright. Like good looks and money, quickness passed her by. She will marry John Thomas (who has mossy teeth in an earnest face) and then I'll be free to sit here and I guess just sing church songs to myself. Although I never was a good singer. Never could carry a tune. I was always better at a man's job. I used to love to milk till I was
110 hooked in the side in '49. Cows are soothing and slow and don't bother you, unless you try to milk them the wrong way.

   I have <u>deliberately</u> turned my back on the house. It is three rooms, just like the one that burned, except the roof is tin; they don't make shingle roofs any more. There are no real windows, just some holes cut in the sides, like the portholes in a ship, but not round and not square, with rawhide holding the shutters up on the outside. This house is in a pasture, too, like the other one. No doubt when Dee sees it she will want to tear it down. She wrote me once that no matter where we
120 "choose" to live, she will manage to come see us. But she will never bring her friends. Maggie and I thought about this and Maggie asked me, "Mama, when did Dee ever *have* any friends?"

   She had a few. <u>Furtive</u> boys in pink shirts hanging about on washday after school. Nervous girls who never laughed. Impressed with her they worshiped the well-turned phrase, the cute shape, the scalding humor that erupted like bubbles in lye. She read to them.

   When she was courting Jimmy T she didn't have much time
130 to pay to us, but turned all her faultfinding power on him. He *flew* to marry a cheap city girl from a family of ignorant flashy people. She hardly had time to recompose herself.

**Pause & Reflect**

---

**Pause & Reflect**

1. Look back at the notes you wrote in the margins. Write an *M* next to the phrases below that describe Maggie. Write a *D* next to the ones describing Dee. **(Clarify)**

thin and homely

confident and independent

insecure and shy

scarred from a fire

ambitious and strong-willed

**MARK IT UP** 2. How does the narrator feel about each of her daughters? Underline details in the story that support your conclusions. **(Draw Conclusions)**

Dee: _____

_____

_____

Maggie: _____

_____

_____

3. What is your opinion of Maggie and Dee so far? **(Evaluate)**

_____

_____

_____

_____

---

WORDS
TO
KNOW

**deliberately** (dĭ-lĭb′ər-ĭt-lē) *adv.* as a result of careful thought
**furtive** (fûr′tĭv) *adj.* sneaky, shifty, or secretive

**When she comes** I will meet—but there they are!

Maggie attempts to make a dash for the house, in her shuffling way, but I stay her with my hand. "Come back here," I say. And she stops and tries to dig a well in the sand with her toe.

140　　It is hard to see them clearly through the strong sun. But even the first glimpse of leg out of the car tells me it is Dee. Her feet were always neat-looking, as if God himself had shaped them with a certain style. From the other side of the car comes a short, stocky man. Hair is all over his head a foot long and hanging from his chin like a kinky mule tail. I hear Maggie suck in her breath. "Uhnnnh," is what it sounds like. Like when you see the wriggling end of a snake just in front of your foot on the road. "Uhnnnh."

Dee next. A dress down to the ground, in this hot weather. 150 A dress so loud it hurts my eyes. There are yellows and oranges enough to throw back the light of the sun. I feel my whole face warming from the heat waves it throws out. Earrings gold, too, and hanging down to her shoulders. Bracelets dangling and making noises when she moves her arm up to shake the folds of the dress out of her armpits. The dress is loose and flows, and as she walks closer, I like it. I hear Maggie go "Uhnnnh" again. It is her sister's hair. It stands straight up like the wool on a sheep. It is black as night and around the edges are two long pigtails that rope about 160 like small lizards disappearing behind her ears.

"Wa-su-zo-Tean-o!" she says, coming on in that gliding way the dress makes her move. The short stocky fellow with the hair to his navel is all grinning and he follows up with "Asalamalakim,[3] my mother and sister!" He moves to hug Maggie but she falls back, right up against the back of my chair. I feel her trembling there and when I look up I see the perspiration falling off her chin.

"Don't get up," says Dee. Since I am stout it takes something of a push. You can see me trying to move a second 170 or two before I make it. She turns, showing white heels through her sandals, and goes back to the car. Out she peeks next with a Polaroid. She stoops down quickly and lines up picture after picture of me sitting there in front of the house

---

3. **Wa-su-zo-Tean-o!** (wä-sōō′zō-tē′nō) . . . **Asalamalakim!** (ə-säl′ə-mə-läk′əm): greetings used by members of the Black Muslims.

with Maggie cowering behind me. She never takes a shot
without making sure the house is included. When a cow comes
nibbling around the edge of the yard she snaps it and me and
Maggie *and* the house. Then she puts the Polaroid in the back
seat of the car, and comes up and kisses me on the forehead.

Meanwhile Asalamalakim is going through motions with
**180** Maggie's hand. Maggie's hand is as limp as a fish, and
probably as cold, despite the sweat, and she keeps trying to
pull it back. It looks like Asalamalakim wants to shake hands
but wants to do it fancy. Or maybe he don't know how people
shake hands. Anyhow, he soon gives up on Maggie.

"Well," I say. "Dee."

"No, Mama," she says. "Not 'Dee,' Wangero Leewanika
Kemanjo!"[4]

"What happened to 'Dee'?" I wanted to know.

"She's dead," Wangero said. "I couldn't bear it any longer,
**190** being named after the people who oppress me."

"You know as well as me you was named after your aunt
Dicie," I said. Dicie is my sister. She named Dee. We called her
"Big Dee" after Dee was born.

"But who was *she* named after?" asked Wangero.

"I guess after Grandma Dee," I said.

"And who was she named after?" asked Wangero.

"Her mother," I said, and saw Wangero was getting tired.
"That's about as far back as I can trace it," I said. Though, in
fact, I probably could have carried it back beyond the Civil
**200** War through the branches.

"Well," said Asalamalakim, "there you are."

"Uhnnnh," I heard Maggie say.

"There I was not," I said, "before 'Dicie' cropped up in our
family, so why should I try to trace it that far back?"

He just stood there grinning, looking down on me like
somebody inspecting a Model A[5] car. Every once in a while he
and Wangero sent eye signals over my head.

"How do you pronounce this name?" I asked.

"You don't have to call me by it if you don't want to," said
**210** Wangero.

---

4. **Wangero Leewanika Kemanjo** (wän-gâr′ō lē-wä-nē′kə kĕ-män′jō).

5. **Model A:** an automobile manufactured by Ford from 1927 to 1931.

WORDS
TO
KNOW

**oppress** (ə-prĕs′) *v.* to keep down by the cruel or unjust
use of power or authority

---

NOTES

READ ALOUD   Lines 179–184

As you read these lines aloud,
try to form a picture of the scene.
Do you think it is funny or sad?
**(Visualize/Connect)**

_____

_____

Everyday Use   **133**

1. How has Dee changed since the last time her mother saw her? **(Clarify)**

_____

_____

_____

2. Why does Dee take so many pictures? **(Cause and Effect)**

_____

_____

_____

_____

**MARK IT UP** 3. How does the narrator feel about Dee's decision to change her name? Circle details on pages 133–134 that help you know this. **(Infer)**

_____

_____

_____

_____

_____

"Why shouldn't I?" I asked. "If that's what you want us to call you, we'll call you."

"I know it might sound awkward at first," said Wangero.

"I'll get used to it," I said. "Ream it out again."

Well, soon we got the name out of the way. Asalamalakim had a name twice as long and three times as hard. After I tripped over it two or three times he told me to just call him Hakim-a-barber.[6] I wanted to ask him was he a barber, but I didn't really think he was, so I didn't ask.

220 "You must belong to those beef-cattle peoples down the road," I said. They said "Asalamalakim" when they met you, too, but they didn't shake hands. Always too busy: feeding the cattle, fixing the fences, putting up salt-lick shelters, throwing down hay. When the white folks poisoned some of the herd the men stayed up all night with rifles in their hands. I walked a mile and a half just to see the sight.

Hakim-a-barber said, "I accept some of their <u>doctrines</u>, but farming and raising cattle is not my style." (They didn't tell me, and I didn't ask, whether Wangero (Dee) had really gone 230 and married him.)

*Pause* **&** **Reflect**

**FOCUS**

During dinner, Dee's actions reveals one reason for her visit. She wants to take mementos from her mother's house.

**MARK IT UP** As you read, underline the words and phrases that show what Dee wants.

**We sat down to eat** and right away he said he didn't eat collards and pork was unclean. Wangero, though, went on through the chitlins and corn bread, the greens and everything else. She talked a blue streak over the sweet potatoes. Everything delighted her. Even the fact that we still used the benches her daddy made for the table when we couldn't 240 afford to buy chairs.

"Oh, Mama!" she cried. Then turned to Hakim-a-barber. "I never knew how lovely these benches are. You can feel the rump prints," she said, running her hands underneath her and along the bench. Then she gave a sigh and her hand closed over Grandma Dee's butter dish. "That's it!" she said. "I

---

6. **Hakim-a-barber** (hä-kē′mə-bär′bər).

WORDS TO KNOW   **doctrine** (dŏk′trĭn) *n.* a principle or rule taught by a religious, political, or philosophical group

knew there was something I wanted to ask you if I could have." She jumped up from the table and went over in the corner where the churn stood, the milk in it clabber[7] by now. She looked at the churn and looked at it.

250 "This churn top is what I need," she said. "Didn't Uncle Buddy whittle it out of a tree you all used to have?"

"Yes," I said.

"Uh huh," she said happily. "And I want the dasher,[8] too."

"Uncle Buddy whittle that, too?" asked the barber.

Dee (Wangero) looked up at me.

"Aunt Dee's first husband whittled the dash," said Maggie so low you almost couldn't hear her. "His name was Henry, but they called him Stash."

"Maggie's brain is like an elephant's," Wangero said, 260 laughing. "I can use the churn top as a centerpiece for the alcove table," she said, sliding a plate over the churn, "and I'll think of something artistic to do with the dasher."

When she finished wrapping the dasher the handle stuck out. I took it for a moment in my hands. You didn't even have to look close to see where hands pushing the dasher up and down to make butter had left a kind of sink in the wood. In fact, there were a lot of small sinks; you could see where thumbs and fingers had sunk into the wood. It was beautiful light yellow wood, from a tree that grew in the yard where 270 Big Dee and Stash had lived.

After dinner Dee (Wangero) went to the trunk at the foot of my bed and started rifling through it. Maggie hung back in the kitchen over the dishpan. Out came Wangero with two quilts. They had been pieced by Grandma Dee and then Big Dee and me had hung them on the quilt frames on the front porch and quilted them. One was in the Lone Star pattern. The other was Walk Around the Mountain. In both of them were scraps of dresses Grandma Dee had worn fifty and more years ago. Bits and pieces of Grandpa Jarrell's Paisley shirts. 280 And one teeny faded blue piece, about the size of a penny matchbox, that was from Great Grandpa Ezra's uniform that he wore in the Civil War.

"Mama," Wangero said sweet as a bird. "Can I have these old quilts?"

**Pause & Reflect**

---

7. **clabber:** milk that has thickened and turned sour.

8. **dasher:** the plunger of a churn, a device formerly used to stir cream or milk to produce butter.

**Pause & Reflect**

1. Review what you underlined as you read. What items does Dee want, and why does she want them? **(Draw Conclusions)**

_____

_____

_____

_____

2. Dee and her mother look at the butter churn from different points of view. What does each woman "see" in the old churn? **(Compare and Contrast)**

Dee sees _____

_____

_____

The narrator sees _____

_____

_____

3. Maggie knows more about the history of the butter churn than Dee because _____

_____

_____

**(Draw Conclusions)**

**FOCUS**

Read to find out how Maggie reacts to Dee's request for the quilts. Will the narrator give Dee what she wants?

**I heard something fall** in the kitchen, and a minute later the kitchen door slammed.

"Why don't you take one or two of the others?" I asked. "These old things was just done by me and Big Dee from some tops your grandma

290  pieced before she died."

"No," said Wangero. "I don't want those. They are stitched around the borders by machine."

"That'll make them last better," I said.

"That's not the point," said Wangero. "These are all pieces of dresses Grandma used to wear. She did all this stitching by hand. Imagine!" She held the quilts securely in her arms, stroking them.

"Some of the pieces, like those lavender ones, come from

300  old clothes her mother handed down to her," I said, moving up to touch the quilts. Dee (Wangero) moved back just enough so that I couldn't reach the quilts. They already belonged to her.

"Imagine!" she breathed again, clutching them closely to her bosom.

"The truth is," I said, "I promised to give them quilts to Maggie, for when she marries John Thomas."

She gasped like a bee had stung her.

"Maggie can't appreciate these quilts!" she said. "She'd

310  probably be backward enough to put them to everyday use."

"I reckon she would," I said. "God knows I been saving 'em for long enough with nobody using 'em. I hope she will!" I didn't want to bring up how I had offered Dee (Wangero) a quilt when she went away to college. Then she had told me they were old-fashioned, out of style.

"But they're *priceless!*" she was saying now, furiously; for she has a temper. "Maggie would put them on the bed and in five years they'd be in rags. Less than that!"

"She can always make some more," I said. "Maggie knows

320  how to quilt."

Dee (Wangero) looked at me with hatred. "You just will not understand. The point is *these* quilts, these quilts!"

"Well," I said, stumped. "What would you do with them?"

"Hang them," she said. As if that was the only thing you *could* do with quilts.

Maggie by now was standing in the door. I could almost hear the sound her feet made as they scraped over each other.

"She can have them, Mama," she said, like somebody used to never winning anything, or having anything reserved for her. "I can 'member Grandma Dee without the quilts."

I looked at her hard. She had filled her bottom lip with checkerberry snuff and it gave her face a kind of dopey, hangdog look. It was Grandma Dee and Big Dee who taught her how to quilt herself. She stood there with her scarred hands hidden in the folds of her skirt. She looked at her sister with something like fear but she wasn't mad at her. This was Maggie's portion. This was the way she knew God to work.

When I looked at her like that something hit me in the top of my head and ran down to the soles of my feet. Just like when I'm in church and the spirit of God touches me and I get happy and shout. I did something I never had done before: hugged Maggie to me, then dragged her on into the room, snatched the quilts out of Miss Wangero's hands and dumped them into Maggie's lap. Maggie just sat there on my bed with her mouth open.

"Take one or two of the others," I said to Dee.

But she turned without a word and went out to Hakim-a-barber.

"You just don't understand," she said, as Maggie and I came out to the car.

"What don't I understand?" I wanted to know.

"Your heritage," she said. And then she turned to Maggie, kissed her, and said, "You ought to try to make something of yourself, too, Maggie. It's really a new day for us. But from the way you and Mama still live you'd never know it."

She put on some sunglasses that hide everything above the tip of her nose and her chin.

Maggie smiled; maybe at the sunglasses. But a real smile, not scared. After we watched the car dust settle I asked Maggie to bring me a dip of snuff. And then the two of us sat there just enjoying, until it was time to go in the house and go to bed.

*Pause & Reflect*

*Pause & Reflect*

1. Why does the narrator give Maggie the quilts instead of Dee? **(Draw Conclusions)**

_____
_____
_____
_____

▸ **MARK IT UP**  2. Maggie gives in to her sister's request without a fight. Why? Underline sentences on this page that support your answer. **(Cause and Effect)**

_____
_____
_____

3. What is your opinion of Mama, the narrator? **(Evaluate)**

_____
_____
_____

✎ **CHALLENGE**

**Minor characters** can often help the reader to understand main characters or issues. What purpose does Hakim-a-barber serve? Review passages about him in the story. Write down in the margins what you learn as a result of his presence in the story. **(Characterization)**

## Wrapping Up

If you are using *The Language of Literature,* you can now move to the questions and activities on pages 513–515 of that book.

# Active Reading SkillBuilder

## Drawing Conclusions

**Drawing conclusions** about a story involves making logical statements about characters, events, and setting. To draw a conclusion, readers need to combine information from the text with their own knowledge and experience. As you read "Everyday Use," record on the chart below important clues about the three women and their conflicts. Then write down any conclusions you can draw as you think about the characters. An example is shown.

| Clues | | |
|---|---|---|
| **The narrator** | **Dee** | **Maggie** |
| —daydreams about being on TV with her successful daughter Dee but knows it would never happen to her | | |
| **Conclusions:** The narrator and her daughter are very different from each other. | **Conclusions:** | **Conclusions:** |

# Literary Analysis SkillBuilder

### Conflict/Resolution

**Conflict,** or the struggle between opposing forces, is the basis of the plot of a story. The main conflict is usually resolved at the end of a story, which is called the **resolution**. For example, the central conflict in "Everyday Use"—who will get the quilts—is resolved in the final paragraphs. On the chart that has been started below, identify additional conflicts you find in this story. Then tell whether or not each conflict listed on the chart is resolved. For each conflict that is resolved, explain how.

| Nature of Conflict | Resolved? If so, how? |
|---|---|
| Dee's conflict with her poverty as a child | Yes. She gets an education, moves away, and surrounds herself with nice things. |
| The mother's conflict with Dee's new life | |
| | |
| | |

# Words to Know SkillBuilder

## Words to Know

deliberately      doctrine      furtive      oppress      sidle

**A.** Find familiar words in the puzzle below. Circle all the ones you can find that go from left to right or top to bottom in the puzzle. Write them down to the right of the puzzle or on a separate sheet of paper.

```
S  E  C  R  E  T  F  I
E  R  P  O  W  E  R  K
B  E  L  I  E  V  E  S
A  S  A  N  E  W  S  C
C  E  N  S  P  Y  O  L
K  N  S  T  H  I  N  K
O  T  R  U  L  E  R  Y
S  I  D  E  O  P  E  N
```

Use ten words from the puzzle to fill in the blanks in the following sentences. If you cannot find a word that makes sense and has the correct meaning, look at the puzzle again. Don't use the same word more than once.

1. To *sidle* is to move toward the _____ . A person

   who sidles is usually not very _____ about it.

2. Behaving *deliberately* requires that one _____

   and is often the result of a _____ .

3. A *doctrine* is similar to a _____ . The doctrines of a

   group reflect what that group _____ .

4. *Furtive* behavior is meant to be _____ . One job

   that requires furtive actions is that of a _____ .

5. People who *oppress* others use _____ to do so,

   and those they oppress almost always _____ it.

**B.** Choose at least **three** of the Words to Know and use each in a descriptive sentence about either Dee or Maggie.

# T.wo Friends

### Guy de Maupassant

**PREVIEW** "Two Friends" takes place in January, 1871. For four months, the city of Paris has been under attack by Prussian, or German, troops. The troops surround the city. German canons, set in the hills of the countryside, shell Paris daily. As the story opens, two old friends happen to meet on the street. They decide to go fishing as they used to before the war. As you will see, their fishing trip takes them to a suburb dangerously close to the Germans.

## Before You Read

If you are using **The Language of Literature**. . .

- Use the information on page 546 of that book to prepare for reading.

- Look at the art on pages 547, 551, and 553. It will help you picture the main **characters** and the **setting** of the story.

## Reading Tips

This story takes place in France, so the names of people and places will be unfamiliar to you. Keep the following points in mind as you read:

- Don't be put off by the difficulty of pronouncing the names. Pronunciation guides are provided for the names of the main characters and places. You only need to keep track of the two main characters.

- Look for details that tell you what these characters care about most. You'll appreciate the story more if you can relate to the characters.

**FOCUS**

In this part of the story, you will be introduced to the two main characters.

**MARK IT UP** As you read, underline any details that help to explain how the two men feel about fishing. Examples are highlighted on page 142.

⑩

**MARK IT UP** KEEP TRACK

As you read, you can use these marks to keep track of your understanding.

✔ ..... I understand.

? ..... I don't understand this.

! ..... Interesting or surprising idea

**Paris was under siege,**[1] in the grip of famine, at its last gasp. There were few sparrows on the rooftops now, and even the sewers were losing some of their inhabitants. The fact is that people were eating anything they could get their hands on.

One bright January morning Monsieur Morissot[2] was strolling dejectedly along one of the outer boulevards, with an empty stomach and his hands in the pockets of his old army trousers. He was a watchmaker by trade and a man who liked to make the most of his leisure. Suddenly, he came upon one of his close friends, and he stopped short. It was Monsieur Sauvage,[3] whom he had got to know on fishing expeditions.

---

1. **siege** (sēj): the surrounding of a city by an enemy army trying to capture it by cutting off supplies and keeping it under attack.

2. **Monsieur Morissot** (mə-syœ′ mô-rē-sō′)

3. **Sauvage** (sō-väzh′)

Every Sunday before the war it was Morissot's custom to set off at the crack of dawn with his bamboo rod in his hand and a tin box slung over his back. He would catch the

**20** Argenteuil⁴ train and get off at Colombes,⁵ from where he would walk to the island of Marante. The minute he reached this land of his dreams he would start to fish—and he would go on fishing till it got dark.

And it was here, every Sunday, that he met a tubby, jolly little man by the name of Sauvage. He was a haberdasher⁶ from the Rue Notre-Dame-de-Lorette, and as <u>fanatical</u> an angler⁷ as Morissot himself. They often spent half the day sitting side by side, rod in hand, with their feet dangling over the water. And they had become firm friends.

**30** There were some days when they hardly spoke to each other. On other occasions they would chat all the time. But they understood each other perfectly without needing to exchange any words, because their tastes were so alike and their feelings identical.

On spring mornings at about ten o'clock, when the <u>rejuvenated</u> sun sent floating over the river that light mist which moves along with the current, warming the backs of the two enthusiastic fishermen with the welcome glow of a new season, Morissot would say to his neighbor:

**40** "Ah! It's grand here, isn't it?"

And Monsieur Sauvage would reply:

"There's nothing I like better."

This simple exchange of words was all that was needed for them to understand each other and confirm their mutual appreciation.

In the autumn towards the close of day, when the sky was blood-red and the water reflected strange shapes of scarlet clouds which reddened the whole river, and the glowing sun set the distant horizon ablaze, making the two friends look as

**50** though they were on fire, and touching with gold the russet leaves which were already trembling with a wintry shudder,

---

4. **Argenteuil** (är-zhän-toe′yə): a suburb of Paris.

5. **Colombes** (kə-lōm′): a suburb of Paris.

6. **haberdasher:** one who sells men's clothing, such as shirts, hats, and gloves.

7. **angler:** fisherman.

WORDS  **fanatical** (fə-năt′ĭ-kəl) *adj.* extremely enthusiastic
TO  **rejuvenated** (rĭ-jōō′və-nā′tĭd) *adj.* made new or young
KNOW  again **rejuvenate** *v.*

Monsieur Sauvage would turn to Morissot with a smile and say:

"What a marvelous sight!"

And Morissot, equally taken up with the wonder of it all, but not taking his eyes off his float, would answer:

"It's better than walking down the boulevards, eh?"

As soon as the two friends had recognized each other, they shook hands warmly, feeling quite emotional over the fact that 60 they had come across each other in such different circumstances. Monsieur Sauvage gave a sigh and remarked:

"What a lot has happened since we last met!"

Morissot, in mournful tones, lamented:

"And what awful weather we've been having! This is the first fine day of the year."

And, indeed, the sky was a cloudless blue, brilliant with light.

They started to walk on together side by side, <u>pensive</u> and melancholy. Then Morissot said:

70 "And what about those fishing trips, eh? There's something worth remembering!"

"When shall we be able to get back to it?" mused Monsieur Sauvage.

They went into a little café and drank a glass of absinthe.[8] Then they resumed their stroll along the boulevards.

Morissot suddenly stopped and said:

"What about another glass of the green stuff, eh?"

"Just as you wish," consented Monsieur Sauvage, and they went into a second bar.

80 When they came out they both felt very fuzzy, as people do when they drink alcohol on an empty stomach. The weather was very mild. A gentle breeze caressed their faces.

Monsieur Sauvage, who felt even more fuddled[9] in this warm air, stopped and said:

"What about it, then? Shall we go?"

"Go where?"

"Fishing!"

"But where can we go?"

---

8. **absinthe:** a syrupy, green alcoholic beverage that has a licorice flavor.

9. **fuddled:** drunk and confused.

WORDS
TO       **pensive** (pĕn′sĭv) *adj.* thoughtful in a wistful or sad way
KNOW

**Two Friends** 143

✎ MARK IT UP  1. Why is it
difficult to live in Paris? Circle
details in the story that help to
explain your answer. (Cause and
Effect)

_____

_____

_____

_____

2. Review what you underlined as
you read. How do the two men
feel about fishing? (Clarify)

_____

_____

_____

_____

3. The fishing spot is beyond
French lines, so the men will not
be under the protection of
French troops. Do you think it is
a good idea for the friends to go
fishing? Why or why not?
(Evaluate)

_____

_____

_____

_____

..............................................

..............................................

..............................................

..............................................

..............................................

..............................................

..............................................

..............................................

**144  The InterActive Reader**

---

"To our island, of course. The French frontline is near
Colombes. I know the colonel in command—fellow called
Dumoulin. I'm sure we'd have no trouble in getting through."

Morissot began to quiver with excitement.

"Right!" he said. "I'm your man!"

And the two friends separated and went off to get their
fishing tackle.

Pause & Reflect

FOCUS
As the friends make
their way to the country-
side, they begin to have
second thoughts.

✎ MARK IT UP  As you
read, circle passages
that describe what the
men fear.

**An hour later** they were striding down
the main road together. They reached
the villa in which the colonel had set up
his headquarters. When he heard their
request, he smiled at their eccentric
enthusiasm but gave them permission.
They set off once again, armed with an
official pass.

They soon crossed the frontline, then went through
Colombes, which had been evacuated, and now found
themselves on the fringe of the area of vineyards which rise in
terraces above the Seine. It was about eleven o'clock.

On the opposite bank they could see the village of
Argenteuil, which looked deserted and dead. The hills of
Orgemont and Sannois dominated the horizon, and the great
plain which stretches as far as Nanterre was empty,
completely empty, with nothing to be seen but its leafless
cherry trees and gray earth.

Pointing towards the high ground Monsieur Sauvage
muttered:

"The Prussians are up there."

And as the two friends gazed at the deserted countryside,
they felt almost paralyzed by the sense of uneasiness which
was creeping through them.

The Prussians! They had never so much as set eyes on
them, but for four months now they had been aware of their
presence on the outskirts of Paris, occupying part of France,
looting, committing atrocities, reducing people to
starvation . . . the invisible yet all-powerful Prussians. As they

WORDS
TO
KNOW

**atrocity** (ə-trŏs′ĭ-tē) n. a very cruel or brutal act

thought of them, a kind of superstitious dread was added to their natural hatred for this unknown, victorious race.

"What if we should happen to run into some of them?" said Morissot nervously.

Monsieur Sauvage gave the sort of reply which showed that cheerful Parisian banter survived in spite of everything.

"Oh, we'll just offer them some nice fish to fry!"

Even so, they were so worried by the silence of the surrounding countryside that they hesitated about going any further.

It was Monsieur Sauvage who finally made up his mind.

"Come on!" he said. "We'll go on—but we must keep a sharp lookout!"

And they scrambled down the slope of one of the vineyards, bent double, crawling on their hands and knees, taking advantage of the cover afforded by the vines, keeping their eyes wide open and their ears on the alert.

All that now separated them from the riverbank was a strip of open ground. They ran across it, and as soon as they reached the river, they crouched amongst the dry rushes.

Morissot pressed his ear to the ground to see if he could detect the sound of marching feet. He could hear nothing. They were alone, completely alone.

*Pause* **&** *Reflect*

**FOCUS**

Read on to learn whether the men enjoy their fishing.

**They told each other** there was nothing to worry about, and started to fish.

Opposite them the deserted island of Marante concealed them from the other bank. The little building which once housed the restaurant was closed and shuttered, and looked as though it had been abandoned for years.

It was Monsieur Sauvage who caught the first fish—a gudgeon.[10] Morissot caught the second, and then, almost without a pause, they jerked up their rods time after time to find a little silvery creature wriggling away on the hook. This really was a miraculous draft of fishes.

---

10. **gudgeon** (gŭj′ən): a small fish related to a carp.

*Pause* **&** Reflect

1. Review the passages that you circled as you read. What are the men afraid of? **(Clarify)**

2. Why don't the men return to the safety of the city? **(Infer)**

3. What do you **predict** will happen on the fishing trip?

160 They carefully placed each fish into a fine-meshed net which was suspended in the water at their feet. And as they did so they were overcome by a delightful sense of joy, the kind of joy you only experience when you resume something you really love after being deprived of it for a long time.

A kindly sun was shedding its warmth across their backs. They were so absorbed that they no longer heard, or thought, or paid the least attention to the outside world. What did anything matter now? They were fishing!

But suddenly, the bank beneath them shook with a dull
170 rumble which seemed to come from underground.

The distant cannon were starting to fire again.

Morissot turned his head, and above the bank, over to the left, he saw the great bulk of Mont Valérien. On the mountainside was a white plume of smoke, showing where the gunpowder had just bellowed out.

Almost immediately another jet of smoke spurted from the fort on the summit, and a few seconds later the rumble of another detonation reached their ears.

Other cannon shots followed, and every now and then the
180 mountain spat out its deadly breath, exhaled its clouds of milky vapor, which rose slowly into the calm sky above.

"There they go again!" said Monsieur Sauvage with a shrug of his shoulders.

Morissot, who was anxiously watching the feather on his float as it bobbed up and down, was suddenly filled with the anger of a peace-loving man for these maniacs who indulge in fighting.

"They've got to be really stupid," he growled, "to go on killing each other like that!"

190 "They're worse than animals," said Monsieur Sauvage.

Morissot, who had just caught another fish, called out:

"And it'll never be any different so long as we have governments!"

"Oh, no," disagreed Monsieur Sauvage. "The Republic[11] would never have declared war . . ."

"Look!" interrupted Morissot. "Under kings you have war against other countries. Under republican governments you have civil war."

And they began to argue, in a calm and friendly way,

---

11. **the Republic:** the Second Republic of France (1848–1852), which was France's first truly representative government.

sorting out all the world's great political problems with the commonsense approach of mild and reasonable men. On one point they were in absolute agreement: mankind would never be free. And as they talked, Mont Valérien went thundering on without respite, demolishing French homes with its cannonades,[12] pounding lives to dust, crushing human beings to pulp, putting an end to so many dreams, to so many long-awaited joys, so much long-expected happiness, tearing into the hearts of all those wives and daughters and mothers with pain and suffering that would never be eased.

"Such is life," said Monsieur Sauvage.

*Pause & Reflect*

**FOCUS**
Read to find out what happens to the two friends.

**"Better to call it death,"** laughed Morissot.

But at that moment they both gave a start, scared by the feeling that somebody had been walking just behind them. They looked round and saw standing above them four men, four tall, bearded men, armed to the teeth, dressed like liveried[13] footmen, with flat military caps on their heads—and rifles which they were pointing straight at the two friends.

The fishing rods dropped from their hands and went floating down the river.

In a matter of seconds they were seized, tied up, hustled along, thrown into a boat and carried across to the island.

Behind the building which they had thought deserted they saw a group of about twenty German soldiers.

A sort of hairy giant who was sitting astride a chair and smoking a large clay pipe asked them in excellent French:

"Well, messieurs, did the fishing go well?"

One of the soldiers placed at the officer's feet the net full of fish which he had been careful to bring along. The Prussian smiled and said:

---

12. **cannonades:** continued firing of cannons.

13. **liveried:** uniformed.

WORDS
TO
KNOW

**respite** (rĕs'pĭt) *n.* a temporary stop; a brief period of rest or relief from activity

---

*Pause & Reflect*

**READ ALOUD** **1.** Read aloud the boxed passage on page 146. Why does Morissot become so angry when he hears the cannons? **(Draw Conclusions)**

_____
_____
_____
_____

**MARK IT UP** **2.** The two friends argue in a friendly way about politics. Circle the passage on this page that tells what the two men agree about. **(Clarify)**

**3.** While the men talk politics, the cannons continue to fire, destroying French lives and property. How do you think the author feels about war? **(Author's Perspective)**

_____
_____
_____
_____

"Well, well! I can see you didn't do badly at all! . . . But I have to deal with a very different matter. Now, listen to me carefully, and don't get alarmed . . . As far as I am concerned you are a couple of spies sent out here to keep an eye on me. I've caught you and I've every right to shoot you. You were obviously pretending to fish as a cover for your real purposes. It's too bad for you that you've fallen into my hands. But war is war . . . Now, since you've come out here past your own 240 lines, you're bound to have a password so you can get back. Just give me that password and I'll spare your lives."

The two friends, ghastly pale, stood there side by side with their hands trembling. They said nothing.

"Nobody will ever get to know about it," continued the officer. "You will go back without any trouble, and the secret will go with you . . . If you refuse to cooperate, you'll die— straight away. So take your choice!"

They stood there motionless, keeping their mouths firmly shut.

250 The Prussian, who was still quite calm, pointed in the direction of the river and said:

"Just think! In five minutes you'll be at the bottom of that river. In five minutes! You must have families. Think of them!"

The rumbling of the cannon was still coming from Mont Valérien.

The two fishermen simply stood there, refusing to speak. The German now gave some orders in his own language. Then he moved his chair some distance away from the 260 prisoners. Twelve men marched up and formed a line twenty yards from them with their rifles at their sides.

"I'll give you one minute to make up your minds," called the officer. "And not two seconds more."

Then he jumped to his feet, went up to the two Frenchmen, took Morissot by the arm, and led him to one side. Then he said to him in a very low voice:

"Quick! Just let me have that password! Your friend won't know you've told me. I'll make it look as though I've taken pity on you both."

270 Morissot said nothing.

The Prussian then dragged Monsieur Sauvage to one side and made the same proposition to him.

Monsieur Sauvage said nothing.

So they were pushed together again, side by side.

It was then that Morissot happened to glance down at the net full of gudgeon which was lying in the grass a few yards away.

A ray of sunlight fell on the heap of glittering fish, which were still quivering with life. As he looked at them he felt a momentary weakness. In spite of his efforts to hold them back, tears filled his eyes.

"Farewell, Monsieur Sauvage," he mumbled.

And Monsieur Sauvage replied:

"Farewell, Monsieur Morissot."

They shook hands, trembling uncontrollably from head to foot.

"Fire!" shouted the officer.

Twelve shots rang out simultaneously.

Monsieur Sauvage fell like a log onto his face. Morissot, who was taller, swayed, spun round, then collapsed on top of his friend, with his face staring up at the sky and the blood welling from where his coat had been burst open across his chest.

The German shouted out more orders. His men went off and came back with some lengths of rope and a few heavy stones which they fastened to the feet of the two bodies. Then they carried them to the riverbank.

All the time Mont Valérien continued to rumble, and now it was capped by a great mountain of smoke.

Two soldiers got hold of Morissot by the head and feet. Two others lifted up Monsieur Sauvage in the same way. The two bodies were swung violently backwards and forwards, then thrown with great force. They curved through the air, then plunged upright into the river, with the stones dragging them down, feet first.

The water spurted up, bubbled, swirled round, then grew calm again, with little waves rippling across to break against the bank. There was just a small amount of blood discoloring the surface.

The officer, still quite unperturbed, said, half aloud:

"Well, now it's the fishes' turn."

As he was going back towards the building, he noticed the net full of gudgeon lying in the grass. He picked it up, looked

**MARK IT UP** WORD POWER

Remember to mark words that you'd like to add to your **Personal Word List.** Later, you can record the words and their meanings beginning on page 316.

1. The German soldiers have spoiled the peaceful scene. What information does the officer want, and why is it important? **(Infer)**

_____

_____

_____

_____

2. What offer does the officer make privately to each man? **(Clarify)**

_____

_____

_____

_____

3. Why don't the friends reveal the password? **(Draw Conclusions)**

_____

_____

_____

_____

CHALLENGE

Maupassant's use of **imagery** in this story highlights the contrast between the peacefulness of nature and the horror of war. Go back through the story and mark all the references to fish. How are the men like the fish? **(Compare and Contrast)**

## Wrapping Up

If you are using *The Language of Literature,* you can now move to the questions and activities on pages 556–558 of that book.

at the fish, then smiled, and called out:

"Wilhelm!"

A soldier came running up. He was wearing a white apron. The Prussian officer threw across to him the catch made by the two executed fishermen, and gave another order:

"Fry me these little creatures—straight away, while they're still alive. They'll be delicious!"

Then he lit his pipe again.

*Translated by Arnold Kellett*

# Active Reading SkillBuilder

### Predicting

A **prediction** is an attempt to determine what will happen next in
you predict, you combine information from the text with your own prior
to make guesses about how the plot will advance. Make an initial prediction
reading the first few paragraphs of "Two Friends." Then adjust your prediction
or make a new prediction as you encounter significant new information. Record
your predictions and adjustments below.

**Initial Prediction:**

**New Prediction/Adjustment:**

**New Prediction/Adjustment:**

**New Prediction/Adjustment:**

# Analysis SkillBuilder

## Situational Irony

Irony is the contrast between what is expected and what actually exists or occurs. Situational irony occurs when a character or reader expects one thing to happen and something entirely different occurs. In short stories, situational irony often takes the form of a surprise ending. The ironic ending to this story, which helps Maupassant express his view of war, comes to many readers as a great blow. In the chart, record the comments about war made by Morissot and Sauvage. These comments help set the stage for the story's ending. An example is given.

| Characters' Comments About War | |
|---|---|
| **Morissot** | **Sauvage** |
| "They've got to be really stupid … to go on killing each other like that!" | |
| | |
| | |
| | |

**Follow Up:** How does the situational irony of the ending in "Two Friends" contribute to your understanding of the story's theme about war?

# Words to Know SkillBuilder

## Words to Know

atrocity      fanatical      pensive      rejuvenated      respite

**A.** Decide which word from the word list belongs in each numbered blank.
Then write the word on the blank line on the right.

In winter, when I'm feeling cold,
I also feel I'm growing old.
In April, I can run and sing,
(1) by the spring.

_____
(1)

He gave in to her spell the day they met
And hasn't lost enthusiasm yet.
He thinks her every sentence is inspired.
He's so (2), he makes me tired.

_____
(2)

I've started playing tennis, golf, and racquetball. I'm tired!
I think I need a (3) from these hobbies I've acquired.

_____
(3)

We caught some trout and fried them up for lunch.
I do not know for sure, but I've a hunch
That though this seems a normal act to me,
The trout might think it an (4).

_____
(4)

The cows in the meadow are silently chewing.
It seems that sad thinking is what they are doing.
They look very (5). They seem to be pondering.
Maybe their minds are, instead, merely wandering.

_____
(5)

**B.** For each phrase in the first column, find the phrase in the second column
that is closest in meaning. Write the letter of that phrase in the blank.

_____ 1. an atrocity nearby             A. crazy for daisies

_____ 2. fanatical about flowers        B. moody Judy

_____ 3. pensive Judith               C. a renewed multitude

_____ 4. a rejuvenated crowd         D. a cause for a pause

_____ 5. a reason for a respite        E. a brutality in this locality

**C.** Write an obituary for either M. Morissot or M. Sauvage that might have been
published after they failed to return from their trip into the countryside and were
presumed dead. Use at least **two** of the Words to Know.

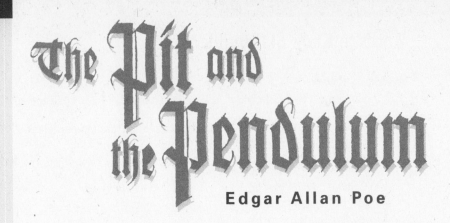

# The Pit and the Pendulum

### Edgar Allan Poe

**PREVIEW** Edgar Allan Poe was a master of the horror story. "The Pit and the Pendulum" is one of his finest tales. It is set in Toledo, a city in Spain, in the early 1800s.

Since the late 15th century, the Inquisition (ĭn′kwĭ-zĭsh′ən) had been a powerful force in Spain. The Inquisition was a court of the Roman Catholic Church. It punished people whose beliefs were opposed to church teachings. The punishments often involved torture—physical or mental. In this story, the narrator is a prisoner of the Inquisition. As the story opens, he is brought into the court to hear the judges pass sentence on him.

IMPIA TORTORUM LONGOS HIC TURBA FURORES
SANGUINIS INNOCUI, NON SATIATA, ALUIT.
SOSPITE NUNC PATRIÂ, FRACTO NUNC FUNERIS ANTRO,
MORS UBI DIRA FUIT VITA SALUSQUE PATENT.
*[Quatrain composed for the gates of a market to be erected upon the site of the Jacobin Club House at Paris.]*

## GUIDE FOR READING

Use this guide for help with unfamiliar words and difficult passages.

**MARK IT UP** **KEEP TRACK**

As you read, you can use these marks to keep track of your understanding.

✔ ..... I understand.

? ..... I don't understand this.

! ..... Interesting or surprising idea

**Impia . . . patent:** Poe uses a Latin quotation to set the mood for the story. The quotation originally marked the spot where bloodthirsty leaders once planned a reign of terror. The quotation is translated as follows: "Here the wicked crowd of tormentors, not satisfied, fed their age-old desire for the blood of innocent people. Now that our homeland is safe, now that the tomb is broken, life and health have taken the place of dread death."

**Jacobin** (jăk'ə-bĭn)**:** belonging to a radical political party in France. During the French Revolution, this party committed acts of terrorism.

FOCUS

The narrator describes the moment in which he hears his death sentence pronounced. He later faints and dimly recalls being taken somewhere far underground.

MARK IT UP  As you read, circle details that help you understand the narrator's state of mind. An example is highlighted.

**I was sick—sick unto death** with that long agony; and when they at length unbound me, and I was permitted to sit, I felt that my senses were leaving me. The sentence—the dread sentence of death—was the last of distinct accentuation which reached my ears. After that, the sound of the inquisitorial voices seemed merged in one dreamy indeterminate hum. It conveyed to my soul the idea of revolution—perhaps from its association in fancy with the burr of a millwheel. This only for a brief period; for presently I heard no more. Yet, for a while, I saw; but with how terrible an exaggeration! I saw the lips of the black-robed judges. They appeared to me white—whiter than the sheet upon which I trace these words—and thin even to grotesqueness; thin with the intensity of their expression of firmness—of immoveable <u>resolution</u>—of stern contempt of human torture. I saw that the decrees of what to me was Fate, were still issuing from those lips. I saw them writhe with a deadly locution. I saw them fashion the syllables of my name; and I shuddered because no sound succeeded. I saw, too, for a few moments of delirious horror, the soft and nearly <u>imperceptible</u> waving of the sable draperies which enwrapped the walls of the apartment. And then my vision fell upon the seven tall candles upon the table. At first they wore the aspect of charity, and seemed white slender angels who would save me; but then, all at once, there came a most deadly nausea over my spirit, and I felt every fiber in my frame thrill as if I had touched the wire of a galvanic battery, while the angel forms became meaningless specters, with heads of flame, and I saw that from them there would be no help. And then there stole into my fancy, like a rich musical note, the thought of what sweet rest there must be in the grave. The thought came gently and <u>stealthily</u>, and it seemed long before it attained full appreciation; but just as my spirit came at length properly to feel and entertain it, the

WORDS
TO
KNOW

**resolution** (rĕz′ə-lōō′shən) *n.* determination
**imperceptible** (ĭm′pər-sĕp′tə-bəl) *adj.* impossible to perceive; unnoticeable
**stealthily** (stĕl′thĭ-lē) *adv.* in a quiet, secretive way

**8–15 After that . . . exaggeration:** The narrator is starting to black out. He no longer hears what the judges are saying. The words run together and seem like the sound a huge wheel might make as it turns and grinds grain. His sense of hearing goes, and then he can only see. His vision is distorted.

✏️ **MARK IT UP** WORD POWER

Mark words that you'd like to add to your **Personal Word List.** After reading, you can record the words and their meanings beginning on page 316.

✏️ **MARK IT UP** Reread Lines 15–22

In this passage, the narrator describes the judges' lips. Circle details in this passage that suggest the judges will have no mercy. **(Locate Details)**

**21–22 I saw them . . . with a deadly locution:** I saw their lips twist **(writhe)** as they pronounced their deadly words **(locution)**.

**23–24 and I shuddered . . . succeeded:** The judges are still speaking. The narrator, though, cannot hear anything. He sees only their moving lips.

**26 apartment:** room.

**26–34 And then . . . help:** The narrator is hallucinating. As he looks at the candles, he first imagines rescuing angels and then phantoms or ghosts **(meaningless specters)**.

**31–32 thrill:** tremble; **galvanic** (găl-văn′ĭk): electric.

**34 fancy:** imagination.

**37 attained . . . appreciation:** was fully understood.

figures of the judges vanished, as if magically, from before me; the tall candles sank into nothingness; their flames went out utterly; the blackness of darkness supervened; all sensations appeared swallowed up in a mad rushing descent as of the soul into Hades. Then silence, and stillness, and night were the universe.

I had swooned; but still will not say that all of consciousness was lost. What of it there remained I will not attempt to define, or even to describe; yet all was not lost. In the deepest slumber—no! In delirium—no! In a swoon—no! In death—no! even in the grave all *is not* lost. Else there is no immortality for man. Arousing from the most profound of slumbers, we break the gossamer web of *some* dream. Yet in a second afterward, (so frail may that web have been) we remember not that we have dreamed. In the return to life from the swoon there are two stages; first, that of the sense of mental or spiritual; secondly, that of the sense of physical, existence. It seems probable that if, upon reaching the second stage, we could recall the impressions of the first, we should find these impressions <u>eloquent</u> in memories of the gulf beyond. And that gulf is—what? How at least shall we distinguish its shadows from those of the tomb? But if the impressions of what I have termed the first stage, are not, at will, recalled, yet, after long interval, do they not come unbidden, while we marvel whence they come? He who has never swooned, is not he who finds strange palaces and wildly familiar faces in coals that glow; is not he who beholds floating in midair the sad visions that the many may not view; is not he who ponders over the perfume of some novel flower—is not he whose brain grows bewildered with the meaning of some musical cadence which has never before arrested his attention.

Amid frequent and thoughtful endeavors to remember; amid earnest struggles to regather some token of the state of seeming nothingness into which my soul had lapsed, there have been moments when I have dreamed of success; there have been brief, very brief periods when I have conjured up remembrances which the <u>lucid</u> reason of a later epoch assures me could have had reference only to that condition of

**39–43 figures of the judges . . . Hades:**
The narrator blacks out here. Everything
disappears, and he senses himself falling
into emptiness.

**43 Hades** (hā′dēz)**:** the underground place of
the dead in Greek mythology.

**45–46 I had swooned . . . not lost:** The
narrator is saying that even though he
blacked out, he still had some awareness.

**53–65 In the return to life . . . coals that
glow:** In reviving from fainting, a person first
has mental images and then is aware of his
or her physical body. The mental images
vanish and are forgotten. It is almost
impossible to remember them. Yet they do
come back on their own when least
expected. For example, in looking at the
glowing coals of a fire, a person might see a
place or a face that flashed through the mind
when he or she was reviving after fainting.

**63 whence:** from where.

**67 novel:** strange; unusual.

**69 cadence** (kād′ns)**:** series of chords.

---

**JOT IT DOWN**   **Reread Lines 41–44**

Why do you think the narrator faints shortly
after hearing "the dread sentence of death"?
**(Infer)**

_____

_____

_____

_____

seeming unconsciousness. These shadows of memory tell, indistinctly, of tall figures that lifted and bore me in silence down—down—still down—till a hideous dizziness oppressed me at the mere idea of the interminableness of the descent. They tell also of a vague horror at my heart, on account of that heart's unnatural stillness. Then comes a sense of sudden motionlessness throughout all things; as if those who bore me (a ghastly train!) had outrun, in their descent, the limits of the limitless, and paused from the wearisomeness of their toil. After this I call to mind flatness and dampness; and that all is *madness*—the madness of a memory which busies itself among forbidden things.

Very suddenly there came back to my soul motion and sound—the tumultuous motion of the heart, and, in my ears, the sound of its beating. Then a pause in which all is blank. Then again sound, and motion, and touch—a tingling sensation pervading my frame. Then the mere consciousness of existence, without thought—a condition which lasted long. Then, very suddenly, *thought,* and shuddering terror, and earnest endeavor to comprehend my true state. Then a strong desire to lapse into insensibility. Then a rushing revival of soul and a successful effort to move. And now a full memory of the trial, of the judges, of the sable draperies, of the sentence, of the sickness, of the swoon. Then entire forgetfulness of all that followed; of all that a later day and much earnestness of endeavor have enabled me vaguely to recall.

**Pause & Reflect**

**FOCUS**

The narrator finds himself in a place of total darkness. He struggles to control his fear and tries to get a sense of his surroundings. Read to find out why he is terrified.

**So far, I had not** opened my eyes. I felt that I lay upon my back, unbound. I reached out my hand, and it fell heavily upon something damp and hard. There I suffered it to remain for many minutes, while I strove to imagine where and *what* I could be. I longed, yet dared not to employ my vision. I dreaded the first glance at objects around me. It was not that

**90–97 Very suddenly there came back . . .
my true state:** The narrator revives
somewhere deep underground. He is
aware first of his heartbeat, then of
sensation, then of his existence, and finally
of his ability to think. He tries to understand
his condition and where he is.
**94 pervading:** spreading throughout.
**98 insensibility** (ĭn-sĕn'sə-bĭl'ĭ-tē):
unconsciousness.

**109 suffered:** allowed.

*Pause* **&** **Reflect**

**1.** Review the details that you circled as you
read. Then cross out the phrase below that
is *not* true of the narrator's state of mind.
**(Infer)**

imagines that the candles might be angels

regards death as a "sweet rest"

recalls nothing after he faints

believes he will be pardoned

**MARK IT UP** **2.** Reread the boxed
passage on page 160. What words and
phrases tell you that the dungeon is far
beneath the ground? Underline them.
**(Evaluate)**

I feared to look upon things horrible, but that I grew aghast lest there should be *nothing* to see. At length, with a wild desperation at heart, I quickly unclosed my eyes. My worst thoughts, then, were confirmed. The blackness of eternal night <u>encompassed</u> me. I struggled for breath. The intensity of the darkness seemed to oppress and stifle me. The atmosphere was intolerably close. I still lay quietly, and made effort to exercise my reason. I brought to mind the inquisitorial proceedings, and attempted from that point to deduce my real condition. The sentence had passed; and it appeared to me that a very long interval of time had since elapsed. Yet not for a moment did I suppose myself actually dead. Such a <u>supposition</u>, notwithstanding what we read in fiction, is altogether inconsistent with real existence;—but where and in what state was I? The condemned to death, I knew, perished usually at the *auto-da-fé,* and one of these had been held on the very night of the day of my trial. Had I been remanded to my dungeon, to await the next sacrifice, which would not take place for many months? This I at once saw could not be. Victims had been in immediate demand. Moreover, my dungeon, as well as all the condemned cells at Toledo, had stone floors, and light was not altogether excluded.

A fearful idea now suddenly drove the blood in torrents upon my heart, and for a brief period, I once more <u>relapsed</u> into insensibility. Upon recovering, I at once started to my feet, trembling convulsively in every fiber. I thrust my arms wildly above and around me in all directions. I felt nothing; yet dreaded to move a step, lest I should be impeded by the walls of the *tomb*. Perspiration burst from every pore and stood in cold big beads on my forehead. The agony of suspense grew at length intolerable, and I cautiously moved forward, with my arms extended, and my eyes straining from their sockets, in the hope of catching some faint ray of light. I proceeded for many paces; but still all was blackness and vacancy. I breathed more freely. It seemed evident that mine was not, at least, the most hideous of fates.

And now, as I still continued to step cautiously onward, there came thronging upon my recollection a thousand vague rumors of the horrors of Toledo. Of the dungeons there had been strange things narrated—fables I had always deemed

---

WORDS
TO
KNOW

**encompass** (ĕn-kŭm′pəs) *v.* to surround; enclose
**supposition** (sŭp′ə-zĭsh′ən) *n.* an opinion or assumption
**relapse** (rĭ-lăps′) *v.* to fall back into a former state

What details suggest the narrator's terror as
he opens his eyes? Circle these details.
**(Locate Details)**

**129 auto-da-fé** (ou′tō-də-fā′) **Portuguese:**
act of faith—a public execution of people
tried by the Inquisition, carried out by the
civil authorities.

**130 remanded:** sent back.

**READ ALOUD** **Lines 139–149**

The narrator is terrified because he may have
been sentenced to "the most hideous of
fates." What is that fate? Check *one* phrase
below. **(Draw Conclusions)**

being burned to death

being buried alive

being eaten by rats

**150–155 And now . . . whisper:** The
narrator gropes his way in the darkness. He
recalls rumors about the terrible things that
happen to prisoners in the dungeons. These
rumors frighten him, and he wonders
whether they might be true.

**151 thronging:** crowding.

them—but yet strange, and too ghastly to repeat, save in a whisper. Was I left to perish of starvation in the subterranean world of darkness; or what fate, perhaps even more fearful, awaited me? That the result would be death, and a death of more than customary bitterness, I knew too well the character of my judges to doubt. The mode and the hour were all that occupied or distracted me.

160

My outstretched hands at length encountered some solid obstruction. It was a wall, seemingly of stone masonry—very smooth, slimy, and cold. I followed it up! stepping with all the careful distrust with which certain antique narratives had inspired me. This process, however, afforded me no means of ascertaining the dimensions of my dungeon; as I might make its circuit, and return to the point whence I set out, without being aware of the fact; so perfectly uniform seemed the wall. I therefore sought the knife which had been in my pocket,

170

when led into the inquisitorial chamber; but it was gone; my clothes had been exchanged for a wrapper of coarse serge. I had thought of forcing the blade in some minute crevice of the masonry, so as to identify my point of departure. The difficulty, nevertheless, was but trivial; although, in the disorder of my fancy, it seemed at first <u>insuperable</u>. I tore a part of the hem from the robe and placed the fragment at full length, and at right angles to the wall. In groping my way around the prison I could not fail to encounter this rag upon completing the circuit. So, at least I thought: but I had not

180

counted upon the extent of the dungeon, or upon my own weakness. The ground was moist and slippery. I staggered onward for some time, when I stumbled and fell. My excessive fatigue induced me to remain prostrate; and sleep soon overtook me as I lay.

*Pause* **&** **Reflect**

**FOCUS**
The narrator continues to explore his dungeon. Read to find out what he discovers.

**Upon awakening,** and stretching forth an arm, I found beside me a loaf and a pitcher with water. I was too much exhausted to reflect upon this

WORDS
TO
KNOW

**insuperable** (ĭn-sōō′pər-ə-bəl) *adj.* impossible to overcome

**162 stone masonry:** stonework.

**171 serge** (sûrj): a woolen cloth.

**183 prostrate** (prŏs´trāt´)**:** lying flat.

## Pause & Reflect

**MARK IT UP** **1.** What does the narrator do to try to measure his dungeon? Write the answer below. Then underline details on page 164 that led you to the answer. **(Summarize)**

_____

_____

_____

_____

**2.** Imagine yourself in the narrator's place. What do you think might happen to you in this dungeon? **(Predict)**

_____

_____

_____

_____

**3.** What do you think the narrator would see if there were light in the dungeon? **(Visualize)**

_____

_____

_____

_____

circumstance, but ate and drank with avidity. Shortly afterward, I resumed my tour around the prison, and with much toil, came at last upon the fragment of the serge. Up to the period when I fell I had counted fifty-two paces, and upon resuming my walk, I counted forty-eight more;—when I arrived at the rag. There were in all, then, a hundred paces; and, admitting two paces to the yard, I presumed the dungeon to be fifty yards in circuit. I had met, however, with many angles in the wall, and thus I could form no guess at the shape of the vault; for vault I could not help supposing it to be.

I had little object—certainly no hope—in these researches; but a vague curiosity prompted me to continue them. Quitting the wall, I resolved to cross the area of the enclosure. At first I proceeded with extreme caution, for the floor, although seemingly of solid material, was treacherous with slime. At length, however, I took courage, and did not hesitate to step firmly; endeavoring to cross in as direct a line as possible. I had advanced some ten or twelve paces in this manner, when the remnant of the torn hem of my robe became entangled between my legs. I stepped on it, and fell violently on my face.

In the confusion attending my fall, I did not immediately apprehend a somewhat startling circumstance, which yet, in a few seconds afterward, and while I still lay prostrate, arrested my attention. It was this—my chin rested upon the floor of the prison, but my lips and the upper portion of my head, although seemingly at a less elevation than the chin, touched nothing. At the same time my forehead seemed bathed in a clammy vapor, and the peculiar smell of decayed fungus arose to my nostrils. I put forward my arm, and shuddered to find that I had fallen at the very brink of a circular pit, whose extent, of course, I had no means of ascertaining at the moment. Groping about the masonry just below the margin, I succeeded in dislodging a small fragment, and let it fall into the abyss. For many seconds I hearkened to its reverberations as it dashed against the sides of the chasm in its descent; at length there was a sullen plunge into water, succeeded by loud echoes. At the same moment there came a sound resembling the quick opening, and as rapid closing of a door

WORDS TO KNOW   **treacherous** (trĕch′ər-əs) *adj.* dangerous

**189 avidity:** eagerness.

**212 apprehend:** become conscious of;
perceive.

**214–219 It was this . . . nostrils:** The
narrator has fallen in such a way that his chin
rests on the floor of the dungeon. The upper
part of his face, however, lies over the edge
of the pit. The dampness of the pit makes his
forehead feel clammy. He smells something
moldy **(decayed fungus)** coming from
the pit.

**224 reverberations** (rĭ-vûr′bə-rā′shənz):
echoes.

**MARK IT UP** **KEEP TRACK**

Remember to use these marks to keep track
of your understanding.

✔ ..... I understand.

? ..... I don't understand this.

! ..... Interesting or surprising idea

**READ ALOUD** **Lines 222–227**

How does the narrator discover that there is
water at the bottom of the pit? **(Clarify)**

_____

_____

_____

_____

overhead, while a faint gleam of light flashed suddenly through the gloom, and as suddenly faded away.

I saw clearly the doom which had been prepared for me, and congratulated myself upon the timely accident by which I had escaped. Another step before my fall, and the world had seen me no more. And the death just avoided, was of that very character which I had regarded as fabulous and frivolous in the tales respecting the Inquisition. To the victims of its tyranny, there was the choice of death with its direst physical agonies, or death with its most hideous moral horrors. I had been reserved for the latter. By long suffering my nerves had been unstrung, until I trembled at the sound of my own voice, and had become in every respect a fitting subject for the species of torture which awaited me.

Shaking in every limb, I groped my way back to the wall; resolving there to perish rather than risk the terrors of the wells, of which my imagination now pictured many in various positions about the dungeon. In other conditions of mind I might have had courage to end my misery at once by a plunge into one of these abysses; but now I was the veriest of cowards. Neither could I forget what I had read of these pits—that the *sudden* extinction of life formed no part of their most horrible plan.

*Pause* **&** *Reflect*

**FOCUS**
Drugged by his torturers, the narrator falls into a deep sleep. When he wakes up, he finds his dungeon lit by a strange light.
**MARK IT UP** As you read, circle any details that describe new things the narrator learns about his dungeon.

**Agitation of spirit** kept me awake for many long hours; but at length I again slumbered. Upon arousing, I found by my side as before, a loaf and a pitcher of water. A burning thirst consumed me, and I emptied the vessel at a draft. It must have been drugged; for scarcely had I drunk, before I became irresistibly drowsy. A deep sleep fell upon me—a sleep like that of death. How long it lasted of course, I know not; but when, once again, I unclosed my eyes, the objects around me were visible. By a wild sulphurous luster, the

**234–236 And the death . . . the Inquisition:** The narrator has heard tales about the tortures of the Inquisition. In these tales, one means of death involves falling into a pit. The narrator had regarded this means of death as an author's invention—not something that could happen in real life.

**235 fabulous** (făb′yə-ləs): like a fable; untrue.

**237 direst** (dī′rĭst): most dreadful.

**249–251 Neither could I forget . . . their most horrible plan:** The narrator fears there might be more pits in his dungeon than the one he has avoided. From what he knows about the Inquisition, he realizes that he would die a slow, painful death if he were to fall into one of these pits.

## Pause & Reflect

1. Why do you think the torturers leave the narrator bread and water? **(Infer)**

_____

_____

_____

_____

✏️ MARK IT UP  2. The narrator discovers a pit in his dungeon. What accident prevents him from falling into the pit? Circle the *two* sentences on page 166 that tell the answer. **(Cause and Effect)**

3. Do you think the torturers have been watching the narrator all the time? *Yes / No,* because_____

_____

_____

_____.

**(Infer)**

**264 sulphurous** (sŭl′fə-rəs) **luster:** fiery glow. Later in the story, the narrator discovers where this light comes from.

**The Pit and the Pendulum   169**

origin of which I could not at first determine, I was enabled to see the extent and aspect of the prison.

In its size I had been greatly mistaken. The whole circuit of its walls did not exceed twenty-five yards. For some minutes this fact occasioned me a world of vain trouble; vain indeed! for what could be of less importance, under the terrible circumstances which environed me, than the mere dimensions of my dungeon? But my soul took a wild interest in trifles, and I busied myself in endeavors to account for the error I had committed in my measurement. The truth at length flashed upon me. In my first attempt at exploration I had counted fifty-two paces, up to the period when I fell; I must then have been within a pace or two of the fragments of serge; in fact, I had nearly performed the circuit of the vault. I then slept, and upon awaking, I must have returned upon my steps—thus supposing the circuit nearly double what it actually was. My confusion of mind prevented me from observing that I began my tour with the wall to the left, and ended it with the wall to the right.

I had been deceived, too, in respect to the shape of the enclosure. In feeling my way around I had found many angles, and thus deduced an idea of great irregularity; so <u>potent</u> is the effect of total darkness upon one arousing from <u>lethargy</u> or sleep! The angles were simply those of a few slight depressions, or niches, at odd intervals. The general shape of the prison was square. What I had taken for masonry seemed now to be iron, or some other metal, in huge plates, whose sutures or joints occasioned the depression. The entire surface of this metallic enclosure was rudely daubed in all the hideous and repulsive devices to which the charnel superstitions of the monks has given rise. The figures of fiends in aspects of menace, with skeleton forms, and other more really fearful images, overspread and disfigured the walls. I observed that the outlines of these monstrosities were sufficiently distinct, but that the colors seemed faded and blurred, as if from the effects of a damp atmosphere. I now noticed the floor, too, which was of stone. In the center yawned the circular pit from whose jaws I had escaped; but it was the only one in the dungeon.

WORDS TO KNOW

**potent** (pōt′nt) *adj.* powerful
**lethargy** (lĕth′ər-jē) *n.* sluggishness; unconsciousness

**MARK IT UP** WORD POWER

Remember to mark words that you'd like to
add to your **Personal Word List.** After reading,
you can record the words and their meanings
beginning on page 316.

**269 occasioned . . . trouble:** caused me a
great deal of useless worry.

**293–295 The entire surface . . . has given
rise:** The narrator notices the walls of the
dungeon are covered with grim drawings.
The drawings represent the monks'
superstitious beliefs about hell. The word
*charnel* means "suggesting or suitable for
receiving the dead."

All this I saw distinctly and by much effort: for my personal condition had been greatly changed during slumber. I now lay upon my back, and at full length, on a species of low framework of wood. To this I was securely bound by a long strap resembling a surcingle. It passed in many convolutions about my limbs and body, leaving at liberty only my head, and my left arm to such extent that I could, by dint of much exertion, supply myself with food from an earthen dish which lay by my side on the floor. I saw, to my horror, that the pitcher had been removed. I say to my horror; for I was consumed with intolerable thirst. This thirst it appeared to be the design of my persecutors to stimulate: for the food in the dish was meat pungently seasoned.

*Pause* & **Reflect**

**FOCUS**

Looking up at the ceiling of the dungeon, the narrator discovers a new horror. A sharp blade is swinging like the pendulum of a clock. Slowly it descends. As you read, notice details that help you visualize the pendulum.

**Looking upward I surveyed** the ceiling of my prison. It was some thirty or forty feet overhead, and constructed much as the side walls. In one of its panels a very singular figure riveted my whole attention. It was the painted figure of Time as he is commonly represented, save that, in lieu of a scythe, he held what, at a casual glance, I supposed to be the pictured image of a huge pendulum such as we see on antique clocks. There was something, however, in the appearance of this machine which caused me to regard it more attentively. While I gazed directly upward at it (for its position was immediately over my own) I fancied that I saw it in motion. In an instant afterward the fancy was confirmed. Its sweep was brief, and of course slow. I watched it for some minutes, somewhat in fear, but more in wonder. Wearied at length with observing its dull movement, I turned my eyes upon the other objects in the cell.

A slight noise attracted my notice, and, looking to the floor, I saw several enormous rats traversing it. They had issued from the well, which lay just within view to my right.

**308 surcingle** (sûr'sĭng'gəl)**:** a band used to tie a pack or a saddle to a horse.
**310 dint:** force.

**322–327 It was the painted figure . . . on antique clocks:** Time is sometimes pictured as an old man who holds a **scythe** (sīth), a tool for mowing or reaping. This tool has a long, curved blade attached to a long, bent handle. The figure of Time painted on the ceiling of the narrator's dungeon holds a pendulum instead of **(in lieu of)** a scythe. A pendulum is something suspended that swings freely back and forth.

## Pause & Reflect

**1.** Review the details you circled as you read. What does the narrator learn about his cell? Cross out the *one* sentence below that does not apply. **(Clarify)**

It forms a square.

The walls are made of metal and painted with images of demons.

The floor is made of wood.

**MARK IT UP** **2.** The narrator discovers that he made a mistake in measuring his dungeon. Why did he make this mistake? Write the answer below. Then underline the details on page 170 that led you to the answer. **(Cause and Effect)**

_____

_____

_____

_____

**READ ALOUD** **3.** Read aloud the boxed passage on page 172. What did the torturers do to the narrator while he was asleep? **(Summarize)**

_____

_____

_____

_____

Even then, while I gazed, they came up in troops, hurriedly, with ravenous eyes, allured by the scent of the meat. From this it required much effort and attention to scare them away.

It might have been half an hour, perhaps even an hour, (for I could take but imperfect note of time) before I again cast my eyes upward. What I then saw confounded and amazed me. The sweep of the pendulum had increased in extent by nearly a yard. As a natural consequence, its velocity was also much greater. But what mainly disturbed me was the idea that it had perceptibly *descended*. I now observed—with what horror it is needless to say—that its nether extremity was formed of a crescent of glittering steel, about a foot in length from horn to horn; the horns upward, and the under edge evidently as keen as that of a razor. Like a razor also, it seemed massy and heavy, tapering from the edge into a solid and broad structure above. It was appended to a weighty rod of brass, and the whole *hissed* as it swung through the air.

I could no longer doubt the doom prepared for me by monkish ingenuity in torture. My cognizance of the pit had become known to the inquisitorial agents—*the pit* whose horrors had been destined for so bold a recusant as myself—*the pit,* typical of hell, and regarded by rumor as the Ultima Thule of all their punishments. The plunge into this pit I had avoided by the merest of accidents, and I knew that surprise, or entrapment into torment, formed an important portion of all the grotesquerie of these dungeon deaths. Having failed to fall, it was no part of the demon plan to hurl me into the abyss; and thus (there being no alternative) a different and a milder destruction awaited me. Milder! I half smiled in my agony as I thought of such application of such a term.

What boots it to tell of the long, long hours of horror more than mortal, during which I counted the rushing vibrations of the steel! Inch by inch—line by line—with a descent only appreciable at intervals that seemed ages—down and still down it came! Days passed—it might have been that many days passed—ere it swept so closely over me as to fan me with its acrid breath. The odor of the sharp steel forced itself into my nostrils. I prayed—I wearied heaven with my prayer for its more speedy descent. I grew frantically mad, and struggled to force myself upward against the sweep of the fearful scimitar. And then I fell suddenly calm, and lay smiling at the glittering death, as a child at some rare bauble.

**356–357 I could no longer doubt . . . in torture:** The narrator realizes that his torturers have devised a cleverly wicked way for him to die. Tied to a wooden frame, he is forced to watch the pendulum as it slowly descends. Eventually, its blade will first wound and then kill him.

**357 ingenuity** (ĭn-jə-noo′ĭ-tē)**:** cleverness, originality; **cognizance** (kŏg′nĭ-zəns)**:** knowledge; awareness.

**359 recusant** (rĕk′yə-zənt)**:** a religious dissenter; heretic.

**360–361 Ultima Thule** (ŭl′tə-mə thoo′lē)**:** according to ancient geographers, the most remote region of the world—here used figuratively to mean "most extreme achievement," "summit."

**364 grotesquerie** (grō-tĕs′kə-rē)**:** something horrible and strange.

**369 what boots it:** what good is it.

**375 acrid** (ăk′rĭd)**:** sharp; pungent.

**375–379 The odor . . . scimitar:** The blade of the pendulum has descended so low that it is very close to the narrator. At times he wishes the blade would just kill him at once and get it over with.

**379 scimitar** (sĭm′ĭ-tər)**:** a curved, single-edged Asian sword.

**READ ALOUD  Lines 373–377**

As you read these lines aloud, notice the details that describe the descending pendulum. What sense do these details appeal to? **(Clarify)**

There was another interval of utter insensibility; it was brief; for, upon again lapsing into life there had been no perceptible descent in the pendulum. But it might have been long; for I knew there were demons who took note of my swoon, and who could have arrested the vibration at pleasure. Upon my recovery, too, I felt very—oh, inexpressibly sick and weak, as if through long inanition. Even amid the agonies of that period, the human nature craved food. With painful effort I outstretched my left arm as far as my bonds permitted, and took possession of the small remnant which had been spared me by the rats. As I put a portion of it within my lips, there rushed to my mind a half formed thought of joy—of hope. Yet what business had *I* with hope? It was, as I say, a half formed thought—man has many such which are never completed. I felt that it was of joy—of hope; but I felt also that it had perished in its formation. In vain I struggled to perfect—to regain it. Long suffering had nearly annihilated all my ordinary powers of mind. I was an imbecile—an idiot.

The vibration of the pendulum was at right angles to my length. I saw that the crescent was designed to cross the region of the heart. It would fray the serge of my robe—it would return and repeat its operations—again—and again. Notwithstanding its terrifically wide sweep (some thirty feet or more) and the hissing vigor of its descent, sufficient to sunder these very walls of iron, still the fraying of my robe would be all that, for several minutes, it would accomplish. And at this thought I paused. I dared not go farther than this reflection. I dwelt upon it with a <u>pertinacity</u> of attention—as if, in so dwelling, I could arrest *here* the descent of the steel. I forced myself to ponder upon the sound of the crescent as it should pass across the garment—upon the peculiar thrilling sensation which the friction of cloth produces on the nerves. I pondered upon all this frivolity until my teeth were on edge.

*Pause* **&** *Reflect*

---

WORDS
TO
KNOW

**pertinacity** (pûr'tn-ăs'ĭ-tē) *n.* a persistent stubbornness

**387 inanition** (ĭn′ə-nĭsh′ən): wasting away from lack of food.

**402–407 It would fray . . . accomplish:** The torture will be drawn out. The blade will cut into the narrator's clothes for many minutes. Only gradually will the blade descend low enough to break the skin.

*Pause* **&** *Reflect*

**1.** The narrator notices that rats are swarming out of the pit in the dungeon. What threat do these rats pose to him? **(Infer)**

_____

_____

_____

_____

**2.** What do you think are the most interesting details about the pendulum? **(Evaluate)**

_____

_____

_____

_____

**3.** As the pendulum descends, what does the narrator focus his thoughts on? Circle one phrase below. **(Clarify)**

the blade cutting his robe

his confession to the judges

the rats biting his fingers

**FOCUS**

The narrator watches
the pendulum as it
descends. Read to find
out what he notices
about the band that
ties him to the wooden
frame.

**Down—steadily down it crept.** I took a
frenzied pleasure in contrasting its
downward with its lateral velocity.
To the right—to the left—far and
wide—with the shriek of a . . . spirit;
to my heart with the stealthy pace
of the tiger! I alternately laughed
and howled as the one or the other idea grew predominant.

Down—certainly, relentlessly down! It vibrated within
three inches of my bosom! I struggled violently, furiously, to
free my left arm. This was free only from the elbow to the
hand. I could reach the latter, from the platter beside me, to
my mouth, with great effort, but no farther. Could I have
broken the fastenings above the elbow, I would have seized
and attempted to arrest the pendulum. I might as well have
attempted to arrest an avalanche!

Down—still unceasingly—still inevitably down! I gasped
and struggled at each vibration. I shrunk convulsively at its
every sweep. My eyes followed its outward or upward whirls
with the eagerness of the most unmeaning despair; they
closed themselves spasmodically at the descent, although
death would have been a relief, oh! how unspeakable! Still I
quivered in every nerve to think how slight a sinking of the
machinery would precipitate that keen, glistening axe upon
my bosom. It was *hope* that prompted the nerve to quiver—
the frame to shrink. It was *hope*—the hope that triumphs on
the rack—that whispers to the death-condemned even in the
dungeons of the Inquisition.

I saw that some ten or twelve vibrations would bring the
steel in actual contact with my robe, and with this
observation there suddenly came over my spirit all the keen,
collected calmness of despair. For the first time during many
hours—or perhaps days—I *thought*. It now occurred to me
that the bandage, or surcingle, which enveloped me, was
*unique*. I was tied by no separate cord. The first stroke of the
razor-like crescent athwart any portion of the band, would so
detach it that it might be unwound from my person by means
of my left hand. But how fearful, in that case, the proximity
of the steel! The result of the slightest struggle how deadly!

MARK IT UP    Reread Lines 415–442

The first three paragraphs in this part begin with the same word. Circle that word each time it appears. Why do you think the author repeats this word at the beginning of these paragraphs? **(Author's Purpose)**

_____

_____

_____

_____

**440–442 It was _hope_ . . . the Inquisition:** The narrator says that even in this terrible situation he still has hope. He compares his situation to that of a prisoner on the rack. The rack is a device for torturing people by gradually stretching their bodies.

**450 athwart:** across.

Was it likely, moreover, that the minions of the torturer had not foreseen and provided for this possibility! Was it probable that the bandage crossed my bosom in the track of the pendulum? Dreading to find my faint, and, as it seemed, my last hope frustrated, I so far elevated my head as to obtain a distinct view of my breast. The surcingle enveloped my limbs and body close in all directions—*save in the path of the destroying crescent.*

**Pause & Reflect**

**FOCUS**
The narrator thinks of a desperate plan to save his life. Read to find out about this plan.

**Scarcely had I dropped my head** back into its original position, when there flashed upon my mind what I cannot better describe than as the unformed half of that idea of deliverance to which I have previously alluded, and of which a moiety only floated indeterminately through my brain when I raised food to my burning lips. The whole thought was now present— feeble, scarcely sane, scarcely definite,—but still entire. I proceeded at once, with the nervous energy of despair, to attempt its execution.

For many hours the immediate vicinity of the low framework upon which I lay, had been literally swarming with rats. They were wild, bold, ravenous; their red eyes glaring upon me as if they waited but for motionlessness on my part to make me their prey. "To what food," I thought, "have they been accustomed in the well?"

They had devoured, in spite of all my efforts to prevent them, all but a small remnant of the contents of the dish. I had fallen into an habitual see-saw, or wave of the hand about the platter, and, at length, the unconscious uniformity of the movement deprived it of effect. In their <u>voracity</u> the vermin frequently fastened their sharp fangs into my fingers. With the particles of the oily and spicy viand which now remained, I thoroughly rubbed the bandage wherever I could reach it; then, raising my hand from the floor, I lay breathlessly still.

WORDS
TO
KNOW

**voracity** (vô-răs′ĭ-tē) *n.* greed for food; ravenousness

**454 minions** (mĭn′yənz): followers; servants.

**459–461 The surcingle . . . _crescent_:** A band is wrapped around the narrator's body, leaving only his chest uncovered. His chest lies directly in the path of the pendulum's blade **(destroying crescent)**.
**460 _save:_** except.

**467 moiety** (moi′ĭ-tē): half.

**477–478 "To what food . . . in the well":** The narrator doesn't answer this question. From hints in the story, though, it is clear that the rats have fed on human flesh down in the pit.

**485 viand** (vī′ənd): food.

## Pause & Reflect

1. What does the narrator notice about the band that ties him to the wooden frame? Circle the sentence below that tells the answer. **(Clarify)**

   It is a chain of iron.

   It consists of several ropes.

   It is one single belt.

2. Imagine yourself in the narrator's situation. Eventually, the blade of the pendulum will descend low enough to slice your heart open. What would you do to try to escape death? **(Connect)**

   _____

   _____

   _____

At first the ravenous animals were startled and terrified at the change—at the cessation of movement. They shrank alarmedly back; many sought the well. But this was only for a moment. I had not counted in vain upon their voracity. Observing that I remained without motion, one or two of the boldest leaped upon the framework, and smelt at the surcingle. This seemed the signal for a general rush. Forth from the well they hurried in fresh troops. They clung to the wood—they overran it, and leaped in hundreds upon my person. The measured movement of the pendulum disturbed them not at all. Avoiding its strokes they busied themselves with the anointed bandage. They pressed—they swarmed upon me in ever accumulating heaps. They writhed upon my throat; their cold lips sought my own; I was half stifled by their thronging pressure; disgust, for which the world has no name, swelled my bosom, and chilled, with a heavy clamminess, my heart. Yet one minute, and I felt that the struggle would be over. Plainly I perceived the loosening of the bandage. I knew that in more than one place it must be already severed. With a more than human resolution I lay *still*.

Nor had I erred in my calculations—nor had I endured in vain. I at length felt that I was *free*. The surcingle hung in ribands from my body. But the stroke of the pendulum already pressed upon my bosom. It had divided the serge of the robe. It had cut through the linen beneath. Twice again it swung, and a sharp sense of pain shot through every nerve. But the moment of escape had arrived. At a wave of my hand my deliverers hurried tumultuously away. With a steady movement—cautious, sidelong, shrinking, and slow—I slid from the embrace of the bandage and beyond the reach of the scimitar. For the moment, at least, *I was free*.

*Pause* **&** **Reflect**

**488 ravenous** (răv′ə-nəs): very hungry; greedy.

**500 writhed** (rī*th*d): twisted.

**509 erred** (ûrd): made a mistake.

**511 ribands** (rĭb′əndz): ribbons.

## Pause & Reflect

**1.** What does the narrator do to free himself from the frame to which he is attached? **(Summarize)**

_____

_____

_____

_____

**MARK IT UP** **2.** What details on pages 180 and 182 help you **visualize** the rats? Circle these details.

**READ ALOUD** **3.** Read aloud the boxed passage on page 182. The narrator stays perfectly still while the rats swarm all over him, even touching his lips. How would you have reacted if you were in the narrator's place? **(Connect)**

_____

_____

_____

_____

520

530

540

550

560

**FOCUS**

The narrator has escaped both the pit and the pendulum. Now he faces a new danger. Read to find out what it is.

**Free!—and in the grasp** of the Inquisition! I had scarcely stepped from my wooden bed of horror upon the stone floor of the prison, when the motion of the hellish machine ceased and I beheld it drawn up, by some invisible force, through the ceiling. This was a lesson which I took desperately to heart. My every motion was undoubtedly watched. Free!—I had but escaped death in one form of agony, to be delivered unto worse than death in some other. With that thought I rolled my eyes nervously around the barriers of iron that hemmed me in. Something unusual—some change which at first I could not appreciate distinctly—it was obvious, had taken place in the apartment. For many minutes in a dreamy and trembling abstraction, I busied myself in vain, unconnected conjecture. During this period, I became aware, for the first time, of the origin of the sulphurous light which illuminated the cell. It proceeded from a fissure, about half an inch in width, extending entirely around the prison at the base of the walls, which thus appeared, and were, completely separated from the floor. I endeavored, but of course in vain, to look through the aperture.

As I arose from the attempt, the mystery of the alteration in the chamber broke at once upon my understanding. I have observed that, although the outlines of the figures upon the walls were sufficiently distinct, yet the colors seemed blurred and indefinite. These colors had now assumed, and were momentarily assuming, a startling and most intense brilliancy, that gave to the spectral and fiendish portraitures an aspect that might have thrilled even firmer nerves than my own. Demon eyes, of a wild and ghastly vivacity, glared upon me in a thousand directions, where none had been visible before, and gleamed with the lurid luster of a fire that I could not force my imagination to regard as unreal.

*Unreal!*—Even while I breathed there came to my nostrils the breath of the vapor of heated iron! A suffocating odor pervaded the prison! A deeper glow settled each moment in the eyes that glared at my agonies! A richer tint of crimson diffused itself over the pictured horrors of blood. I panted! I gasped for breath! There could be no doubt of the design of

MARK IT UP | **KEEP TRACK**

Remember to use these marks to keep track of your understanding.

✔ ..... I understand.

**?** ..... I don't understand this.

**!** ..... Interesting or surprising idea

**534–535 For many minutes . . . conjecture:** For a while the narrator is lost in thought. He is trying to think of explanations for the change in the shape of the dungeon.

**535 abstraction:** absentmindedness; **conjecture:** guesswork; speculation.

**536–542 During this period. . . through the aperture:** The light in the dungeon comes through a crack **(fissure)** at the bottom of the walls. This crack separates the walls from the floor of the dungeon. The light may be from the fire that is burning the walls.

**542 aperture** (ăp′ər-chər)**:** opening.

**547–550 These colors . . . than my own:** The colors are becoming brighter and more vivid because of the extreme heat that is burning the walls.

**551 vivacity** (vĭ-văs′ĭ-tē)**:** liveliness.

**560 design:** intent.

my tormentors—oh! most unrelenting! oh! most demoniac of men! I shrank from the glowing metal to the center of the cell. Amid the thought of the fiery destruction that impended, the idea of the coolness of the well came over my soul like balm. I rushed to its deadly brink. I threw my straining vision below. The glare from the enkindled roof illumined its inmost recesses. Yet, for a wild moment, did my spirit refuse to comprehend the meaning of what I saw. At length it forced— it wrestled its way into my soul—it burned itself in upon my shuddering reason.—Oh! for a voice to speak!—oh! horror!—oh! any horror but this! With a shriek, I rushed from the margin, and buried my face in my hands—weeping bitterly.

The heat rapidly increased, and once again I looked up, shuddering as with a fit of the ague. There had been a second change in the cell—and now the change was obviously in the *form*. As before, it was in vain that I, at first, endeavored to appreciate or understand what was taking place. But not long was I left in doubt. The Inquisitorial vengeance had been hurried by my two-fold escape, and there was to be no more dallying with the King of Terrors. The room had been square. I saw that two of its iron angles were now acute—two, consequently, obtuse. The fearful difference quickly increased with a low rumbling or moaning sound. In an instant the apartment had shifted its form into that of a lozenge. But the alteration stopped not here—I neither hoped nor desired it to stop. I could have clasped the red walls to my bosom as a garment of eternal peace. "Death," I said, "any death but that of the pit!" Fool! might I have not known that *into the pit* it was the object of the burning iron to urge me? Could I resist its glow? or, if even that, could I withstand its pressure? And now, flatter and flatter grew the lozenge, with a rapidity that left me no time for contemplation. Its center, and of course, its greatest width, came just over the yawning gulf. I shrank back—but the closing walls pressed me resistlessly onward. At length for my seared and writhing body there was no longer an inch of foothold on the firm floor of the prison. I struggled no more, but the agony of my soul found vent in one loud, long, and final scream of despair. I felt that I tottered upon the brink—I averted my eyes—

**563–565 Amid the thought. . . like balm:** The walls are red hot, and at first the water at the bottom of the pit seems to the narrator like a welcome relief.

**565 balm** (bäm): a soothing ointment.

📖 **READ ALOUD**  **Lines 565–573**

Read aloud the boxed passage in a way that expresses the narrator's horror. What do you think he sees at the bottom of the pit? **(Draw Conclusions)**

_____

_____

_____

_____

**575 the ague** (ā′gyo͞o): a feverish illness.

**584–585 In an instant . . . lozenge:** The walls of the dungeon have changed in shape from a square to a diamond **(lozenge)**. The walls are moving closer together and eventually will crush and burn the narrator.

There was a <u>discordant</u> hum of human voices! There was a loud blast of many trumpets! There was a harsh grating as of a thousand thunders! The fiery walls rushed back! An outstretched arm caught my own as I fell, fainting, into the abyss. It was that of General Lasalle. The French army had entered Toledo. The Inquisition was in the hands of its enemies.

*Pause* **&** **Reflect**

---

**discordant** (dĭ-skôr′dnt) *adj.* marked by a harsh mixture of sounds

**603–606 An outstretched arm . . .**
**enemies:** The French army has defeated the Spanish troops at Toledo. The general of the French army arrives in time to grab the narrator as he is about to topple down into the pit.

*Pause* **&** *Reflect*

✎ MARK IT UP **1.** The walls of the narrator's dungeon change in two ways. What are these ways? Write the answer below. Then circle details on pages 184 and 186 that led you to your answer. **(Clarify)**

_____

_____

_____

_____

**2.** The narrator is saved at the end of the story. Does this ending seem realistic? *Yes / No,* because_____

_____

_____

_____.

**(Evaluate)**

✎ CHALLENGE

**Mood** is the feeling, or atmosphere, that a writer creates for the reader. In this story, Poe creates a mood of horror. Review passages in the story that describe the various tortures the narrator suffers. In these passages, mark examples of vivid descriptive language. How do these words and phrases help to create a sense of horror? **(Analyze)**

## Wrapping Up

If you are using **The Language of Literature,** you can now move to the questions and activities on pages 575–577 of that book.

# Active Reading Skillbuilder

## Visualizing

Readers can better understand a story if they **visualize,** or mentally picture, what is being described. As you read this story, use the following chart to write down details about the characters, events, and setting that you can vividly picture in your mind. Examples are shown.

| Details I Can Visualize | | |
|---|---|---|
| **Characters** | **Events** | **Setting** |
| "I saw the lips of the black-robed judges. They appeared to me white . . . and thin." (lines 15–18) | "tall figures that lifted and bore me in silence down—down—still down" (lines 79–80) | "The ground was moist and slippery." (line 181) |

# Literary Analysis Skillbuilder

### Suspense

**Suspense** is the excitement or tension readers feel as they become involved in a story. Poe builds suspense in this story by using a frightening setting, strange complications of plot, and a first-person narrator who describes his mental state at each turn of events. Imagine you are creating a soundtrack for a film of this story. First, identify the moments of greatest suspense where the music should be most dramatic. Then on the line graph, list events and mark their level of suspense. Examples are shown below.

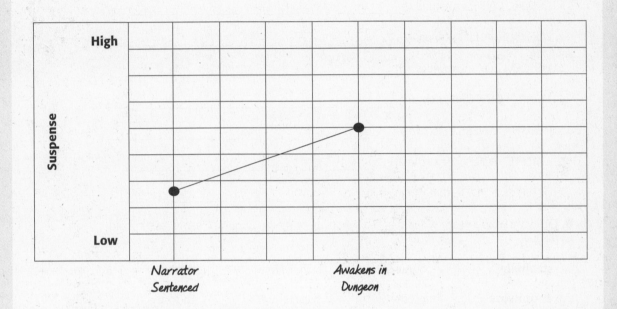

# Words to Know SkillBuilder

## Words to Know

| | | | | |
|---|---|---|---|---|
| discordant | imperceptible | lucid | relapse | supposition |
| eloquent | insuperable | pertinacity | resolution | treacherous |
| encompass | lethargy | potent | stealthily | voracity |

**A.** Complete each of the following analogies by using the correct Word to Know. Remember that the second pair of words in an analogy should have the same relationship as the first pair.

1. COLOR : GARISH : : sound : _____

2. LARGE : SMALL : : noticeable : _____

3. VICTORY : JOY : : tiredness : _____

4. MURKY : OBSCURE : : clear : _____

5. HEALTH : ILLNESS : : recovery : _____

6. ATHLETE : AGILE : : speechmaker : _____

7. DETERMINE : DETERMINATION : : resolve : _____

**B.** Circle the word in each group that is a synonym, or means about the same, as the bold-faced word.

1. **stealthily**     obviously     secretively     alertly

2. **encompass**     uncover     direct     enclose

3. **insuperable**     unbeatable     suffering     attainable

4. **supposition**     promise     assumption     question

5. **treacherous**     hazardous     sly     slippery

6. **potent**     dense     determined     powerful

7. **voracity**     filth     engaging     greed

8. **pertinacity**     indifference     obstinacy     pleasantness

**C.** Imagine that you had been in the pit described in "The Pit and the Pendulum." Write a diary entry that tells what happened and how you reacted. Use at least **five** of the Words to Know.

# FROM
# NIGHT

## Elie Wiesel

## MEMOIR

### Before You Read
If you are using **The Language of Literature**...

- Use the information on page 593 of that book to prepare for reading.

- Look at the photograph of concentration camp survivors on page 594. What does it reveal about these men and their experience?

### Reading Tips
This selection is an excerpt from *Night*, the **memoir** of a man who spent his teenage years in concentration camps. At the time described in this excerpt, the writer had been in concentration camps for almost one year.

- As you begin reading, you may feel as if you are entering into the middle of the story. Keep reading. You will soon get caught up in the action.

- Imagine yourself in the author's position. What might you be thinking or feeling?

- Think about the **author's purpose** for sharing his experiences. What does he want you to understand or learn from his experiences?

**PREVIEW** *Night* is the story of one Jewish teenager's actual experiences in concentration camps during World War II. In 1944, 15-year-old Elie Wiesel[1] and his family were arrested. Wiesel and his father were transported together from their home in Romania to a series of concentration camps in Poland. This excerpt from Wiesel's **memoir** describes one of his early experiences with the "selection" process. During a "selection," weak or sickly prisoners were separated out from the group and put to death. Would Wiesel and his father survive the cut?

**FOCUS**
Wiesel learns that a selection is soon to take place. Those who fail the test will be killed and cremated (burned to ashes) in huge furnaces.

**MARK IT UP** As you read, circle details that describe the selection process. An example is highlighted.

**The SS[2] gave us** a fine New Year's gift. We had just come back from work. As soon as we had passed through the door of the camp, we sensed something different in the air. Roll call did not take so long as usual. The evening soup was given out with great speed and swallowed down at once in anguish.

I was no longer in the same block[3] as my father. I had been transferred to another unit, the building one, where, twelve hours a day, I had to drag heavy blocks of stone about. The head of my new block was a German Jew, small of

**MARK IT UP** **KEEP TRACK**
As you read, you can use these marks to keep track of your understanding.

✔ ..... I understand.

? ..... I don't understand this.

! ..... Interesting or surprising

---

1. **Elie Wiesel** (ĕl'ē vē-zĕl').
2. **SS:** an elite military unit of the Nazi party that served as Hitler's personal guard and as a special security force.
3. **block:** prisoners were assigned to different units or groups, called blocks, and housed in large buildings often referred to as cell blocks.

<u>stature</u>, with piercing eyes. He told us that evening that no one would be allowed to go out after the evening soup. And soon a terrible word was circulating—selection.

We knew what that meant. An SS man would examine us. Whenever he found a weak one, a *musulman* as we called them, he would write his number down: good for the

20 crematory.[4]

After soup, we gathered together between the beds. The veterans said:

"You're lucky to have been brought here so late. This camp is paradise today, compared with what it was like two years ago. Buna[5] was a real hell then. There was no water, no blankets, less soup and bread. At night we slept almost naked, and it was below thirty degrees. The corpses were collected in hundreds every day. The work was hard. Today, this is a little paradise. The Kapos[6] had orders to kill a certain number of

30 prisoners every day. And every week—selection. A merciless selection. . . . Yes, you're lucky."

"Stop it! Be quiet!" I begged. "You can tell your stories tomorrow or on some other day."

They burst out laughing. They were not veterans for nothing.

"Are you scared? So were we scared. And there was plenty to be scared of in those days."

The old men stayed in their corner, dumb, motionless, haunted. Some were praying.

40 An hour's delay. In an hour, we should know the verdict— death or a reprieve.

And my father? Suddenly I remembered him. How would he pass the selection? He had aged so much. . . .

The head of our block had never been outside concentration camps since 1933. He had already been through all the slaughterhouses, all the factories of death. At about

---

4. **crematory** (krē′mə-tôr′ē): a furnace for the burning of corpses.

5. **Buna** (boo′nə): a forced-labor camp in Poland, near the Auschwitz concentration camp.

6. **Kapos** (kä′pōz): the prisoners who served as foremen, or heads, of each building or cell block.

WORDS
TO
KNOW

**stature** (stăch′ər) *n.* a person's height

nine o'clock, he took up his position in our midst: "Achtung!"[7]

There was instant silence.

50    "Listen carefully to what I am going to say." (For the first time, I heard his voice quiver.) "In a few moments the selection will begin. You must get completely undressed. Then one by one you go before the SS doctors. I hope you will all succeed in getting through. But you must help your own chances. Before you go into the next room, move about in some way so that you give yourselves a little color. Don't walk slowly, run! Run as if the devil were after you! Don't look at the SS. Run, straight in front of you!"

He broke off for a moment, then added:

60    "And, the essential thing, don't be afraid!"

Here was a piece of advice we should have liked very much to be able to follow.

Pause & Reflect

FOCUS
Will both Wiesel and his father pass the test? Read to find out what happens during the selection.

**I got undressed,** leaving my clothes on the bed. There was no danger of anyone stealing them this evening.

Tibi and Yossi,[8] who had changed their unit at the same time as I had, came up to me and said:

"Let's keep together. We shall be stronger."

70    Yossi was murmuring something between his teeth. He must have been praying. I had never realized that Yossi was a believer. I had even always thought the reverse. Tibi was silent, very pale. All the prisoners in the block stood naked between the beds. This must be how one stands at the last judgment.

"They're coming!"

There were three SS officers standing around the <u>notorious</u>

---

7. **Achtung!** (äкн-tŏŏng′) *German:* Attention!

8. **Tibi** (tĭb′ē) **and Yossi** (yō′sē): two young Czech brothers in Wiesel's block at Buna who become his friends.

WORDS
TO
KNOW

**notorious** (nō-tôr′ē-əs) *adj.* having a widely known, usually very bad reputation

Pause & Reflect

MARK IT UP    1. Review the details that you circled as you read. Star the passage on page 194 that explains who will be selected. (Locate Specific Details)

2. The head of Wiesel's block offers his men specific tips for passing the selection. **Summarize** his advice.

_____
_____
_____
_____

3. Wiesel is afraid that his father might not pass the selection. Why does he think his father might be selected? (Clarify)

_____
_____
_____
_____

4. If you were in Wiesel's situation, what might be your thoughts or feelings at this time? (Connect)

_____
_____
_____
_____

Dr. Mengele,[9] who had received us at Birkenau.[10] The head of the block, with an attempt at a smile, asked us:

80 "Ready?"

Yes, we were ready. So were the SS doctors. Dr. Mengele was holding a list in his hand: our numbers. He made a sign to the head of the block: "We can begin!" As if this were a game!

The first to go by were the "officials" of the block: *Stubenaelteste*,[11] Kapos, foremen, all in perfect physical condition of course! Then came the ordinary prisoners' turn. Dr. Mengele took stock of them from head to foot. Every now and then, he wrote a number down. One single thought filled

90 my mind: not to let my number be taken; not to show my left arm.

There were only Tibi and Yossi in front of me. They passed. I had time to notice that Mengele had not written their numbers down. Someone pushed me. It was my turn. I ran without looking back. My head was spinning: you're too thin, you're too weak, you're too thin, you're good for the furnace. . . . The race seemed <u>interminable</u>. I thought I had been running for years. . . . You're too thin, you're too weak. . . . At last I had arrived exhausted. When I regained

100 my breath, I questioned Yossi and Tibi:

"Was I written down?"

"No," said Yossi. He added, smiling: "In any case, he couldn't have written you down, you were running too fast. . . ."

I began to laugh. I was glad. I would have liked to kiss him. At that moment, what did the others matter! I hadn't been written down.

Those whose numbers had been noted stood apart, abandoned by the whole world. Some were weeping in silence.

110 The SS officers went away. The head of the block appeared, his face reflecting the general weariness.

---

9. **Dr. Mengele** (mĕng′ə-lə): Josef Mengele, a German doctor who personally selected nearly half a million prisoners to die in gas chambers at Auschwitz. He also performed inhuman medical experiments on inmates.

10. **Birkenau** (bîr′kə-nou): a large section of the Auschwitz concentration camp.

11. *Stubenaelteste* (shtōō′bən-ĕl′tə-stə) *German:* a rank of Kapos; literally "elders of the rooms."

WORDS
TO
KNOW

**interminable** (ĭn-tûr′mə-nə-bəl) *adj.* endless or seemingly endless

"Everything went off all right. Don't worry. Nothing is going to happen to anyone. To anyone."

Again he tried to smile. A poor, <u>emaciated</u>, dried-up Jew questioned him avidly in a trembling voice:

"But . . . but, *Blockaelteste*,[12] they did write me down!"

The head of the block let his anger break out. What! Did someone refuse to believe him!

"What's the matter now? Am I telling lies then? I tell you 120 once and for all, nothing's going to happen to you! To anyone! You're wallowing in your own despair, you fool!"

The bell rang, a signal that the selection had been completed throughout the camp.

With all my might I began to run to Block 36. I met my father on the way. He came up to me:

"Well? So you passed?"

"Yes. And you?"

"Me too."

How we breathed again, now! My father had brought me a 130 present—half a ration of bread obtained in exchange for a piece of rubber, found at the warehouse, which would do to sole a shoe.

The bell. Already we must separate, go to bed. Everything was regulated by the bell. It gave me orders, and I automatically obeyed them. I hated it. Whenever I dreamed of a better world, I could only imagine a universe with no bells.

## Pause & Reflect

**FOCUS**

Several days later, about ten prisoners, including Wiesel's 140 father, are ordered to stay behind when the rest go to work. Read to find out if Wiesel's father escapes a second selection.

**Several days had elapsed.** We no longer thought about the selection. We went to work as usual, loading heavy stones into railway wagons. Rations had become more meager: this was the only change.

We had risen before dawn, as on

12. *Blockaelteste* (blôk´ĕl´tə-stə) *German*: a rank of Kapos; literally "elders of the building."

WORDS TO KNOW

**emaciated** (ĭ-mā´shē-ā-tĭd) *adj.* extremely thin, especially as a result of starvation **emaciate** *v.*

## Pause & Reflect

**MARK IT UP** 1. What does Wiesel worry about as he stands in line for the selection? Underline the passages on page 196 that describe his worries. **(Locate Specific Details)**

2. What happens during the selection? **(Clarify)**

_____

_____

_____

_____

3. After the selection, one prisoner is terrified because his name was written down. Why do you think the head of the block responds in anger? **(Cause and Effect)**

_____

_____

_____

_____

every day. We had received the black coffee, the ration of bread. We were about to set out for the yard as usual. The head of the block arrived, running.

"Silence for a moment. I have a list of numbers here. I'm going to read them to you. Those whose numbers I call won't be going to work this morning; they'll stay behind in the camp."

150  And, in a soft voice, he read out about ten numbers. We had understood. These were numbers chosen at the selection. Dr. Mengele had not forgotten.

The head of the block went toward his room. Ten prisoners surrounded him, hanging onto his clothes:

"Save us! You promised . . . ! We want to go to the yard. We're strong enough to work. We're good workers. We can . . . we will . . . ."

He tried to calm them to reassure them about their fate, to
160  explain to them that the fact that they were staying behind in the camp did not mean much, had no tragic significance.

"After all, I stay here myself every day," he added.

It was a somewhat feeble argument. He realized it, and without another word went and shut himself up in his room.

The bell had just rung.

"Form up!"

It scarcely mattered now that the work was hard. The essential thing was to be as far away as possible from the block, from the crucible[13] of death, from the center of hell.

170  I saw my father running toward me. I became frightened all of a sudden.

"What's the matter?"

Out of breath, he could hardly open his mouth.

"Me, too . . . me, too . . . ! They told me to stay behind in the camp."

They had written down his number without his being aware of it.

"What will happen?" I asked in anguish.

But it was he who tried to reassure me.

180  "It isn't certain yet. There's still a chance of escape. They're going to do another selection today . . . a decisive selection."

I was silent.

---

13. **crucible** (krōō′sə-bəl): a severe test or trial.

He felt that his time was short. He spoke quickly. He would have liked to say so many things. His speech grew confused; his voice choked. He knew that I would have to go in a few moments. He would have to stay behind alone, so very alone.

"Look, take this knife," he said to me. "I don't need it any longer. It might be useful to you. And take this spoon as well. Don't sell them. Quickly! Go on. Take what I'm giving you!"

190 The inheritance.

"Don't talk like that, Father." (I felt that I would break into sobs.) "I don't want you to say that. Keep the spoon and knife. You need them as much as I do. We shall see each other again this evening, after work."

He looked at me with his tired eyes, veiled with despair. He went on:

"I'm asking this of you. . . . Take them. Do as I ask, my son. We have no time. . . . Do as your father asks."

Our Kapo yelled that we should start.

200 The unit set out toward the camp gate. Left, right! I bit my lips. My father had stayed by the block, leaning against the wall. Then he began to run, to catch up with us. Perhaps he had forgotten something he wanted to say to me. . . . But we were marching too quickly . . . Left, right!

We were already at the gate. They counted us, to the <u>din</u> of military music. We were outside.

### *Pause* & Reflect

**FOCUS**

Read on to learn whether Wiesel's father passes the second selection test.

210 **The whole day,** I wandered about as if sleepwalking. Now and then Tibi and Yossi would throw me a brotherly word. The Kapo, too, tried to reassure me. He had given me easier work today. I felt sick at heart. How well they were treating me! Like an orphan! I thought: even now, my father is still helping me.

I did not know myself what I wanted—for the day to pass quickly or not. I was afraid of finding myself alone that night. How good it would be to die here!

WORDS
TO
KNOW

**din** (dĭn) *n.* a jumble of loud noises

*Pause* & Reflect

1. Why are Wiesel and his father so surprised that the father's number has been called for a second selection? **(Clarify)**

_____

_____

_____

_____

**READ ALOUD** 2. Read aloud the boxed passage. Wiesel's father gives him the knife and spoon because\_\_\_\_\_

_____

_____.

Wiesel does not want to take them because_____

_____

_____.

**(Cause and Effect)**

3. Wiesel describes the block as "the crucible of death . . . the center of hell" (line 169). What do these metaphors reveal about his feelings? **(Infer)**

_____

_____

_____

_____

4. What do you think will happen to Wiesel's father? **(Predict)**

_____

_____

_____

_____

MARK IT UP   2. When Wiesel is waiting for news, the other prisoners are very considerate. Why? Write the answer below. Then underline the passage on page 199 that led you to that answer. **(Draw Conclusions)**

_____

_____

_____

_____

CHALLENGE

**Tone** is the attitude a writer takes toward a subject. For example, the writer's tone may be objective, bitter, serious, or amused. How would you describe Wiesel's tone in this selection? Mark passages that help you know this. **(Analyze Style)**

## Wrapping Up

If you are using **The Language of Literature,** you can now move to the questions and activities on pages 600–601 of that book.

At last we began the return journey. How I longed for orders to run!

The military march. The gate. The camp.

220   I ran to Block 36.

Were there still miracles on this earth? He was alive. He had escaped the second selection. He had been able to prove that he was still useful. . . . I gave him back his knife and spoon.

Pause **&** Reflect

# Active Reading SkillBuilder

## Connecting

Readers often compare what they are reading with their own knowledge and experience. Sometimes they also imagine themselves in a situation similar to that of a character or person in a piece of writing. In these ways, readers are **connecting** with what they are reading. In the chart below, keep notes of your mental and emotional reactions to events and conversations related by Wiesel. Then write some of your reflections on the piece itself and on the Holocaust in general. An example has been done.

| Event/Conversation | Mental and Emotional Reaction |
|---|---|
| Wiesel had to work 12 hours every day dragging heavy stones. | I would hate such a life. I'm not sure I could do it. |
| | |
| | |

**Reflections:**

# Literary Analysis SkillBuilder

## Style

**Style** is the particular way a piece of literature is written. It has to do with *how* something is said, not *what* is said. Style is created through a writer's choice of words, sentence structure, tone, imagery, and dialogue. For example, in the first paragraph Wiesel uses several short sentences and simple words to create a direct, plain style. Choose a brief passage from this excerpt. Identify the elements of its style using the five categories in the chart below. Then briefly describe the overall style of the passage.

| Passage beginning _____ Lines: _____ | |
|---|---|
| **Word Choice** | |
| **Sentence Structure** | |
| **Tone** | |
| **Imagery** | |
| **Dialogue** | |

**Style:** _____

_____

# Words to Know SkillBuilder

## Words to Know

din          emaciated          interminable          notorious          stature

**A.** Decide which word from the word list belongs in each numbered blank.
Then write the word on the blank line on the right.

An old lady who had to live in a shoe
Had a whole lot of children within.
And the noise from this brood,
In its most playful mood,
Created a terrible (1).

_____
(1)

As you know, it's been said in a poem you have read,
In that myth Mother Goose once created,
There was almost no food.
So, one might conclude
That the children were (2).

_____
(2)

That wasn't their fate. They just had to wait
An (3) time at each meal.
If a plate has to go
All the way from the toe,
It won't quickly arrive at the heel!

_____
(3)

Now, all of the tots had their own assigned spots,
Which began, as was right, with the smallest.
He got his food first;
You can tell it was worst
For the child whose (4) was tallest.

_____
(4)

There was waiting and noise and an excess of toys,
And that shoe was most often uproarious.
But the woman did not
Give her kiddies a swat.
It's unfair she's become so (5).

_____
(5)

**B.** Use at least **one** of the Words to Know in writing a description of a visual
image you had while reading "Night."

## Before You Read

If you are using *The Language of Literature* . . .

- Use the information on page 645 of that book to prepare for reading.

- Look at the photo on page 647 to get an idea of an artilleryman in action. Then look at the photo on page 648. What feelings are expressed in that photo?

## Reading Tips

Although both poems are about the experience of war, each one has a unique **style**. In "The Artilleryman's Vision," the lines are long, and there is no complete stop until the end of the poem. By contrast, "look at this)" has short lines and few words. The punctuation and capitalization are not used in the usual way. As you read, use the following strategies to help you understand each poem.

- Read each poem aloud two or three times. Read the first poem in a way that expresses the drama of war. Read the second poem at a slower pace. As you reread each poem, answer the Pause & Reflect questions.

- In each poem, try to imagine the **speaker**, or the voice that talks to the reader. What sort of person is the speaker? What situation is he describing?

**PREVIEW** "The Artilleryman's Vision" was first published in 1865. The poet imagines how a soldier might be affected in the future by his experience in the Civil War. The **speaker** in the poem served in the artillery, the division of the army that operates the cannons. Although the war has been over for several years, the speaker still relives the experience in his mind. The poem "look at this)"—published in 1926—presents the fragmented thoughts of a soldier who has lost a good friend in World War I.

## The Artilleryman's Vision

### Walt Whitman

**FOCUS**

As the speaker lies in bed in his peaceful home, he has a sudden "vision" of himself back on a Civil War battlefield.

**MARK IT UP** As you read, underline details that help bring the sights and sounds of the battle to life. An example is highlighted on page 205.

While my wife at my side lies slumbering, and the wars
    are over long,
And my head on the pillow rests at home, and the
    vacant midnight passes,
And through the stillness, through the dark, I hear, just
    hear, the breath of my infant,
There in the room as I wake from sleep this vision
    presses upon me;
5  The engagement[1] opens there and then in fantasy
    unreal,

---

1. **engagement:** battle.

The skirmishers[2] begin, they crawl cautiously ahead, I hear the irregular snap! snap!

I hear the sounds of the different missiles, the short *t-h-t! t-h-t!* of the rifle balls,

I see the shells exploding leaving small white clouds, I hear the great shells shrieking as they pass,

The grape[3] like the hum and whirr of wind through the trees, (tumultuous[4] now the contest rages,)

All the scenes at the batteries[5] rise in detail before me again,

The crashing and smoking, the pride of the men in their pieces,

The chief-gunner ranges and sights his piece[6] and selects a fuse of the right time,

After firing I see him lean aside and look eagerly off to note the effect;

Elsewhere I hear the cry of a regiment charging, (the young colonel leads himself this time with brandish'd[7] sword,)

I see the gaps cut by the enemy's volleys[8], (quickly fill'd up, no delay,)[9]

I breathe the suffocating smoke, then the flat clouds hover low concealing all;

Now a strange lull for a few seconds, not a shot fired on either side,

Then resumed the chaos louder than ever, with eager calls and orders of officers,

While from some distant part of the field the wind wafts to my ears a shout of applause, (some special success,)

---

2. **skirmishers:** soldiers sent out in advance of a main attack.

3. **grape:** grapeshot—small iron balls shot in a bunch from a cannon.

4. **tumultuous** (to͞o-mŭl′cho͞o-əs): noisy and confusing.

5. **batteries:** groups of cannons.

6. **ranges and sights his piece:** The gunner is aiming the cannon at the target.

7. **brandish'd:** raised and waving.

8. **volleys:** groups of cannonballs fired at the same time.

9. **quickly . . . delay:** As the attacking soldiers are cut down by enemy gunfire, new soldiers take their places.

MARK IT UP **KEEP TRACK**

As you read, you can use these marks to keep track of your understanding.

✔ ..... I understand.

? ..... I don't understand this.

! ..... Interesting or surprising idea

MARK IT UP **WORD POWER**

Mark words that you'd like to add to your **Personal Word List.** After reading, you can record the words and their meanings beginning on page 316.

Pause & Reflect

MARK IT UP  **1.** Review the details that you underlined as you read. Star the details that you find most vivid or memorable. **(Evaluate)**

**2.** In line 20 the speaker feels "devilish exultation" and "the old mad joy." In your own words, explain what you think he means. **(Analyze Speaker)**

_____

_____

_____

_____

READ ALOUD  **3.** Read aloud the boxed passage. Circle two phrases below that describe the speaker's experience. **(Infer)**

Feels excited during battle

Goes out of his way to help the wounded

Notices what happens around him

Tries to run from battle

20 And ever the sound of the cannon far or near, (rousing[10] even in dreams a devilish exultation[11] and all the old mad joy in the depths of my soul,)

And ever the hastening of infantry shifting positions, batteries, cavalry, moving hither and thither,

(The falling, dying, I heed not, the wounded dripping and red I heed not, some to the rear are hobbling,)

Grime, heat, rush, aide-de-camps[12] galloping by or on a full run,

With the patter of small arms, the warning *s-s-t* of the rifles, (these in my vision I hear or see,)

25 And bombs bursting in air, and at night the vari-color'd rockets.

Pause & Reflect

---

10. **rousing:** awakening.
11. **exultation** (ek′səl-tā′shən): rejoicing or celebrating.
12. **aide-de-camps** (ād′dĭ-kămps′): assistants to military commanders.

**206**  The InterActive Reader

# look at this)

## E. E. Cummings

**FOCUS**

The speaker in this poem is struggling to come to terms with the loss of his friend.

**MARK IT UP** As you read, circle words that reveal the speaker's feelings about his dead comrade.

look at this)
a 75[1] done
this nobody would
have believed
would they no
kidding this was my particular

pal
funny aint
it we was
buddies
i used to

know
him lift the
poor cuss
tenderly this side up handle

with care
fragile
and send him home

to his old mother in
a new nice pine box

(collect[2]

### Pause & Reflect

**Pause & Reflect**

1. How did the speaker's friend die? (Clarify)

2. Review the words you circled as you read. How would you describe the speaker's feelings about his friend? (Analyze Speaker)

**READ ALOUD** 3. Read aloud lines 15–21. What scene is being described here? (Infer)

**CHALLENGE**

Though E. E. Cummings and Walt Whitman lived in different centuries, both were famous for breaking the "rules" of poetry. Which of the two poems do you think is more effective in conveying its message? Support your opinion with examples from the poems. (Evaluate)

## Wrapping Up

If you are using *The Language of Literature,* you can now move to the questions and activities on pages 649–651 of that book.

---

1. **75:** a 75-millimeter cannon.

2. **collect:** To send something collect means that the receiver will pay the shipping charges. When the mother receives her son's body, she will "pay" with her grief.

# Active Reading SkillBuilder

## Comparing and Contrasting Speakers

In poetry, the speaker is the voice that "talks" to the reader. The speakers in these
two poems have both fought in a war. Their experiences and reactions
differ in some ways, however. Reread each poem. Think about the kind of person
the speaker seems to be and the attitude he has toward war. Use the chart below
to **compare and contrast the two speakers** and their experiences of war.
Two examples are given.

| Speakers in "The Artilleryman's Vision" and "look at this)" | |
|---|---|
| **Similarities** | **Differences** |
| Both speakers experienced battle. | Only the first speaker describes the battle in great detail. |

# Literary Analysis SkillBuilder

## Tone and Diction

**Tone** is the attitude a writer takes toward a subject. One way in which writers create tone is through **diction,** or word choice. For example, a piece of writing with a positive tone might include such words as *strong, best,* or *promising.* Decide which of the following words best describe the tone of each poem. More than one word may apply.

- serious
- anxious
- playful
- shocked
- bitter
- sad
- proud
- excited

Write the words you've chosen in the chart below. Then record examples of diction from each poem that contribute to each tone you have identified. Two examples are given.

| "The Artilleryman's Vision" | "look at this)" |
|---|---|

| Tone: | Tone: |
|---|---|
| Diction:     *"great shells shrieking"* (line 8) | Diction:     *"a 75 done this nobody would have believed"* (lines 2–4) |

## Before You Read

If you are using **The Language of Literature** . . .

- Use the information on pages 682–689 of that book to prepare for reading.

- Examine the art throughout pages 692–712.

## Reading Tips

Shakespeare wrote this play about four hundred years ago. The play, therefore, includes some words no longer used in English and other words whose meanings have changed since Shakespeare's time.

- You don't have to understand every word to make sense of this play. Read for general meaning and keep moving. Pause at the end of a line only if you come upon a mark of punctuation.

- Use the Guide for Reading, beginning on page 213, to help you understand unfamiliar words and difficult lines and passages.

- Try reading some lines aloud and listen to their rhythmic patterns.

- As you meet the **characters** in this play, notice ways in which they remind you of the people you know.

from

# The Tragedy of

# JULIUS CAESAR

# William Shakespeare

PREVIEW You are about to read Act One of *Julius Caesar*. Written probably in the late 1590s, Shakespeare's **drama** is based on real people and events from Roman history. Julius Caesar, who died in Rome in 44 B.C., was a great general. His military victories made him popular with the people of Rome. They granted him a title no one had ever held before in Rome—dictator for life. Some of the senators, however, saw Caesar as a threat to the Roman republic. He was in control of the government. The senators feared he wanted to be king.

As the play begins, Caesar stands at the height of his powers. He does not know that several senators are plotting to end his rule—and his life.

# CHARACTERS

**Julius Caesar**
   (jool' yəs sē' zər)

**TRIUMVIRS AFTER THE DEATH OF JULIUS CAESAR**

**Octavius Caesar**
   (ök-tā' vē-əs sē' zər)

**Marcus Antonius**
   (mär' kəs ăn-tō' nē-əs)

**M. Aemilius Lepidus**
   (ə-mēl' yəs lĕp' ĭ-dəs)

**SENATORS**

**Cicero** (sĭs' ə-rō)
**Publius** (pŏŏ' blē-əs)
**Popilius Lena**
   (pō-pĭl' ē-əs lē' nə)

**CONSPIRATORS AGAINST JULIUS CAESAR**

**Marcus Brutus**
   (mär' kəs broo' təs)
**Cassius** (kăsh' əs)
**Casca** (kăs' kə)
**Trebonius** (trə-bō' nē -əs)
**Ligarius** (lĭ-gär' ē-əs)
**Decius Brutus**
   (dē' shəs broo' təs)
**Metellus Cimber**
   (mə-tĕl' əs cĭm' bər)
**Cinna** (sĭn' ə)

**FRIENDS TO BRUTUS AND CASSIUS**

**Lucilius** (loo-sĭ' lē-əs)
**Titinius** (tī-tĭn' ē-əs)
**Messala** (məs-ä' lə)
**Young Cato** (kā' tō)
**Volumnius** (və-loom' nē-əs)

**Flavius and Marullus**,
   (flā' vē-əs)
   and (mə-rool' əs),
   Tribunes of the people

**Artemidorus of Cnidos**
   (är' tə-mə-dôr' əs), a
   teacher of Rhetoric

**A Soothsayer**
**Cinna,** a poet
**Another Poet**

**SERVANTS TO BRUTUS**

**Varro** (vär' ō)
**Clitus** (clĭ' təs)
**Claudius** (clô' dē-əs)
**Strato** (strā' tō)
**Lucius** (loo' shəs)
**Dardanius** (där-dō' nē-əs)

**Pindarus** (pĭn-dar' əs),
   servant to Cassius
**Calpurnia** (kal-pûr' nē-ə),
   wife to Caesar
**Portia** (pôr' shə), wife to
   Brutus
**The Ghost of Caesar**
**Senators, Citizens, Guards,**
   **Attendants, Servants, etc.**

**MARK IT UP** **KEEP TRACK**

As you read, you can use these marks to keep track of your understanding.

✓ ..... I understand.

? ..... I don't understand this.

! ..... Interesting or surprising idea

**READ ALOUD**

Read aloud the names of the characters in this play. Note that several characters are conspirators, or those who are plotting in secret against Julius Caesar. One character is supernatural—the Ghost of Caesar.

TIME: **44** B.C.

PLACE: **Rome; the camp near Sardis; the plains of Philipi**

# SCENE I    A STREET IN ROME.

**PREVIEW** The play begins on February 15, the religious feast of Lupercal (lōō′ pər-kāl). Today the people have a particular reason for celebrating. Julius Caesar has just returned to Rome after a long civil war in which he defeated the forces of Pompey, his rival for power. Caesar now has the opportunity to take full control of Rome.

In this opening scene, a group of workmen, in their best clothes, celebrate in the streets. They are joyful over Caesar's victory. The workers meet Flavius (flā′ vē-əs) and Marullus (mə-rōōl′ əs), two tribunes—government officials—who supported Pompey. The tribunes express their anger at the celebration, and one worker responds with puns. Finally, the two tribunes scatter the crowd.

**FOCUS**

Read to find out about the conflict between the two tribunes and the crowd of workers.

**MARK IT UP** As you read, underline details that help you understand how the crowd feels about Caesar and how they celebrate his victory. An example is highlighted on page 214.

> **Flavius.** Hence! home, you idle creatures, get you
>     home!
>   Is this a holiday? What, know you not,
>   Being mechanical, you ought not walk
>   Upon a laboring day without the sign
> 5   Of your profession? Speak, what trade art thou?

**First Commoner.** Why, sir, a carpenter.

**Marullus.** Where is thy leather apron and thy rule?
    What dost thou with thy best apparel on?
    You, sir, what trade are you?

10 **Second Commoner.** Truly sir, in respect of a fine
    workman I am but, as you would say, a cobbler.

**Marullus.** But what trade art thou? Answer me
    directly.

**Second Commoner.** A trade, sir, that I hope I may
    use with a safe conscience, which is indeed, sir, a
15    mender of bad soles.

**Flavius.** What trade, thou knave? Thou naughty
    knave, what trade?

Use this guide for help with unfamiliar words and difficult passages.

**2–5 What, know . . . profession:** Since you are workers **(mechanical)**, you should be carrying the tools of your trade **(sign / Of your profession)**.

**10–27** In this conversation, the **cobbler** (shoemaker) makes several puns, which all go over the head of Marullus. Imagine the workmen laughing, as Marullus gets angrier and angrier, wondering what's so funny. Marullus is insulted because he thinks the commoner is refusing to answer his question. The comic misunderstanding is based on two different meanings of the word **cobbler** in Shakespeare's time: a specific meaning—"a person who repairs shoes"—and a general one—"any clumsy worker."

**16–18** Marullus accuses the commoner of being a wicked, sly person **(naughty knave)**, but the commoner begs Marullus not to be angry with him **(be not out with me)**. *Out* can mean both "angry" and "having worn-out shoes"; therefore *mend you* can mean "improve your character" or "repair your shoes."

✎ **MARK IT UP** WORD POWER

Mark words that you'd like to add to your **Personal Word List.** After reading, you can record the words and their meanings beginning on page 316.

✎ **JOT IT DOWN** Reread Lines 1–5

How would you describe Flavius' attitude toward the workers? **(Infer)**

_____

_____

_____

_____

**Second Commoner.** Nay, I beseech you, sir, be not out
  with me. Yet if you be out, sir, I can mend you.

**Marullus.** What mean'st thou by that? Mend me, thou
  saucy fellow?

20 **Second Commoner.** Why, sir, cobble you.

**Flavius.** Thou art a cobbler, art thou?

**Second Commoner.** Truly, sir, all that I live by is with
  the awl. I meddle with no tradesman's matters nor
  women's matters, but with all. I am indeed, sir, a
25  surgeon to old shoes. When they are in great
  danger, I recover them. As proper men as ever trod
  upon neat's leather have gone upon my handiwork.

**Flavius.** But wherefore art not in thy shop today?
  Why dost thou lead these men about the streets?

30 **Second Commoner.** Truly, sir, to wear out their shoes,
  to get myself into more work. But indeed, sir, we
  make holiday to see Caesar and to rejoice in his
  triumph.

**Marullus.** Wherefore rejoice? What conquest brings he
  home?
35  What tributaries follow him to Rome
  To grace in captive bonds his chariot wheels?
  You blocks, you stones, you worse than senseless
  things!
  O you hard hearts, you cruel men of Rome!
  Knew you not Pompey? Many a time and oft
40  Have you climbed up to walls and battlements,
  To tow'rs and windows, yea, to chimney tops,
  Your infants in your arms, and there have sat
  The livelong day, with patient expectation,
  To see great Pompey pass the streets of Rome.
45  And when you saw his chariot but appear,
  Have you not made an universal shout,
  That Tiber trembled underneath her banks
  To hear the replication of your sounds
  Made in her concave shores?
50  And do you now put on your best attire?
  And do you now cull out a holiday?
  And do you now strew flowers in his way
  That comes in triumph over Pompey's blood?
  Be gone!

**19** Marullus thinks the cobbler means "I can mend your behavior." He accuses the cobbler of being disrespectful **(saucy)**.

**23–24** The cobbler puns on the words *awl* (a shoemaker's tool) and *all*, which sound alike.

**27 neat's leather:** calfskin, used to make expensive shoes. The cobbler means that even rich people come to him for shoes.
**28 wherefore:** why.

**33 triumph:** Caesar's victory procession into Rome after defeating the sons of Pompey.
**35–36 What . . . wheels:** What captured prisoners march chained to the wheels of his chariot?

**39 Pompey:** a former Roman ruler defeated by Caesar in 48 B.C. Pompey was murdered a year after his defeat.
**41 chimney tops:** Shakespeare is describing his own London, not Rome.

**47 Tiber:** a river that runs through Rome.
**48 replication:** echo.

**50–54** In previous years, the crowd celebrated Pompey's victories. Now it celebrates the man who returns in triumph after defeating Pompey's sons **(Pompey's blood)** in Spain; **cull out:** select.

**READ ALOUD** Lines 50–54

Use the volume and tone of your voice to convey Marullus' anger at the crowd. What repeated phrase helps to convey that anger?

_____

_____

55    Run to your houses, fall upon your knees,
Pray to the gods to intermit the plague
That needs must light on this ingratitude.

**Flavius.** Go, go, good countrymen, and for this fault
Assemble all the poor men of your sort;
60    Draw them to Tiber banks, and weep your tears
Into the channel, till the lowest stream
Do kiss the most exalted shores of all.

[*Exeunt all the* Commoners.]

See, whe'r their basest metal be not moved.
They vanish tongue-tied in their guiltiness.
65    Go you down that way towards the Capitol;
This way will I. Disrobe the images
If you do find them decked with ceremonies.

**Marullus.** May we do so?
You know it is the feast of Lupercal.

70  **Flavius.** It is no matter. Let no images
Be hung with Caesar's trophies. I'll about
And drive away the vulgar from the streets.
So do you too, where you perceive them thick.

These growing feathers plucked from Caesar's wing
75    Will make him fly an ordinary pitch,
Who else would soar above the view of men
And keep us all in servile fearfulness.

[*Exeunt.*]

*Pause* & *Reflect*

**56–57 intermit . . . ingratitude:** hold back the deadly illness that might be just punishment for your behavior.

**60–62 weep . . . of all:** weep into the Tiber River until it overflows.

**Exeunt** (Latin)**:** They leave.

**63** Flavius and Marullus are now alone, having shamed the workers into leaving the street. Flavius says that they will now see if they have touched **(moved)** the workers' poor characters **(basest metal)**.

**66–67 Disrobe . . . ceremonies:** Strip the statues of any decorations you find on them.

**71–73 I'll about . . . thick:** I'll go around and scatter the rest of the commoners **(the vulgar)**. Do the same yourself wherever they are forming a crowd.

**74–77 These . . . fearfulness:** Flavius compares Caesar to a soaring falcon. He hopes that turning away some of Caesar's supporters **(growing feathers)** will prevent him from becoming too powerful; **ordinary pitch:** the usual height at which a bird flies above the ground.

## Pause & Reflect

1. Review the details that you underlined as you read. The crowd once cheered for Pompey. Now it celebrates his rival, Caesar, who has just defeated Pompey's sons. What can you conclude about the crowd? **(Draw Conclusions)**

_____

_____

_____

_____

2. Review the boxed passage on page 216. Flavius compares Caesar to a falcon that will soar in the sky unless his wings are clipped. What does Flavius think of Caesar? **(Infer)**

_____

_____

_____

3. What do you think might happen to the tribunes for removing the decorations from the statues? **(Predict)**

_____

_____

_____

# SCENE 2   A PUBLIC PLACE IN ROME.

PREVIEW As Caesar attends the traditional race at the festival of Lupercal, a soothsayer warns him to beware of the ides of March, or March 15. When Caesar leaves, Cassius tries to turn Brutus against Caesar by using flattery, examples of Caesar's weaknesses, and sarcasm about Caesar's power. Caesar passes by again, expressing his distrust of Cassius. Cassius and Brutus learn of Caesar's rejection of a crown the people of Rome have offered him. They agree to meet again to discuss what to do about Caesar.

> **FOCUS**
>
> In this scene, you meet Caesar and several other important characters. As you read, notice how Caesar is clearly in command.

[*A flourish of trumpets announces the approach of Caesar. A large crowd of* Commoners *has assembled; a* Soothsayer *is among them. Enter* Caesar, *his wife* Calpurnia, Portia, Decius, Cicero, Brutus, Cassius, Casca, *and* Antony, *who is stripped for running in the games.*]

**Caesar.** Calpurnia.

**Casca.**　　　　　　Peace, ho! Caesar speaks.

**Caesar.**　　　　　　　　　　　　　Calpurnia.

**Calpurnia.** Here, my lord.

**Caesar.** Stand you directly in Antonius' way
　　When he doth run his course. Antonius.

5　**Antony.** Caesar, my lord?

**Caesar.** Forget not in your speed, Antonius,
　　To touch Calpurnia; for our elders say
　　The barren, touched in this holy chase,
　　Shake off their sterile curse.

　　**Antony.**　　　　　　　　I shall remember.

10　When Caesar says "Do this," it is performed.

**Caesar.** Set on, and leave no ceremony out.

[*Flourish of trumpets.* Caesar *starts to leave.*]

**Soothsayer.** Caesar!

**Caesar.** Ha! Who calls?

**Casca.** Bid every noise be still. Peace yet again!

15　**Caesar.** Who is it in the press that calls on me?
　　I hear a tongue shriller than all the music
　　Cry "Caesar!" Speak. Caesar is turned to hear.

**3–9 Stand . . . curse:** Antony **(Antonius)** is about to run in a race that is part of the Lupercal celebration. Caesar refers to the superstition that a **sterile** woman (one unable to bear children) can become fertile if touched by one of the racers. Caesar has not produced a male heir. He, therefore, is eager for his wife Calpurnia to **shake off** her **sterile curse** and bear him a son.

**11 set on:** proceed.

**12–14** Remember that the crowd is cheering constantly. The **soothsayer** (fortuneteller), who calls out Caesar's name can hardly be heard. Casca tells the crowd to quiet down.
**15 press:** crowd.

**READ ALOUD**  **Lines 9–10**

What do these lines tell you about Antony's attitude toward Caesar? **(Infer)**

_____

_____

_____

_____

**Soothsayer.** Beware the ides of March.

**Caesar.**                                    What man is that?

**Brutus.** A soothsayer bids you beware the ides of March.

20    **Caesar.** Set him before me; let me see his face.

**Cassius.** Fellow, come from the throng; look upon
        Caesar.

**Caesar.** What say'st thou to me now? Speak once again.

**Soothsayer.** Beware the ides of March.

**Caesar.** He is a dreamer; let us leave him. Pass.

[*Trumpets sound. Exeunt all but* Brutus *and* Cassius.]

Pause **&** Reflect

FOCUS

Brutus and Cassius are alone together. Cassius
wants to find out why Brutus has been avoiding
him. Read to find out why Brutus has been keeping
to himself.

25    **Cassius.** Will you go see the order of the course?

**Brutus.** Not I.

**Cassius.** I pray you do.

**Brutus.** I am not gamesome. I do lack some part
        Of that quick spirit that is in Antony.
30      Let me not hinder, Cassius, your desires.
        I'll leave you.

**Cassius.** Brutus, I do observe you now of late;
        I have not from your eyes that gentleness
        And show of love as I was wont to have.
35      You bear too stubborn and too strange a hand
        Over your friend that loves you.

**Brutus.**                                    Cassius,
        Be not deceived. If I have veiled my look,
        I turn the trouble of my countenance
        Merely upon myself. Vexed I am
40      Of late with passions of some difference,
        Conceptions only proper to myself,

**18 ides:** the middle day of the month.

**25–28** Cassius asks if Brutus is going to watch the race **(the order of the course)**, but Brutus says he is not fond of sports **(gamesome)**.

**32–34 I do observe . . . to have:** Lately I haven't seen the friendliness in your face that I used to see **(was wont to have)**.

**38–47 I turn . . . other men:** I have been frowning at myself, not at you. I have been troubled **(Vexed)** lately by mixed emotions **(passions of some difference)**. They are personal matters that are, perhaps, marring my good manners. I hope my friends won't interpret **(construe)** my actions as anything more than my own private concerns.

Which give some soil, perhaps, to my behaviors;
But let not therefore my good friends be grieved
(Among which number, Cassius, be you one)
45 Nor construe any further my neglect
Than that poor Brutus, with himself at war,
forgets the shows of love to other men.

**Cassius.** Then, Brutus, I have much mistook your
passion,
By means whereof this breast of mine hath buried
50 Thoughts of great value, worthy cogitations.
Tell me, good Brutus, can you see your face?

**Brutus.** No, Cassius, for the eye sees not itself
But by reflection, by some other things.

**Cassius.** 'Tis just.
55 And it is very much lamented, Brutus,
That you have no such mirrors as will turn
Your hidden worthiness into your eye,
That you might see your shadow. I have heard
Where many of the best respect in Rome
60 (Except immortal Caesar), speaking of Brutus
And groaning underneath this age's yoke,
Have wished that noble Brutus had his eyes.

**Brutus.** Into what dangers would you lead me, Cassius,
That you would have me seek into myself
65 For that which is not in me?

**Cassius.** Therefore, good Brutus, be prepared to hear;
And since you know you cannot see yourself
So well as by reflection, I, your glass,
Will modestly discover to yourself
70 That of yourself which you yet know not of.
And be not jealous on me, gentle Brutus.
Were I a common laugher, or did use
To stale with ordinary oaths my love
To every new protester; if you know
75 That I do fawn on men and hug them hard,
And after scandal them; or if you know
That I profess myself in banqueting
To all the rout, then hold me dangerous.

*Pause & Reflect*

**48–50 I have . . . cogitations:** I have misunderstood your feelings. As a result, I have kept important thoughts to myself.

**54 'Tis just:** That's right.

**55–62 it is . . . eyes:** It is too bad you don't have a mirror that would reflect **(turn)** your inner qualities **(hidden worthiness)**. In fact, many respected citizens suffering under Caesar's rule **(this age's yoke)** have wished that Brutus could see himself as they see him. Cassius says the phrase "immortal Caesar" in a sarcastic way. He implies that Caesar is not really a god, even though he may think so.

**66–70 Therefore . . . not of:** Listen, Brutus, since you cannot see yourself, I will be your mirror **(glass)** and show you what you truly are.

**71 jealous on me:** suspicious of me; **gentle:** noble.

**72–78 Were I . . . dangerous:** Cassius reminds Brutus that he (Cassius) is worthy of trust. Cassius says he is not a fool **(common laugher)** or someone who pretends to be everyone's friend. Moreover, he does not show friendship and then talk evil about his friends **(scandal them)** behind their backs. Nor does he at a large dinner **(in banqueting)** try to win over the people **(all the rout)**.

## Pause & Reflect

**READ ALOUD** **1.** Read aloud the boxed passage on page 222. Brutus has been avoiding Cassius because he is troubled within. What do you think Brutus' war with himself is about? **(Infer)**

_____

_____

_____

**2.** In lines 58–62 of this scene, Cassius tells Brutus that many people in Rome wish that he (Brutus) could see himself as they see him. What is Cassius trying to tell Brutus? Check the answer below. **(Draw Conclusions)**

that Brutus has hidden faults

that Brutus should support Caesar

that the people really want Brutus to be their leader

**3.** In lines 68–70 of this scene, Cassius tells Brutus that he will serve as his mirror to show Brutus his inner self. Do you think a true friend can show you what you are like inside? _Yes / No_, because_____

_____

_____

_____.

Cassius is filled with envy toward Caesar. He resents
the fact that some Romans are hailing Caesar as a
god. To show that Caesar is not a god, Cassius
describes the two times when Caesar almost died.
Read to find out about these times.

[*Flourish and shout.*]

**Brutus.** What means this shouting? I do fear the people
80  Choose Caesar for their king.

**Cassius.**                              Ay, do you fear it?
Then must I think you would not have it so.

**Brutus.** I would not, Cassius, yet I love him well.
But wherefore do you hold me here so long?
What is it that you would impart to me?
85  If it be aught toward the general good,
Set honor in one eye and death i' the other,
And I will look on both indifferently;
For let the gods so speed me as I love
The name of honor more than I fear death.

90  **Cassius.** I know that virtue to be in you, Brutus,
As well as I do know your outward favor.
Well, honor is the subject of my story.
I cannot tell what you and other men
Think of this life, but for my single self,
95  I had as lief not be as live to be
In awe of such a thing as I myself.
I was born free as Caesar, so were you;
We both have fed as well, and we can both
Endure the winter's cold as well as he.
100  For once, upon a raw and gusty day,
The troubled Tiber chafing with her shores,
Caesar said to me, "Dar'st thou, Cassius, now
Leap in with me into this angry flood
And swim to yonder point?" Upon the word,
105  Accoutered as I was, I plunged in
And bade him follow. So indeed he did.
The torrent roared, and we did buffet it
With lusty sinews, throwing it aside
And stemming it with hearts of controversy.
110  But ere we could arrive the point proposed,
Caesar cried, "Help me, Cassius, or I sink!"

**79–80 I do fear . . . for their king:** Rome had been a republic for almost 500 years. Many Romans hated the idea of being ruled by a king instead of their representatives in the Senate. The thought that Caesar might be named king horrifies people such as Brutus.

**80–81 Ay do you . . . it so:** Imagine Cassius blurting out these lines, maybe a little more eagerly than he had intended. He is trying to find a meaning in Brutus' words that may or may not be there.

**85–87 If it . . . indifferently:** If what you have in mind concerns the good of Rome **(the general good)**, I will not let the fear of death prevent me from doing the honorable thing.

**88 speed:** give good fortune to.

**91 outward favor:** physical appearance.

**95–96 I had . . . I myself:** I would rather not live, than to live in awe of someone no better than I am.

**READ ALOUD** Lines 82–89

What person does Brutus love?

_____

What value does Brutus love?

_____

**(Clarify)**

**101 troubled . . . shores:** The Tiber River was rising in the middle of a storm.

**105 Accoutered:** fully armed.

**107–109 we did . . . controversy:** We fought the tide with strong muscles **(lusty sinews),** conquering it with our spirit of competition **(hearts of controversy).**

**110 ere:** before.

I, as Aeneas, our great ancestor,
Did from the flames of Troy upon his shoulder
The old Anchises bear, so from the waves of Tiber
115 Did I the tired Caesar. And this man
Is now become a god, and Cassius is
A wretched creature and must bend his body
If Caesar carelessly but nod on him.

He had a fever when he was in Spain,
120 And when the fit was on him, I did mark
How he did shake. 'Tis true, this god did shake.
His coward lips did from their color fly,
And that same eye whose bend doth awe the world
Did lose his luster. I did hear him groan.
125 Ay, and that tongue of his that bade the Romans
Mark him and write his speeches in their books,
Alas, it cried, "Give me some drink, Titinius,"
As a sick girl! Ye gods! it doth amaze me
A man of such a feeble temper should
130 So get the start of the majestic world
And bear the palm alone.

**Pause & Reflect**

FOCUS

Cassius and Brutus again hear the crowd shouting,
apparently cheering Caesar. Cassius continues to try
to win over Brutus. He appeals to Brutus' manhood
and his pride in an ancestor. As you read, notice
these appeals.

[*Shout. Flourish.*]

**Brutus.** Another general shout?
    I do believe that these applauses are
    For some new honors that are heaped on Caesar.

135 **Cassius.** Why, man, he doth bestride the narrow
        world
    Like a Colossus, and we petty men
    Walk under his huge legs and peep about
    To find ourselves dishonorable graves.

**112–115 I, as Aeneas . . . Caesar:** Aeneas (ĭ-nē′ əs), the mythological founder of Rome, carried his father, Anchises (ăn-kī′ sēz), out of the burning city of Troy. Cassius says he carried Caesar out of the water when Caesar could no longer swim in the raging river.

**117 bend his body:** bow.

**122 His coward . . . fly:** His lips turned pale.

**123 bend:** glance.

**125–131 that tongue . . . alone:** The same tongue that told the Romans to memorize his speeches cried out in the tone of a sick girl. I'm amazed that such a weak man should get ahead of the rest of the world and appear as the victor **(bear the palm)** all by himself. (A palm leaf was a symbol of victory in war.)

**132–134 Another . . . on Caesar:** The shouts of the crowd are coming from off-stage. Brutus is troubled by this cheering for Caesar, worried about where it might lead.

**135–136 he doth . . . Colossus:** Cassius compares Caesar to the Colossus, the huge statue of the Greek god Apollo at Rhodes. The statue supposedly spanned the entrance to the harbor and was so high that ships could sail through the space between its legs.

*Pause & Reflect*

**1.** Cassius tells Brutus that he once saved Caesar's life by _____

_____

_____

_____ .

**(Clarify)**

**MARK IT UP** **2.** Reread the boxed passage on page 226. Circle details in these lines that describe Caesar's weakness while suffering from a fever.

Men at some time are masters of their fates.
140 The fault, dear Brutus, is not in our stars,
But in ourselves, that we are underlings.
"Brutus," and "Caesar." What should be in that
"Caesar"?
Why should that name be sounded more than yours?
Write them together: yours is as fair a name.
145 Sound them, it doth become the mouth as well.
Weigh them, it is as heavy. Conjure with 'em:
"Brutus" will start a spirit as soon as "Caesar."
Now in the names of all the gods at once,
Upon what meat doth this our Caesar feed
150 That he is grown so great? Age, thou are shamed!
Rome, thou hast lost the breed of noble bloods!

When went there by an age since the great Flood
But it was famed with more than with one man?
When could they say (till now) that talked of Rome
155 That her wide walls encompassed but one man?
Now is it Rome indeed, and room enough,
When there is in it but one only man!

O, you and I have heard our fathers say
There was a Brutus once that would have brooked
160 The eternal devil to keep his state in Rome
As easily as a king.

**Brutus.** That you do love me I am nothing jealous.
What you would work me to, I have some aim.
How I have thought of this, and of these times,
165 I shall recount hereafter. For this present,
I would not (so with love I might entreat you)
Be any further moved. What you have said
I will consider; what you have to say
I will with patience hear, and find a time
170 Both meet to hear and answer such high things.
Till then, my noble friend, chew upon this:

Brutus had rather be a villager
Than to repute himself a son of Rome
Under these hard conditions as this time
175 Is like to lay upon us.

**Cassius.**                 I am glad
That my weak words have struck but thus much show
Of fire from Brutus.

*Pause & Reflect*

**140–141 The fault . . . underlings:** It is not the stars that have determined our fate; we are inferiors through our own fault.

**146 Conjure:** call up spirits.

**150 Age . . . shamed:** It is a shameful time **(Age)** in which to be living. Cassius complains that Rome has lost its honor now that Caesar is the only man celebrated there.

**159–161 There was . . . a king:** Cassius is referring to an ancestor of Brutus who expelled the last king of Rome, Tarquin; **brooked:** permitted.
**162 am nothing jealous:** am sure.
**163 have some aim:** can guess.
**164–167 How I have . . . moved:** I will tell you later **(recount hereafter)** my thoughts about this topic. For now, I ask you as a friend not to try to convince me further.

**170 meet:** appropriate.

**172–175** Brutus is making a very strong statement, one that stuns Cassius. He says that he'd rather become a barbarian and give up the honor of being a Roman citizen than live in Rome as the subject of a king; **repute himself:** present himself as.

## Pause & Reflect

**MARK IT UP** **1.** Review lines 152–157 on page 228. Then circle the phrase "one man" each time it appears. Why do you think Cassius repeats this phrase? **(Analyze)**

**2.** In lines 159–161 on page 228, Cassius refers to Brutus' ancestor who expelled a tyrant from Rome. Imagine you are in Brutus' situation. How would you feel if Cassius appealed to your pride in an ancestor? **(Connect)**

_____

_____

_____

_____

**READ ALOUD** **3.** Read aloud lines 172–175 on page 228. What do you think Brutus might be prepared to do? **(Predict)**

_____

_____

_____

_____

The private conversation between Cassius and
Brutus is now over. Caesar and his followers return
from the market place. Caesar is very upset over
something that happened to him. He notices Cassius
and comments to Antony about him.

MARK IT UP   As you read, circle details that help you
understand why Caesar distrusts Cassius.

[*Voices and Music are heard approaching.*]

**Brutus.** The games are done, and Caesar is returning.

**Cassius.** As they pass by, pluck Casca by the sleeve,
180    And he will (after his sour fashion) tell you
What hath proceeded worthy note today.

[*Reenter* Caesar *and his train of followers.*]

**Brutus.** I will do so. But look you, Cassius!
The angry spot doth glow on Caesar's brow,
And all the rest look like a chidden train.
185    Calpurnia's cheek is pale, and Cicero
Looks with such ferret and such fiery eyes
As we have seen him in the Capitol,
Being crossed in conference by some senators.

**Cassius.** Casca will tell us what the matter is.

[Caesar *looks at* Cassius *and turns to* Antony.]

190    **Caesar.** Antonius.

**Antony.** Caesar?

**Caesar.** Let me have men about me that are fat,
Sleek-headed men, and such as sleep o' nights.
Yond Cassius has a lean and hungry look;
195    He thinks too much, such men are dangerous.

**Antony.** Fear him not, Caesar, he's not dangerous.
He is a noble Roman, and well given.

**Caesar.** Would he were fatter! But I fear him not.
Yet if my name were liable to fear,
200    I do not know the man I should avoid
So soon as that spare Cassius. He reads much,
He is a great observer, and he looks
Quite through the deeds of men. He loves no plays
As thou dost, Antony; he hears no music.
205    Seldom he smiles, and smiles in such a sort
As if he mocked himself and scorned his spirit

**181 worthy note:** worth remembering.

**184 chidden train:** a group of followers who have been scolded.

**185–188 Cicero . . . senators:** Cicero was a highly respected senator. Brutus says he has the angry look of a **ferret** (a fierce little animal), the look he gets when other senators disagree with him at the Capitol.

**190–214** Brutus and Cassius take Casca aside. The conversation Caesar has with Antony is not heard by any of the other characters around them.

**197 well given:** Antony says that Cassius, despite his appearance, is a supporter of Caesar.

**200–203 I do not . . . of men:** Caesar labels Cassius dangerous and, at the same time, one who can see through people and understand their secrets.

That could be moved to smile at anything.
Such men as he be never at heart's ease
Whiles they behold a greater than themselves,
210 And therefore are they very dangerous.
I rather tell thee what is to be feared
Than what I fear, for always I am Caesar.
Come on my right hand, for this ear is deaf,
And tell me truly what thou think'st of him.

**Pause & Reflect**

FOCUS

Brutus, Cassius, and Casca remain on stage. Casca
reveals what happened in the market place to upset
Caesar.

MARK IT UP  As you read, underline details that
suggest how Caesar really feels about becoming
king.

[*Trumpets sound. Exeunt* Caesar *and all his train except*
Casca, *who stays behind.*]

215 **Casca.** You pulled me by the cloak. Would you speak
with me?

**Brutus.** Ay, Casca. Tell us what hath chanced today
That Caesar looks so sad.

**Casca.** Why, you were with him, were you not?

**Brutus.** I should not then ask Casca what had
chanced.

220 **Casca.** Why, there was a crown offered him; and
being offered him, he put it by with the back of his
hand, thus. And then the people fell a-shouting.

**Brutus.** What was the second noise for?

**Casca.** Why, for that too.

225 **Cassius.** They shouted thrice. What was the last cry
for?

**Casca.** Why, for that too.

**Brutus.** Was the crown offered him thrice?

**Casca.** Ay, marry, was't! and he put it by thrice, every

**1.** Review the details you circled as you read. Why does Caesar distrust Cassius? **(Summarize)**

_____

_____

_____

_____

**MARK IT UP** **2.** According to Caesar, how does Cassius differ from Antony? Star the lines on page 230 that tell the answer. **(Compare and Contrast)**

**3.** Based on Caesar's comments about Cassius, how would you rate Caesar as a judge of character? *Good / Poor*, because _____

_____

_____

_____.

**(Evaluate)**

**216 hath chanced:** has happened.

**217 sad:** serious.

**221 put it by:** pushed it aside.

**228 Ay, marry, was't:** Yes, indeed, it was. *Marry* was a mild oath used in Shakespeare's time (but not in ancient Rome). The word means "by the Virgin Mary."

**230** time gentler than other; and at every putting-by mine honest neighbors shouted.

**Cassius.** Who offered him the crown?

**Casca.** Why, Antony.

**Brutus.** Tell us the manner of it, gentle Casca.

**Casca.** I can as well be hanged as tell the manner of it.
**235** It was mere foolery; I did not mark it. I saw Mark
Antony offer him a crown—yet 'twas not a crown
neither, 'twas one of these coronets—and, as I told
you, he put it by once. But for all that, to my
thinking, he would fain have had it. Then he offered
**240** it to him again; then he put it by again; but to my
thinking, he was very loath to lay his fingers off it.
And then he offered it the third time. He put it the
third time by; and still as he refused it, the rabblement
hooted, and clapped their chapped hands, and
**245** threw up their sweaty nightcaps, and uttered such a
deal of stinking breath because Caesar refused the
crown that it had, almost, choked Caesar; for he
swounded and fell down at it. And for mine own
part, I durst not laugh, for fear of opening my lips
**250** and receiving the bad air.

**Cassius.** But soft, I pray you. What, did Caesar
swound?

**Casca.** He fell down in the market place and foamed
at mouth and was speechless.

**Brutus.** 'Tis very like. He hath the falling sickness.

**255** **Cassius.** No, Caesar hath not it; but you, and I,
And honest Casca, we have the falling sickness.

**Casca.** I know not what you mean by that, but I am
sure Caesar fell down. If the tag-rag people did not
clap him and hiss him, according as he pleased and
**260** displeased them, as they use to do the players in
the theater, I am no true man.

**Brutus.** What said he when he came unto himself?

**Casca.** Marry, before he fell down, when he perceived
the common herd was glad he refused the crown, he
**265** plucked me ope his doublet and offered them his
throat to cut. An I had been a man of any occupation,

**237 coronets:** small crowns made out of laurel branches twisted together. A coronet was less of an honor than the kind of crown a king would wear.

**239 fain:** gladly.

**241 loath:** reluctant.

**243 rabblement:** unruly crowd.

**245 nightcaps:** close-fitting caps.

**248 swounded:** fainted.

**251 soft:** Wait a moment.

**252–254** There is some historical evidence that Caesar had epilepsy. In Shakespeare's time, this illness was known as the falling sickness (because someone having an epileptic seizure is likely to fall to the floor).

**256** Cassius sarcastically uses the phrase *falling sickness* to refer to the tendency to bow down before Caesar.

**263–268** Casca reports that before Caesar fell down he tried to win the crowd's approval. To do so, he pretended not to want the crown. He opened his jacket **(ope his doublet)** and exposed his throat to the crowd. He said in effect that if anyone in the crowd thought Caesar wanted the crown, that person should step forward and cut Caesar's throat. Casca says that if he had been one of the laborers **(a man of any occupation)** in the crowd, he would have done just that—slit Caesar's throat.

> **MARK IT UP**  **Reread Lines 234–250**
>
> Circle words and phrases that reveal Casca's low opinion of the crowd. **(Analyze)**

if I would not have taken him at a word I
would I might go to hell among the rogues. And so
he fell. When he came to himself again, he said, if

270 he had done or said anything amiss, he desired their
worships to think it was his infirmity. Three or four
wenches where I stood cried, "Alas, good soul!" and
forgave him with all their hearts. But there's no heed
to be taken of them. If Caesar had stabbed their

275 mothers, they would have done no less.

**Brutus.** And after that, he came thus sad away?

**Casca.** Ay.

**Cassius.** Did Cicero say anything?

**Casca.** Ay, he spoke Greek.

280 **Cassius.** To what effect?

**Casca.** Nay, an I tell you that, I'll ne'er look you i' the
face again. But those that understood him smiled at
one another and shook their heads; but for mine
own part, it was Greek to me. I could tell you more

285 news, too. Marullus and Flavius, for pulling scarfs
off Caesar's images, are put to silence. Fare you well.
There was more foolery yet, if I could remember it.

**Cassius.** Will you sup with me tonight, Casca?

**Casca.** No, I am promised forth.

290 **Cassius.** Will you dine with me tomorrow?

**Casca.** Ay, if I be alive, and your mind hold, and your
dinner worth eating.

**Cassius.** Good. I will expect you.

**Casca.** Do so. Farewell both.

[*Exit.*]

*Pause* & *Reflect*

**270 amiss:** wrong.

**271 infirmity:** sickness.

**272 wenches:** common women.

**273–275 But there's no heed . . . done no less:** Casca says it doesn't mean anything that some women in the crowd pitied Caesar. They forgave him for what he said while he was having a seizure. These women would have forgiven him even if he had done something terrible, such as stab their mothers.

**286 put to silence:** This may mean that the two tribunes have been put to death or that they have been barred from public life.

**289 I am promised forth:** I have another appointment.

## Pause & Reflect

**1.** What happened to Caesar after he refused the crown three times? **(Clarify)**

_____

_____

_____

_____

**2.** Review the details you underlined as you read. Do you think Julius Caesar really wants to be king? *Yes / No,* because _____

_____

_____

_____ .

**(Infer)**

### CHALLENGE

In Scene 1, the crowd is represented by the commoners who talk to Flavius and Marullus. In scene 2, Casca expresses his disgust with the crowd. The crowd functions as a **character** in this play. How would you describe this character? What are its positive or negative traits? **(Analyze)**

295 **Brutus.** What a blunt fellow is this grown to be!
He was quick mettle when he went to school.

**Cassius.** So is he now in execution
Of any bold or noble enterprise,
However he puts on this tardy form.
300 This rudeness is a sauce to his good wit,
Which gives men stomach to digest his words
With better appetite.

**Brutus.** And so it is. For this time I will leave you.
Tomorrow, if you please to speak with me,
305 I will come home to you; or if you will,
Come home to me, and I will wait for you.

**Cassius.** I will do so. Till then, think of the world.

[*Exit* Brutus.]

Well, Brutus, thou art noble; yet I see
Thy honorable mettle may be wrought
310 From that it is disposed. Therefore it is meet
That noble minds keep ever with their likes;
For who so firm that cannot be seduced?
Caesar doth bear me hard, but he loves Brutus.
If I were Brutus now and he were Cassius,
315 He should not humor me. I will this night,
In several hands, in at his windows throw,
As if they came from several citizens,
Writing, all tending to the great opinion
That Rome holds of his name; wherein obscurely
320 Caesar's ambition shall be glanced at.
And after this let Caesar seat him sure,
For we will shake him, or worse days endure.

[*Exit.*]

*Pause* **&** **Reflect**

**296 quick mettle:** clever, intelligent.

**297–302 So is . . . appetite:** Cassius says that Casca can still be intelligent in carrying out an important project. He only pretends to be slow **(tardy)**. His rude manner makes people more willing to accept **(digest)** the things he says.

**309–310 Thy . . . disposed:** Your honorable nature can be manipulated **(wrought)** into something not quite so honorable.

**313 bear me hard:** hold a grudge against me.

**315 He should . . . me:** I wouldn't let him get away with fooling me.

**315–320 I will . . . glanced at:** Cassius plans to leave letters at Brutus' home that appear to be from concerned citizens of Rome. These letters will suggest that Caesar really wants to be king.

**322 we will . . . endure:** We will remove Caesar from his high position or suffer the consequences.

## Pause & Reflect

**READ ALOUD** **1.** Read aloud the boxed passage on page 238. What does Cassius really think of Brutus? **(Summarize)**

_____

_____

_____

_____

**2.** What does Cassius plan to do to trick Brutus into joining the conspiracy? **(Clarify)**

_____

_____

_____

_____

.......................................................

.......................................................

.......................................................

.......................................................

.......................................................

.......................................................

## CHALLENGE

One way that Shakespeare reveals Brutus' character is through the use of a **foil**. A foil is a character who provides a striking contrast to another character. How does Cassius serve as a foil for Brutus? How would you contrast their motives for opposing Caesar? Which character do you admire more, and why? Cite details from Scene 2 to support your views. **(Compare and Contrast)**

.......................................................

.......................................................

.......................................................

# SCENE 3    A STREET IN ROME.

**PREVIEW**  It is the night of March 14. Amid violent thunder and lightning, a terrified Casca fears that the storm and other strange events are signs of terrible events to come. Cassius interprets the storm as a sign that Caesar must be overthrown. Cassius and Casca agree that Caesar's rise to power must be stopped by any means. Cinna, another plotter, enters, and they discuss how to persuade Brutus to follow their plan.

**FOCUS**

Casca tells Cicero about several unnatural events witnessed in Rome.
**MARK IT UP**  As you read, circle details that tell you about these unnatural events.

[*Thunder and lightning. Enter, from opposite sides,* Casca, *with his sword drawn, and* Cicero.]

**Cicero.** Good even, Casca. Brought you Caesar home?
   Why are you breathless? and why stare you so?

**Casca.** Are not you moved when all the sway of earth
   Shakes like a thing unfirm? O Cicero,
5   I have seen tempests when the scolding winds
   Have rived the knotty oaks, and I have seen
   The ambitious ocean swell and rage and foam
   To be exalted with the threat'ning clouds;
   But never till tonight, never till now,
10   Did I go through a tempest dropping fire.
   Either there is a civil strife in heaven,
   Or else the world, too saucy with the gods,
   Incenses them to send destruction.

**Cicero.** Why, saw you anything more wonderful?

15 **Casca.** A common slave—you know him well by
      sight—
   Held up his left hand, which did flame and burn
   Like twenty torches joined; and yet his hand,
   Not sensible of fire, remained unscorched.
   Besides—I ha' not since put up my sword—
20   Against the Capitol I met a lion,
   Who glared upon me, and went surly by

MARK IT UP **KEEP TRACK**

Remember to use these marks to
keep track of your understanding.

✔ ..... I understand.

? ..... I don't understand this.

! ..... Interesting or surprising idea

**3 sway of earth:** the natural order of
things.
**5 tempests:** storms.
**6 rived:** torn.

**8 To be exalted with:** to raise themselves
to the level of.

**11–13 Either . . . destruction:** Such a
terrible storm could be caused by only two
things—a civil war (strife) in heaven or angry
gods destroying the world.
**14 saw . . . wonderful:** Did you see
anything else that was strange?

**18 Not sensible of fire:** not feeling the fire.
**19–20 I ha' not . . . lion:** I haven't put my
sword back into its scabbard since I saw a
lion at the Capitol building.

Without annoying me. And there were drawn
Upon a heap a hundred ghastly women,
Transformed with their fear, who swore they saw
25    Men, all in fire, walk up and down the streets.
And yesterday the bird of night did sit
Even at noonday upon the market place,
Hooting and shrieking. When these prodigies
Do so conjointly meet, let not men say,
30    "These are their reasons, they are natural,"
For I believe they are portentous things
Unto the climate that they point upon.

**Cicero.** Indeed it is a strange-disposed time.
But men may construe things after their fashion,
35    Clean from the purpose of the things themselves.
Comes Caesar to the Capitol tomorrow?

**Casca.** He doth, for he did bid Antonius
Send word to you he would be there tomorrow.

**Cicero.** Good night then, Casca. This disturbed sky
40    Is not to walk in.

**Casca.**                    Farewell, Cicero.

[*Exit* Cicero.]

*Pause* **&** *Reflect*

FOCUS

As Cicero hurries away, Cassius enters. He and
Casca discuss the terrible storm. Cassius' reaction to
the storm is different from Casca's. Read to find out
about Cassius' reaction and his views on suicide.

[*Enter* Cassius.]

**Cassius.** Who's there?

**Casca.**                    A Roman.

**Cassius.**                                        Casca, by your voice.

**Casca.** Your ear is good. Cassius, what night is this!

**Cassius.** A very pleasing night to honest men.

**Casca.** Who ever knew the heavens menace so?

45    **Cassius.** Those that have known the earth so full of
faults.

**22 annoying:** physically harming.

**22–23 drawn / Upon:** huddled together.

**26 bird of night:** the owl, usually seen only at night.

**28–32 When these . . . upon:** When strange events **(prodigies)** like these happen at the same time **(conjointly meet)**, no one should say there are natural explanations for them. I believe they are bad omens **(portentous things)** for the place where they happen.

**33–35 Indeed . . . themselves:** Cicero does not accept Casca's superstitious explanation of events. He agrees that the times are strange. But he says people can interpret events the way they want to, no matter what actually causes the events.

**41 Who's there?:** Cassius probably has his sword out. Remember, with no light other than moonlight, it could be dangerous to come upon a stranger in the street.

---

*Pause* **&** *Reflect*

**READ ALOUD** **1.** Review the details you circled as you read. Then cross out the phrase below that does *not* identify one of the unnatural events witnessed in Rome. **(Clarify)**

a lion stalking the streets

a flaming, yet unburned, hand

a storm dropping fire

a lark eating an owl

**2.** Casca believes that the unnatural events are omens, or signs, that something terrible will occur. What might that terrible event be? **(Predict)**

_____

_____

_____

_____

For my part, I have walked about the streets,
Submitting me unto the perilous night,
And, thus unbraced, Casca, as you see,
Have bared my bosom to the thunder-stone;
50    And when the cross blue lightning seemed to open
The breast of heaven, I did present myself
Even in the aim and very flash of it.

**Casca.** But wherefore did you so much tempt the
    heavens?
It is the part of men to fear and tremble
55    When the most mighty gods by tokens send
Such dreadful heralds to astonish us.

**Cassius.** You are dull, Casca, and those sparks of life
That should be in a Roman you do want,
Or else you use not. You look pale, and gaze,
60    And put on fear, and cast yourself in wonder,
To see the strange impatience of the heavens.
But if you would consider the true cause
Why all these fires, why all these gliding ghosts,
Why birds and beasts, from quality and kind;
65    Why old men fool and children calculate;
Why all these things change from their ordinance,
Their natures, and preformed faculties,
To monstrous quality, why, you shall find
That heaven hath infused them with these spirits
70    To make them instruments of fear and warning
Unto some monstrous state.

> Now could I, Casca, name to thee a man
> Most like this dreadful night
> That thunders, lightens, opens graves, and roars
> 75    As doth the lion in the Capitol;
> A man no mightier than thyself or me
> In personal action, yet prodigious grown
> And fearful, as these strange eruptions are.

**Casca.** 'Tis Caesar that you mean. Is it not, Cassius?

80    **Cassius.** Let it be who it is. For Romans now
Have thews and limbs like to their ancestors.
But woe the while! our fathers' minds are dead,
And we are governed with our mothers' spirits,
Our yoke and sufferance show us womanish.

**46–52 For my part . . . flash of it:** Cassius brags that he offered himself to the dangerous night, with his coat open **(unbraced)**, exposing his chest to the thunder and lightning.

**54–56 It is . . . astonish us:** Men are supposed to tremble when the gods use signs **(tokens)** to send frightening messengers **(heralds)** to scare us.

**58 want:** lack.

**62–71** Cassius says there is a reason for all the unnatural occurrences. He then lists some of the wonders. Ghosts have appeared. Birds and beasts have acted against their natures **(from quality and kind)**. Old people who should be wise are acting like fools. Children who should be unknowing are predicting the future **(calculate)**. Things have changed their natures and have grown frightening **(change from their oridinance / Their natures, and preformed faculties)**. Cassius then says that the gods **(heaven)** have done these things to warn the Romans of an evil condition in the state.

**READ ALOUD  Lines 72–78**

As you say these lines, stress the powerful verbs—*thunders, lightens, opens,* and *roars.* To whom does Cassius refer in these lines?

**77 prodigious grown:** become enormous and threatening.

**80–84 Romans . . . womanish:** Modern Romans have muscles **(thews)** and limbs like our ancestors, but we have the minds of our mothers, not our fathers. Our acceptance of a dictator **(yoke and sufferance)** shows us to be like women, not like men. (In Shakespeare's time—and in ancient Rome— women were considered weak creatures.)

**Casca.** Indeed, they say the senators tomorrow
    Mean to establish Caesar as king,
    And he shall wear his crown by sea and land
    In every place save here in Italy.

**Cassius.** I know where I will wear this dagger then;
    Cassius from bondage will deliver Cassius.
    Therein, ye gods, you make the weak most strong;
    Therein, ye gods, you tyrants do defeat.
    Nor stony tower, nor walls of beaten brass,
    Nor airless dungeon, nor strong links of iron,
    Can be retentive to the strength of spirit;
    But life, being weary of these worldly bars,
    Never lacks power to dismiss itself.

    If I know this, know all the world besides,
    That part of tyranny that I do bear
    I can shake off at pleasure.

[*Thunder still.*]

**Casca.**                 So can I.
    So every bondman in his own hand bears
    The power to cancel his captivity.

**Cassius.** And why should Caesar be a tyrant then?
    Poor man! I know he would not be a wolf
    But that he sees the Romans are but sheep;
    He were no lion, were not Romans hinds.
    Those that with haste will make a mighty fire
    Begin it with weak straws. What trash is Rome,
    What rubbish and what offal, when it serves
    For the base matter to illuminate
    So vile a thing as Caesar! But, O grief,
    Where hast thou led me? I, perhaps, speak this
    Before a willing bondman. Then I know
    My answer must be made. But I am armed,
    And dangers are to me indifferent.

**Casca.** You speak to Casca, and to such a man
    That is no fleering telltale. Hold, my hand.
    Be factious for redress of all these griefs,
    And I will set this foot of mine as far
    As who goes farthest.

**87–88 he shall . . . Italy:** The senators will make Caesar the king of all Roman territories except **(save)** Rome itself **(Italy)**, since Romans would never let their own land be ruled by a king.

**89–90 I know . . . deliver Cassius:** I will free myself from slavery **(bondage)** by killing myself **(wear this dagger)**.

**91–97** Cassius shouts these lines toward the sky, trying to be heard over the thunder. Only through suicide, he says angrily, do the gods make the weak strong and able to defeat tyrants. The strong spirit cannot be imprisoned by tower, metal walls, dungeons, or iron chains. The reason is that one can always commit suicide **(life . . . Never lacks power to dismiss itself)**.

**103–111 And why . . . as Caesar:** Cassius goes into a tirade about Caesar, saying things for which he could be put to death. He says the only reason for Caesar's strength is the weakness of the Romans. They are female deer **(hinds)** and trash **(offal)** for allowing such a person as Caesar to come to power.

**111–113 But, O . . . bondman:** Cassius pretends that he did not mean to speak so freely. Maybe, he says, he has been speaking to a happy slave **(willing bondman)** of Caesar.

**117 fleering telltale:** sneering tattletale.
**118–120 Be factious . . . farthest:** Form a group, or faction, to correct **(redress)** these wrongs, and I will go as far as any other man.

---

📖 **READ ALOUD  Lines 89–97**

Cassius considers suicide a(n) (circle one) *cowardly / honorable* act because

_____

_____

_____

_____ .

**(Cause and Effect)**

**Cassius.**                                    There's a bargain made.
Now know you, Casca, I have moved already
Some certain of the noblest-minded Romans
To undergo with me an enterprise
Of honorable-dangerous consequence;
125    And I do know, by this they stay for me
In Pompey's Porch; for now, this fearful night,
There is no stir or walking in the streets,
And the complexion of the element
In favor's like the work we have in hand,
130    Most bloody, fiery, and most terrible.

*Pause* **&** *Reflect*

**FOCUS**

Read to find out why the conspirators value Brutus.

[*Enter* Cinna.]

**Casca.** Stand close awhile, for here comes one in haste.

**Cassius.** 'Tis Cinna. I do know him by his gait.
He is a friend. Cinna, where haste you so?

**Cinna.** To find out you. Who's that? Metellus Cimber?

135    **Cassius.** No, it is Casca, one incorporate
To our attempts. Am I not stayed for, Cinna?

**Cinna.** I am glad on't. What a fearful night is this!
There's two or three of us have seen strange sights.

**Cassius.** Am I not stayed for? Tell me.

**Cinna.**                                    Yes, you are.
140    O Cassius, if you could
But win the noble Brutus to our party—

**Cassius.** Be you content. Good Cinna, take this paper
And look you lay it in the praetor's chair,
Where Brutus may but find it, and throw this
145    In at his window. Set this up with wax
Upon old Brutus' statue. All this done,
Repair to Pompey's Porch, where you shall find us.
Is Decius Brutus and Trebonius there?

**125–126 by this . . . Porch:** Right now, they wait **(stay)** for me at the entrance to the theater Pompey built.

**128–130 the complexion . . . terrible:** The sky **(element)** looks like the work we have ahead of us—bloody, full of fire, and terrible.

**131 close:** hidden.

**132 gait:** manner of walking.

**135–136 it is . . . stayed for:** This is Casca, who is now part of our plan **(incorporate / To our attempts)**. Are they waiting for me?

**142–146** Cassius gives Cinna several notes addressed to Brutus, along with instructions about where each note should be placed.

**143 lay it . . . chair:** Place this paper in the judge's **(praetor's)** seat.

**146 old Brutus:** Lucius Junius Brutus, who was Marcus Brutus' ancestor.

**147 Pompey's Porch:** the entrance to a theater built by Pompey.

**148 Decius Brutus** (dē'shəs broo'təs)**:** This conspirator is not Marcus Brutus, whom Cassius is trying to win over.

## Pause & Reflect

1. How does Cassius react to the storm? Circle the two words below that describe his reaction. **(Clarify)**

   terrified          unafraid

   amazed          defiant

2. Reread lines 104–106 on page 246. According to Cassius, how have the Romans made it easy for Caesar to become a tyrant, or an all-powerful ruler? **(Draw Conclusions)**

   _____

   _____

   _____

   _____

**Cinna.** All but Metellus Cimber, and he's gone
150    To seek you at your house. Well, I will hie
       And so bestow these papers as you bade me.

**Cassius.** That done, repair to Pompey's Theater.

[*Exit* Cinna.]

       Come, Casca, you and I will yet ere day
       See Brutus at his house. Three parts of him
155    Is ours already, and the man entire
       Upon the next encounter yields him ours.

**Casca.** O, he sits high in all the people's hearts,
       And that which would appear offense in us,
       His countenance, like richest alchemy,
160    Will change to virtue and to worthiness.

**Cassius.** Him and his worth and our great need of
          him
       You have right well conceited. Let us go,
       For it is after midnight, and ere day
       We will awake him and be sure of him.

[*Exeunt.*]

*Pause* & *Reflect*

**150–151 I will . . . bade me:** I'll hurry **(hie)** to place **(bestow)** these papers as you instructed me.

**154–156 Three parts . . . yields him ours:** We've already won over three parts of Brutus. The next time we meet him, he will be ours completely.

**157–160 he sits . . . worthiness:** The people love Brutus. What would seem offensive if we did it will, like magic **(alchemy)**, become good and worthy because of his involvement.

**162 conceited:** judged.

*Pause* & *Reflect*

READ ALOUD **1.** Read aloud the boxed passage on page 250. Why does Casca feel that the conspirators need Brutus? **(Infer)**

_____

_____

_____

_____

**2.** Do you think Cassius' plans can be successful without Brutus? *Yes / No,* because_____

_____

_____

_____.

**(Connect)**

CHALLENGE

**External conflict** occurs when a character is pitted against an outside force, such as another character, a physical obstacle, or an aspect of nature or society. **Internal conflict** occurs when the struggle takes place within a character. Identify the conflicts in Act One, and classify each one as external or internal. Which conflict do you think will be most important as this play unfolds, and why?

## Moving On

If you are using *The Language of Literature,* you can move to page 714 of that book to continue reading *Julius Caesar.* As you do so, continue to be an active reader. Ask yourself the kinds of questions you found in this lesson.

# Active Reading SkillBuilder

## Understanding Shakespeare's Plays

The English language has changed a great deal since Shakespeare's time. Therefore, Shakespeare's way of saying things can be difficult for you to understand. You may find the play easier to follow if you keep track of the characters as you read. List each important character that you meet in Act One in the correct column of the chart that follows. An example is shown.

| Characters in *The Tragedy of Julius Caesar*, Act One | | |
|---|---|---|
| **Pro-Caesar** | **Anti-Caesar** | **Neutral** |
| Mark Antony | | |

# Literary Analysis Skillbuilder

## Blank Verse

**Blank verse** is unrhymed lines of poetry written in iambic pentameter. These lines contain five unstressed syllables each followed by a stressed syllable. Shakespeare chose blank verse for his plays because it imitates the rhythms of natural speech. However, some of his characters speak in prose. He also uses rhymed lines of iambic pentameter to stress a point or to signal that a scene or act is about to end. In the chart below, record two blank verse passages from Act One. Mark the unstressed ( ˘ ) and stressed ( ´ ) syllables to show that the passage is written in blank verse. An example is shown.

| Blank-Verse Passages |
|---|
| These grówĭng féathĕrs plúckĕd frŏm Cáesăr's wíng<br><br>Wĭll máke hĭm flý ăn órdĭnáry pítch,<br><br>(Scene 1, lines 74–75) |
|  |
|  |

**Follow Up:** Examine the use of prose in Act One, Scene 1. Why do you think Shakespeare had the commoners speak in prose? _____

_____

## Before You Read

If you are using *The Language of Literature* . . .

- Use the information on page 822 of that book to prepare for reading.

- Look at the art and read the quotes displayed on pages 823–831. What do you **predict** this story will be about?

## Reading Tips

This story contains many long sentences that are rich with **descriptive details**. For this reason, you may find the story difficult to read. Here are some strategies that can help you understand this story.

- Begin slowly, taking time to picture the **characters** and **setting** in your mind. You may need to reread some of the long or difficult sentences in order to understand them.

- As you read, ask yourself questions about what is happening and why. Such questions can help keep your reading on track.

---

✏️ **MARK IT UP** KEEP TRACK

As you read, you can use these marks to keep track of your understanding.

✔ ..... I understand.

? ..... I don't understand this.

! ..... Interesting or surprising idea

---

# A White Heron
## Sarah Orne Jewett

**PREVIEW** "A White Heron" is set in rural New England in the late 1800s. Nine-year-old Sylvia is walking home to her grandmother's farm when she meets a friendly young stranger with a gun. The man explains that he is hunting birds to add to his collection. He adds that he is offering a reward to anyone who can help him find a rare white heron, a tall, graceful water bird. Sylvia likes the young man and knows her grandmother could use the money. Will Sylvia help the man get his heart's desire, or will she keep the heron's nest a secret?

---

**FOCUS**

Read to find out where Sylvia comes from and how her life has changed since moving to her grandmother's farm.

✏️ **MARK IT UP** As you read, underline details that help you understand Sylvia. Examples are highlighted.

🔟

**The woods were already filled** with shadows one June evening, just before eight o'clock, though a bright sunset still glimmered faintly among the trunks of the trees. A little girl was driving home her cow, a plodding, dilatory,[1] provoking creature in her behavior, but a valued companion for all that. They were going away from whatever light there was, and striking deep into the woods, but their feet were familiar with the path, and it was no matter whether their eyes could see it or not.

There was hardly a night the summer through when the old cow could be found waiting at the pasture bars;[2] on the contrary, it was her greatest pleasure to hide herself away among the high huckleberry bushes, and though she wore a

---

1. **dilatory** (dĭl′ə-tôr′ē): tending to postpone or delay.
2. **pasture bars:** the fence that surrounds the land set aside for the cows to use for grazing.

loud bell she had made the discovery that if one stood
perfectly still it would not ring. So Sylvia had to hunt for her
until she found her, and call Co'! Co'! with never an
20 answering Moo, until her childish patience was quite spent. If
the creature had not given good milk and plenty of it, the case
would have seemed very different to her owners. Besides,
Sylvia had all the time there was, and very little use to make
of it. Sometimes in pleasant weather it was a consolation to
look upon the cow's pranks as an intelligent attempt to play
hide-and-seek, and as the child had no playmates she lent
herself to this amusement with a good deal of zest. Though
this chase had been so long that the wary animal herself had
given an unusual signal of her whereabouts, Sylvia had only
30 laughed when she came upon Mistress Moolly at the swamp-
side, and urged her affectionately homeward with a twig of
birch leaves. The old cow was not inclined to wander farther;
she even turned in the right direction for once as they left the
pasture, and stepped along the road at a good pace. She was
quite ready to be milked now, and seldom stopped to browse.
Sylvia wondered what her grandmother would say because
they were so late. It was a great while since she had left home
at half past five o'clock, but everybody knew the difficulty of
making this errand a short one. Mrs. Tilley had chased the
40 hornéd torment too many summer evenings herself to blame
anyone else for lingering, and was only thankful as she waited
that she had Sylvia, nowadays, to give such valuable
assistance. The good woman suspected that Sylvia loitered
occasionally on her own account; there never was such a child
for straying about out-of-doors since the world was made!
Everybody said that it was a good change for a little maid
who had tried to grow for eight years in a crowded
manufacturing town, but, as for Sylvia herself, it seemed as if
she never had been alive at all before she came to live at the
50 farm. She thought often with wistful compassion of a
wretched geranium that belonged to a town neighbor.

"'Afraid of folks,'" old Mrs. Tilley said to herself with a
smile after she had made the unlikely choice of Sylvia from
her daughter's houseful of children and was returning to the
farm. "'Afraid of folks,' they said! I guess she won't be
troubled no great with 'em up to the old place!" When they
reached the door of the lonely house and stopped to unlock it,
and the cat came to purr loudly and rub against them, a

A White Heron **255**

deserted pussy, indeed, but fat with young robins, Sylvia
60 whispered that this was a beautiful place to live in, and she
never should wish to go home.

The companions followed the shady wood-road, the cow
taking slow steps and the child very fast ones. The cow
stopped long at the brook to drink, as if the pasture were not
half a swamp, and Sylvia stood still and waited, letting her
bare feet cool themselves in the shoal³ water, while the great
twilight moths struck softly against her. She waded on
through the brook as the cow moved away, and listened to the
thrushes with a heart that beat fast with pleasure. There was a
70 stirring in the great boughs overhead. They were full of little
birds and beasts that seemed to be wide-awake, and going
about their world, or else saying good night to each other in
sleepy twitters. Sylvia herself felt sleepy as she walked along.
However, it was not much farther to the house, and the air
was soft and sweet. She was not often in the woods so late as
this, and it made her feel as if she were a part of the gray
shadows and the moving leaves. She was just thinking how
long it seemed since she first came to the farm a year ago, and
wondering if everything went on in the noisy town just the
80 same as when she was there; the thought of the great red-
faced boy who used to chase and frighten her made her hurry
along the path to escape from the shadow of the trees.

**Pause & Reflect**

### Pause & Reflect

1. Where does Sylvia come from and how does she feel about moving to her grandmother's farm? **(Clarify)**

_____

_____

_____

_____

2. Review the details you underlined that tell about Sylvia. Then circle three words or phrases below that describe her. **(Evaluate)**

| | |
|---|---|
| shy | outgoing |
| unhappy | often alone |
| rebellious | nature-lover |

✏ **MARK IT UP** 3. How does Sylvia feel about the woods and the creatures that live there? Write your answer below. Then circle details on pages 255–256 that support your answer. **(Infer)**

_____

_____

_____

_____

**FOCUS**
On her way home, Sylvia encounters a stranger. She takes him home to spend the night at her grandmother's house.
✏ **MARK IT UP** As you read, circle passages that describe the stranger.

90

**Suddenly this little woods-girl** is horror-stricken to hear a clear whistle not very far away. Not a bird's whistle, which would have a sort of friendliness, but a boy's whistle, determined, and somewhat aggressive. Sylvia left the cow to whatever sad fate might await her, and stepped <u>discreetly</u> aside into the bushes, but she was just too late. The enemy had discovered her, and called out in a very cheerful

---

3. **shoal** (shōl): shallow.

WORDS
TO
KNOW
**discreetly** (dĭ-skrēt′lē) *adv.* in a manner showing good judgment; cautiously

and persuasive tone, "Halloa, little girl, how far is it to the road?" and trembling Sylvia answered almost inaudibly, "A good ways."

She did not dare to look boldly at the tall young man, who carried a gun over his shoulder, but she came out of her bush and again followed the cow, while he walked alongside.

100 "I have been hunting for some birds," the stranger said kindly, "and I have lost my way and need a friend very much. Don't be afraid," he added gallantly. "Speak up and tell me what your name is, and whether you think I can spend the night at your house, and go out gunning early in the morning."

Sylvia was more alarmed than before. Would not her grandmother consider her much to blame? But who could have foreseen such an accident as this? It did not seem to be her fault, and she hung her head as if the stem of it were broken, but managed to answer "Sylvy" with much effort when her companion again asked her name.

110 Mrs. Tilley was standing in the doorway when the trio came into view. The cow gave a loud moo by way of explanation.

"Yes, you'd better speak up for yourself, you old trial! Where'd she tucked herself away this time, Sylvy?" But Sylvia kept an awed silence; she knew by instinct that her grandmother did not comprehend the gravity[4] of the situation. She must be mistaking the stranger for one of the farmer lads of the region.

The young man stood his gun beside the door, and dropped 120 a lumpy game bag beside it; then he bade Mrs. Tilley good evening, and repeated his wayfarer's[5] story, and asked if he could have a night's lodging.

"Put me anywhere you like," he said. "I must be off early in the morning, before day; but I am very hungry, indeed. You can give me some milk at any rate, that's plain."

"Dear sakes, yes," responded the hostess, whose long slumbering hospitality seemed to be easily awakened. "You might fare better if you went out to the main road a mile or so, but you're welcome to what we've got. I'll milk right off,

---

4. **gravity:** seriousness or importance.

5. **wayfarer:** a person who travels, especially on foot.

**130** and you make yourself at home. You can sleep on husks or feathers,"[6] she proffered graciously. "I raised them all myself. There's good pasturing for geese just below here toward the ma'sh.[7] Now step round and set a plate for the gentleman, Sylvy!" And Sylvia promptly stepped. She was glad to have something to do, and she was hungry herself.

It was a surprise to find so clean and comfortable a little dwelling in this New England wilderness. The young man had known the horrors of its most primitive housekeeping and the dreary <u>squalor</u> of that level of society which does not rebel at **140** the companionship of hens. This was the best thrift of an old-fashioned farmstead, though on such a small scale that it seemed like a hermitage.[8] He listened eagerly to the old woman's quaint talk, he watched Sylvia's pale face and shining gray eyes with ever-growing enthusiasm, and insisted that this was the best supper he had eaten for a month, and afterward, the new-made friends sat down in the doorway together while the moon came up.

Soon it would be berry time, and Sylvia was a great help at picking. The cow was a good milker, though a plaguy[9] thing **150** to keep track of, the hostess gossiped frankly, adding presently that she had buried four children, so Sylvia's mother and a son (who might be dead) in California were all the children she had left. "Dan, my boy, was a great hand to go gunning," she explained sadly. "I never wanted for pa'tridges[10] or gray squer'ls[11] while he was to home. He's been a great wand'rer, I expect, and he's no hand to write letters.[12] There, I don't blame him; I'd ha' seen the world myself if it had been so I could.

"Sylvia takes after him," the grandmother continued **160** affectionately, after a minute's pause. "There ain't a foot o'

---

6. **husks or feathers:** Mattresses of this era were often stuffed with corn husks or bird feathers.

7. **ma'sh:** dialect for marsh, a low-lying wetland.

8. **hermitage:** place where a hermit, or recluse, lives.

9. **plaguy** (plā′gē): annoying; bothersome.

10. **pa'tridges:** dialect for *partridges*, a game bird related to the pheasant.

11. **squer'ls:** dialect for *squirrels*.

12. **he's no hand to write letters:** an informal way of saying that he's not one to write letters or that he has no interest in writing letters.

WORDS
TO
KNOW

**squalor** (skwŏl′ər) *n.* a filthy and wretched condition

ground she don't know her way over, and the wild creatur's counts her one o' themselves. Squer'ls she'll tame to come an' feed right out o' her hands, and all sorts o' birds. Last winter she got the jaybirds to bangeing[13] here, and I believe she'd 'a' scanted herself[14] of her own meals to have plenty to throw out amongst 'em if I hadn't kep' watch. Anything but crows, I tell her, I'm willin' to help support—though Dan he had a tamed one o' them that did seem to have reason same as folks. It was round here a good spell after he went away. Dan an' his father they didn't hitch[15]—but he never held up his head ag'in after Dan had dared him an' gone off."

The guest did not notice this hint of family sorrows in his eager interest in something else.

### Pause & Reflect

**FOCUS**

The stranger reveals that he has a collection of birds, which he killed and stuffed. He then offers a reward to anyone who helps him find the rare white heron.

**MARK IT UP** As you read, jot down in the margin what Sylvia already knows about the white heron.

"**So Sylvy knows all** about birds, does she?" he exclaimed, as he looked round at the little girl who sat, very demure but increasingly sleepy, in the moonlight. "I am making a collection of birds myself. I have been at it ever since I was a boy." (Mrs. Tilley smiled.) "There are two or three very rare ones I have been hunting for these five years. I mean to get them on my own ground if they can be found."

"Do you cage 'em up?" asked Mrs. Tilley doubtfully, in response to this enthusiastic announcement.

"Oh no, they're stuffed and preserved, dozens and dozens of them," said the ornithologist,[16] "and I have shot or snared every one myself. I caught a glimpse of a white heron a few miles from here on Saturday, and I have followed it in this direction. They have never been found in this district at all. The little white heron, it is," and he turned again to look at Sylvia with the hope of discovering that the rare bird was one of her acquaintances.

---

13. **bangeing** (băn′jĭng): New England colloquial term meaning gathering or lounging about in groups.

14. **scanted herself**: deprived herself.

15. **didn't hitch**: didn't get along.

16. **ornithologist** (ôr′nə-thŏl′ə-jĭst): one who studies birds.

### Pause & Reflect

1. Review the passages you circled as you read. What do you learn about the stranger? **(Clarify)**

_____

_____

_____

_____

2. Why do you think Sylvia is so worried about the stranger, who is referred to as "the enemy"? **(Draw Conclusions)**

_____

_____

_____

_____

3. What questions or thoughts do you have about the stranger so far? **(Question)**

_____

_____

_____

_____

**Pause & Reflect**

READ ALOUD  **1.** Read aloud the boxed passage. Is the stranger trying to persuade Sylvia to help him? Try reading this passage in several ways before you decide. **(Infer)**

_____

_____

**2.** Why is the young man so interested in finding the white heron? **(Clarify)**

_____

_____

_____

_____

**3.** Review the notes that you made as you read. What does Sylvia know about the heron? **(Clarify)**

_____

_____

_____

_____

**4.** If you were in Sylvia's position, would you help the man find the heron? Give your reasons. **(Connect)**

_____

_____

_____

_____

But Sylvia was watching a hop-toad in the narrow footpath.

"You would know the heron if you saw it," the stranger continued eagerly. "A queer tall white bird with soft feathers and long thin legs. And it would have a nest perhaps in the top of a high tree, made of sticks, something like a hawk's nest."

Sylvia's heart gave a wild beat; she knew that strange white bird, and had once stolen softly near where it stood in some bright green swamp grass, away over at the other side of the woods. There was an open place where the sunshine always seemed strangely yellow and hot, where tall, nodding rushes[17] grew, and her grandmother had warned her that she might sink in the soft black mud underneath and never be heard of more. Not far beyond were the salt marshes,[18] and just this side the sea itself, which Sylvia wondered and dreamed much about, but never had seen, whose great voice could sometimes be heard above the noise of the woods on stormy nights.

"I can't think of anything I should like so much as to find that heron's nest," the handsome stranger was saying. "I would give ten dollars to anybody who could show it to me," he added desperately, "and I mean to spend my whole vacation hunting for it if need be. Perhaps it was only migrating,[19] or had been chased out of its own region by some bird of prey."

Mrs. Tilley gave amazed attention to all this, but Sylvia still watched the toad, not divining,[20] as she might have done at some calmer time, that the creature wished to get to its hole under the doorstep, and was much hindered by the unusual spectators at that hour of the evening. No amount of thought, that night, could decide how many wished-for treasures the ten dollars, so lightly spoken of, would buy.

**Pause & Reflect**

---

17. **rushes:** tall, stiff marsh plants. Rush stems are often used to make baskets or mats.

18. **salt marsh:** a marsh that is flooded with sea water.

19. **migrating:** moving from one region of the country to another, especially seasonally.

20. **divining** (dĭ-vī′ĭng): guessing.

FOCUS
The next day, Sylvia joins the young man in his search for the white heron. Read to find out whether she helps the man find the bird.
230

**The next day the young sportsman** hovered about the woods, and Sylvia kept him company, having lost her first fear of the friendly lad, who proved to be most kind and sympathetic. He told her many things about the birds and what they knew and where they lived and what they did with themselves. And he gave her a jackknife, which she thought as great a treasure as if she were a desert islander. All day long he did not once make her troubled or afraid except when he brought down some unsuspecting singing creature from its bough. Sylvia would have liked him vastly better without his gun; she could not understand why he

240 killed the very birds he seemed to like so much. But as the day waned, Sylvia still watched the young man with loving admiration. She had never seen anybody so charming and delightful; the woman's heart, asleep in the child, was vaguely thrilled by a dream of love. Some premonition[21] of that great power stirred and swayed these young creatures who traversed the solemn woodlands with soft-footed silent care. They stopped to listen to a bird's song; they pressed forward again eagerly, parting the branches—speaking to each other rarely and in whispers; the young man going first and Sylvia

250 following, fascinated, a few steps behind, with her gray eyes dark with excitement.

She grieved because the longed-for white heron was elusive, but she did not lead the guest, she only followed, and there was no such thing as speaking first. The sound of her own unquestioned voice would have terrified her—it was hard enough to answer yes or no when there was need of that. At last evening began to fall, and they drove the cow home together, and Sylvia smiled with pleasure when they came to the place where she heard the whistle and was afraid only the

260 night before.

*Pause* & *Reflect*

*Pause* & *Reflect*

**MARK IT UP** **1.** How have Sylvia's feelings about the young man changed? Answer the question below. Then circle details on page 261 that support your answer. **(Cause and Effect)**

_____
_____
_____
_____

**2.** Sylvia joins the man in his hunt for the white heron but doesn't share what she knows about the bird. Circle two sentences below that help to explain her silence. **(Infer)**

She is still afraid of the young man.

She is too shy to talk.

She has no idea where the white heron is.

She doesn't want the young man to leave her.

21. **premonition:** a sense that something will happen; forewarning

WORDS
TO
KNOW

**traverse** (trə-vûrs') v. to travel or pass across, over, or through
**elusive** (ĭ-lōō'sĭv) adj. hard to catch or discover

**FOCUS**

Sylvia thinks she will
help the man find the
white heron. She
sneaks out of her
house to climb the
great pine tree that
allows her to "see all
the world." As you
read, judge for yourself
whether she is brave or
foolish.

**Half a mile from home,** at the farther edge
of the woods, where the land was
highest, a great pine tree stood, the last
of its generation. Whether it was left for
a boundary mark, or for what reason,
no one could say; the woodchoppers
who had felled its mates were dead and
gone long ago, and a whole forest of
sturdy trees, pines and oaks and maples,
had grown again. But the stately head
of this old pine towered above them all
and made a landmark for sea and shore miles and miles away.
Sylvia knew it well. She had always believed that whoever
climbed to the top of it could see the ocean; and the little girl
had often laid her hand on the great rough trunk and looked
up wistfully at those dark boughs that the wind always
stirred, no matter how hot and still the air might be below.
Now she thought of the tree with a new excitement, for why,
if one climbed it at break of day, could not one see all the
world, and easily discover whence the white heron flew, and
mark the place, and find the hidden nest?

What a spirit of adventure, what wild ambition! What
fancied triumph and delight and glory for the later morning
when she could make known the secret! It was almost too real
and too great for the childish heart to bear.

All night the door of the little house stood open and the
whippoorwills came and sang upon the very step. The young
sportsman and his old hostess were sound asleep, but Sylvia's
great design[22] kept her broad awake and watching. She forgot
to think of sleep. The short summer night seemed as long as
the winter darkness, and at last, when the whippoorwills
ceased, and she was afraid the morning would after all come
too soon, she stole out of the house and followed the pasture
path through the woods, hastening toward the open ground
beyond, listening with a sense of comfort and companionship
to the drowsy twitter of a half-awakened bird, whose perch
she had jarred in passing. Alas, if the great wave of human
interest which flooded for the first time this dull little life
should sweep away the satisfactions of an existence heart to

22. **design:** plan or secretive scheme.

300 heart with nature and the dumb life of the forest![23]

There was the huge tree asleep yet in the paling moonlight, and small and silly Sylvia began with utmost bravery to mount to the top of it, with tingling, eager blood coursing the channels of her whole frame, with her bare feet and fingers, that pinched and held like bird's claws to the monstrous ladder reaching up, up, almost to the sky itself. First she must mount the white oak tree that grew alongside, where she was almost lost among the dark branches and the green leaves heavy and wet with dew; a bird fluttered off its nest, and a

310 red squirrel ran to and fro and scolded pettishly[23] at the harmless housebreaker. Sylvia felt her way easily. She had often climbed there, and knew that higher still one of the oak's upper branches chafed against the pine trunk, just where its lower boughs were set close together. There, when she made the dangerous pass from one tree to the other, the great enterprise would really begin.

She crept out along the swaying oak limb at last, and took the daring step across into the old pine tree. The way was harder than she thought; she must reach far and hold fast, the

320 sharp dry twigs caught and held her and scratched her like angry talons, the pitch made her thin little fingers clumsy and stiff as she went round and round the tree's great stem, higher and higher upward. The sparrows and robins in the woods below were beginning to wake and twitter to the dawn, yet it seemed much lighter there aloft in the pine tree, and the child knew she must hurry if her project were to be of any use.

The tree seemed to lengthen itself out as she went up, and to reach farther and farther upward. It was like a great mainmast to the voyaging earth; it must truly have been

330 amazed that morning through all its <u>ponderous</u> frame as it felt this determined spark of human spirit wending its way from higher branch to branch. Who knows how steadily the least twigs held themselves to advantage this light, weak creature on her way! The old pine must have loved his new dependent.

MARK IT UP WORD POWER

Remember to mark words that you'd like to add to your **Personal Word List**. Later, you can record the words and their meanings beginning on page 316.

---

23. **Alas, if the . . . of the forest:** The narrator calls attention to what Sylvia might lose. Her interest in the young man (**great wave of human interest**) might interfere with her close relationship with nature (**heart to heart with nature**).

24. **pettishly:** crossly; irritably.

WORDS
TO
KNOW
**ponderous** (pŏn′dər-əs) *adj.* very heavy; bulky

## Pause & Reflect

✎ **MARK IT UP** **1.** Why does Sylvia climb the great pine tree? Underline the passages on page 263 that give the answer. **(Clarify)**

**2.** Complete this sentence as if you were Sylvia: As I climbed the great pine tree I felt _____

_____

_____

_____ .

**(Draw Conclusions)**

**3.** Do you think Sylvia's action is brave or foolish? Give your reasons. **(Make Judgments)**

_____

_____

_____

_____

More than all the hawks, and bats, and moths, and even the sweet-voiced thrushes, was the brave, beating heart of the solitary gray-eyed child. And the tree stood still and frowned away the winds that June morning while the dawn grew bright in the east.

## Pause & Reflect

340 **FOCUS**
At the top of the tree, Sylvia discovers that she can see all the way to the sea. She observes many wonderful sights, including the white heron's nest.

✎ **MARK IT UP** As you read, circle details that describe how Sylvia feels about this experience.

**Sylvia's face was like a pale star,** if one had seen it from the ground, when the last thorny bough was past, and she stood trembling and tired but wholly triumphant, high in the treetop. Yes, there was the sea with the dawning sun making a golden dazzle over it, and toward that glorious east flew two hawks with slow-moving pinions.[25]

350 How low they looked in the air from that height when one had only seen them before far up, and dark against the blue sky. Their gray feathers were as soft as moths; they seemed only a little way from the tree, and Sylvia felt as if she too could go flying away among the clouds. Westward, the woodlands and farms reached miles and miles into the distance; here and there were church steeples, and white villages; truly it was a vast and awesome world!

The birds sang louder and louder. At last the sun came up bewilderingly bright. Sylvia could see the white sails of ships

360 out at sea, and the clouds that were purple and rose-colored and yellow at first began to fade away. Where was the white heron's nest in the sea of green branches, and was this wonderful sight and pageant of the world the only reward for having climbed to such a giddy[26] height? Now look down again, Sylvia, where the green marsh is set among the shining birches and dark hemlocks;[27] there where you saw the white heron once you will see him again; look, look! a white spot of him like a single floating feather comes up from the dead hemlock and grows larger, and rises, and comes close at last,

370 and goes by the landmark pine with steady sweep of wing and

_____

25. **pinions** (pĭn′yənz): a bird's wings.

26. **giddy:** dizzying, light-headed.

27. **hemlocks:** evergreen trees with small cones and short, flat leaves.

outstretched slender neck and crested head. And wait! wait!
do not move a foot or a finger, little girl, do not send an
arrow of light and consciousness from your two eager eyes,
for the heron has perched on a pine bough not far beyond
yours, and cries back to his mate on the nest and plumes his
feathers[28] for the new day!

The child gives a long sigh a minute later when a company
of shouting catbirds[29] comes also to the tree, and vexed by
their fluttering and lawlessness, the solemn heron goes away.
380 She knows his secret now, the wild, light, slender bird that
floats and wavers, and goes back like an arrow presently to
his home in the green world beneath. Then Sylvia, well
satisfied, makes her perilous way down again, not daring to
look far below the branch she stands on, ready to cry
sometimes because her fingers ache and her lamed[30] feet slip.
Wondering over and over again what the stranger would say
to her, and what he would think when she told him how to
find his way straight to the heron's nest.

*Pause* & *Reflect*

FOCUS

390 Read the rest of the
story to find out if
Sylvia will keep the
location of the heron's
nest a secret.

**"Sylvy, Sylvy!"** called the busy old
grandmother again and again, but
nobody answered, and the small husk
bed was empty, and Sylvia had
disappeared.

The guest waked from a dream, and
remembering his day's pleasure hurried to dress himself that it
might sooner begin. He was sure from the way the shy little
girl looked once or twice yesterday that she had at least seen
the white heron, and now she must really be made to tell.
Here she comes now, paler than ever, and her worn old frock
400 is torn and tattered, and smeared with pine pitch. The
grandmother and the sportsman stand in the door together
and question her, and the splendid moment has come to speak
of the dead hemlock tree by the green marsh.

But Sylvia does not speak after all, though the old
grandmother fretfully rebukes her, and the young man's kind,

---

28. **plumes his feathers:** cleans and smoothes his feathers with his bill; preens.

29. **catbirds:** gray songbirds. Catbirds make mewing sounds like that of cats.

30. **lamed:** disabled, as from soreness.

*Pause* & **Reflect**

1. List at least three things Sylvia
sees from the top of the great
pine tree. **(Clarify)**

_____

_____

_____

_____

2. Review the details that you
circled as you read. How does
Sylvia feel when she looks out
from the top of the pine tree?
**(Draw Conclusions)**

_____

_____

_____

_____

READ ALOUD **3.** Read
aloud the boxed passage on
this page. What is the heron's
"secret" that Sylvia now
understands? **(Infer)**

_____

_____

_____

_____

4. Will Sylvia help the man find the
heron or will she keep its nest a
secret? Write your prediction.
**(Predict)**

_____

_____

_____

**1.** Why does Sylvia keep the white heron's location a secret? Underline details on page 266 that support your answer. **(Infer)**

_____

_____

_____

**2.** Do you think Sylvia ever regrets her decision? Give your reasons. **(Make Judgments)**

_____

_____

_____

_____

**3.** What would you have done in Sylvia's place? **(Connect)**

_____

_____

_____

_____

**CHALLENGE**

In lines 427–430, the **narrator** speaks directly to the reader. Find and mark other passages in the story where the **narrator** interrupts the flow of the story to present a warning or comment to the reader. What purpose do these interruptions serve? In your judgment, how do such comments affect the reader? **(Writer's Style)**

## Wrapping Up

If you are using **The Language of Literature,** you can now move to the questions and activities on pages 833–835 of that book.

---

appealing eyes are looking straight in her own. He can make them rich with money; he has promised it, and they are poor now. He is so well worth making happy, and he waits to hear the story she can tell.

410 No, she must keep silence! What is it that suddenly forbids her and makes her dumb? Has she been nine years growing and now, when the great world for the first time puts out a hand to her, must she thrust it aside for a bird's sake? The murmur of the pine's green branches is in her ears, she remembers how the white heron came flying through the golden air and how they watched the sea and the morning together, and Sylvia cannot speak; she cannot tell the heron's secret and give its life away.

Dear loyalty, that suffered a sharp pang as the guest went 420 away disappointed later in the day, that could have served and followed him and loved him as a dog loves! Many a night Sylvia heard the echo of his whistle haunting the pasture path as she came home with the loitering cow. She forgot even her sorrow at the sharp report[31] of his gun and the sight of thrushes and sparrows dropping silent to the ground, their songs hushed and their pretty feathers stained and wet with blood. Were the birds better friends than their hunter might have been—who can tell? Whatever treasures were lost to her, woodlands and summertime, remember! Bring your gifts and 430 graces and tell your secrets to this lonely country child!

**Pause & Reflect**

---

31. **report:** explosive noise.

# Active Reading SkillBuilder

## Questioning

Readers can better understand a work of literature by making observations and asking themselves questions. **Questioning** can help readers uncover reasons behind events and characters' feelings. While reading this story, ask yourself the following questions: Why do characters behave as they do? What is the central conflict in the story? What is the significance of events? Are any objects, places, or events symbols? On the chart below, record your questions about unclear or important points in the story. Then use information in the text to help answer these questions. An example is shown.

| Questions | Answers |
|---|---|
| Why is Sylvia so "horror-stricken" to hear a boy's whistle? | She is afraid of people. She is not used to meeting strangers. |
| | |
| | |
| | |
| | |

# Literary Analysis SkillBuilder

## Symbol

A **symbol** is a person, place, or object that represents something beyond itself. Symbols have the power to communicate complicated, emotionally rich ideas. For example, the symbol of the geranium in this story represents Sylvia's feelings about life in town. Use the following chart to analyze the meaning of two other symbols from nature that Jewett uses in "A White Heron." Briefly explain what you think each symbol means. Cite evidence from the text to support your interpretation.

| Symbol | What You Think It Means | Evidence You Find in the Story |
|---|---|---|
| white heron | | |
| old pine tree | | |

**Follow Up:** Share your interpretations of these symbols with classmates; discuss how effective you find Jewett's use of symbols.

# Words to Know SkillBuilder

## Words to Know

| discreetly | elusive | ponderous | squalor | traverse |

**A.** Decide which word from the word list belongs in each numbered blank.
Then write the word on the blank line on the right.

Because the swamp is scary, you might want to cross it fleetly,
But it is filled with quicksand, so you'd better step (1). _____ (1)

The elephant's surely a (2) beast.
With each step it takes, it can flatten at least _____ (2)
A half dozen tulips. So be on your guard,
In case one decides to (3) your back yard. _____ (3)

If you don't clean the parrot's cage,
She just might fly into a rage.
She hates to live in (4), and _____ (4)
Might bite your good-for-nothing hand.

The hunter searches hard, but rarely spies _____ (5)
The most (5) of the butterflies.

**B.** Fill in each blank with the correct word from the word list.

1. Santa's reindeer can fly because they are as light as feathers. Donner is not

   _____.

2. We must keep our get-togethers top secret. If you don't want to blow my cover,

   you must arrange to meet me _____.

3. My sisters aren't a bit alike. The shorter one lives in a clean, well-lighted, tidy

   place, and the taller, in _____.

4. The bully, who was cruelly nasty but always managed to escape from any adult

   in authority, was both abusive and _____.

5. My pickup has better traction going backwards; so when I got stuck in mud,

   I decided to reverse the truck to _____ the muck.

**C.** Write a diary entry that Sylvia might have written to explain her decision after she realized she could not reveal the whereabouts of the white heron. Use at least **two** of the Words to Know.

## Before You Read
If you are using **The Language of Literature,** study the information on page 838 of that book to prepare for reading.

## Reading Tips
This **poem** is written in an easy-going, conversational style. The poem may look simple, but it is challenging and rich in meaning.

• When you reach the end of a line, don't pause in your reading unless you come upon a mark of punctuation. Take in complete sentences at a time.

• Use the author's images to **visualize** the birch trees, the subject of the poem. Ask yourself what they might represent to the **speaker.**

---

### ✎ MARK IT UP KEEP TRACK

As you read, you can use these marks to keep track of your understanding.

✔ ..... I understand.

? ..... I don't understand this.

! ..... Interesting or surprising idea

---

# Birches

## Robert Frost

**PREVIEW** Robert Frost (1874–1963) is regarded as one of America's greatest poets of the 20th century. In many of his poems, he creates realistic pictures of the New England landscape. In "Birches," for example, he describes the birch trees of the New England countryside. These tall, delicate trees have slender white trunks that can be easily bent. The speaker of the poem is an adult who recalls the boyhood pleasure of climbing birch trees and swinging on them.

Imagine you are climbing a birch tree. When you get close to the top of the tree, you might decide to swing on it. To do so, you would jump into the air while holding on to the tip of the trunk or a thick branch. The trunk or branch would bend downward and carry you safely to the ground.

---

### FOCUS

The speaker observes bent birch trees and first imagines that a boy has swung on them. It's more likely, though, that the trees were bent by a winter ice storm. The speaker then imagines such a storm and its effects on the birch trees.

✎ MARK IT UP As you read, circle details that help you visualize these effects. An example is highlighted.

---

When I see birches bend to left and right
Across the lines of straighter darker trees,
I like to think some boy's been swinging them.
But swinging doesn't bend them down to stay
5   As ice-storms do. Often you must have seen them
Loaded with ice a sunny winter morning

After a rain. They click upon themselves
As the breeze rises, and turn many-colored
As the stir cracks and crazes their enamel.[1]
Soon the sun's warmth makes them shed crystal shells
Shattering and avalanching on the snow-crust—[2]
Such heaps of broken glass to sweep away
You'd think the inner dome of heaven had fallen.
They are dragged to the withered bracken by the load,[3]
And they seem not to break; though once they are bowed
So low for long, they never right themselves:
You may see their trunks arching in the woods
Years afterwards, trailing their leaves on the ground
Like girls on hands and knees that throw their hair
Before them over their heads to dry in the sun.

**Pause & Reflect**

**MARK IT UP** WORD POWER

Mark words that you'd like to add to your **Personal Word List.** After reading, you can record the words and their meanings beginning on page 316.

**Pause & Reflect**

**1.** Review the details you circled as you read. Then circle the word or phrase that completes the following sentence: An ice storm bends birch trees *for a short time / forever.* (**Cause and Effect**)

**READ ALOUD** **2.** Read aloud the boxed passage on this page. These lines describe the birch trees covered with ice. Check the sentence below that applies to these trees. (**Analyze Images**)

They give off colors and rhythmical sounds.

They look ordinary and are still.

They seem lifeless and decaying.

**FOCUS**

The speaker again tells about the boy introduced in line 3. The speaker prefers to imagine that it was the boy—not an ice storm—that caused the birches to be bent. Read to find out how the boy goes about swinging on birches.

But I was going to say when Truth broke in
With all her matter-of-fact about the ice-storm
I should prefer to have some boy bend them
As he went out and in to fetch the cows—
Some boy too far from town to learn baseball,
Whose only play was what he found himself,
Summer or winter, and could play alone.

1. **As the stir . . . enamel:** On a winter morning, the breeze makes the branches of the birch trees move and hit one another. The coating of ice on the branches cracks and reflects light in unusual ways.

2. **Shattering . . . on the snow-crust:** The ice covering the birch trees is warmed by the sun and begins to melt. Countless pieces of ice fall from the trees and break when they hit the snow-covered ground; **avalanching:** falling in a large mass.

3. **They are dragged . . . load:** The word *they* refers to the birch trees, not to the "heaps of broken glass"; **withered bracken:** large, coarse ferns that have dried up.

1. Why does the boy like to swing on birches? Check the phrase below that tells the answer. (Clarify)

to show off to his friends

to practice for a baseball team

to amuse himself

to upset his father

READ ALOUD 2. Read aloud the boxed passage on this page. What do you mainly need to be a good swinger of birches? (circle one) *Physical strength / Timing and skill* because_____

_____

_____.

(Infer)

3. Describe an activity from your childhood that swinging on birches calls to mind. (Connect)

_____

_____

_____

_____

One by one he subdued his father's trees
By riding them down over and over again
30 Until he took the stiffness out of them,
And not one but hung limp, not one was left
For him to conquer. He learned all there was
To learn about not launching out too soon
And so not carrying the tree away
35 Clear to the ground. He always kept his poise
To the top branches, climbing carefully
With the same pains you use to fill a cup
Up to the brim, and even above the brim.
Then he flung outward, feet first, with a swish,
40 Kicking his way down through the air to the ground.

*Pause* **&** *Reflect*

FOCUS

The speaker wants to be "a swinger of birches" again. Read to find out why.

So was I once myself a swinger of birches.
And so I dream of going back to be.
It's when I'm weary of considerations,[4]
And life is too much like a pathless wood
45 Where your face burns and tickles with the cobwebs
Broken across it, and one eye is weeping
From a twig's having lashed across it open.
I'd like to get away from earth awhile
And then come back to it and begin over.
50 May no fate willfully[5] misunderstand me
And half grant what I wish and snatch me away
Not to return. Earth's the right place for love:
I don't know where it's likely to go better.

_____

4. **considerations:** thoughts.

5. **willfully:** intentionally; on purpose.

I'd like to go by climbing a birch tree,
And climb black branches up a snow-white trunk
*Toward* heaven, till the tree could bear no more,
But dipped its top and set me down again.
That would be good both going and coming back.
One could do worse than be a swinger of birches.

55

Pause **&** Reflect

*Pause* **&** *Reflect*

**1.** Why does the speaker want to be "a swinger of birches" again? Circle the phrase below that tells the answer. **(Infer)**

to bend the birch trees again

to escape troubles for a while

to leave the earth forever

**MARK IT UP** **2.** In lines 43–47, the speaker compares life to "a pathless wood" that confuses the traveler. What details suggest the pain and troubles of life? Circle these details. **(Supporting Details)**

**READ ALOUD** **3.** Read aloud the boxed passage on this page, which describes the speaker's attitude toward living on earth. How would you describe this attitude? **(Infer)**

_____

_____

_____

_____

**CHALLENGE**

Mark lines in the poem that suggest what the birch trees represent to the speaker. How do they function as a **symbol** in this poem? What message about life does this symbol help to express? **(Analyze)**

## Wrapping Up

If you are using *The Language of Literature,* you can now move to the questions and activities on pages 841–842 of that book.

# Active Reading SkillBuilder

## Analyzing Images

**Imagery** refers to the words and phrases that a writer uses to re-create vivid sensory experiences for the reader. An image may appeal to one or more of the five senses: sight, smell, hearing, touch, and taste. While reading "Birches," use the following chart to record your observations about the images in the poem. An example is shown.

| "Birches" | Images of Sight | Images of Sound or Touch |
|---|---|---|
| Lines 1–20 | an ice storm's bending of birches— "Loaded with ice a sunny winter morning" (line 6) | |
| Lines 21–40 | | |
| Lines 41–59 | | |

# Literary Analysis SkillBuilder

### Figurative Language

**Figurative language** communicates ideas beyond the literal meanings of the words. Figurative language includes specific figures of speech, such as similes and metaphors. Both **similes** and **metaphors** make comparisons. Similes use the word *like* or *as,* while metaphors do not. On the chart below, record examples of figurative language in "Birches." Identify each example as a simile or a metaphor. Then list the two things that are compared. An example has been provided for you.

| Figurative Language | Figure of Speech | Things Compared |
|---|---|---|
| "And life is too much like a pathless wood "(line 44) | simile | life and a wood without a path |
|  |  |  |
|  |  |  |
|  |  |  |

**Follow Up:** Write your own metaphor and simile to add to Frost's description of the wintry scene. Compare your figures of speech with those of your classmates.

## Before You Read

If you are using **The Language of Literature** . . .

- Use the information on pages 1018–1019 of that book to prepare for reading.

- Look at the photographs and film clips on pages 1018 through 1060.

## Reading Tips

This **drama** is made up of brief scenes, separated by **odes,** or poems. The actors who performed the scenes wore masks and costumes and spoke the **dialogue.** The Chorus—a group of about 15 members—sang and danced the poems to music. These poems commented on the action of the play. Sometimes, the leader of the Chorus took part in the dialogue.

- When you read the **dialogue,** put yourself in the place of the character speaking. Read some of the lines aloud—by yourself or with a partner.

- When you come to the lines of the Chorus, slow down. Try to grasp the overall sense, but don't worry if there are some lines you can't understand. You can return to them later for close study.

- Use the Guide for Reading, beginning on page 279, to help you understand difficult lines and passages.

*FROM* # ANTIGONE

## SOPHOCLES

*TRANSLATED BY* DUDLEY FITTS
AND ROBERT FITZGERALD

**PREVIEW** You are about to read the opening sections of *Antigone.*[1] Sophocles[2] (496–406 B.C.) was one of the great dramatists of ancient Greece. He and other Greek playwrights often based their dramas on stories from mythology. According to Greek myth, Antigone and her sister Ismene (ĭs-mē′nē) are the daughters of Oedipus (ĕd′ə-pəs), who once was king of Thebes. He unknowingly killed his father and then married his mother. Upon discovering this horrible truth, Oedipus blinded himself and left Thebes forever. His two daughters, Antigone and Ismene, looked after him until his death.

When Oedipus' sons Eteocles (ē-tē′ə-klēz) and Polyneices (pŏl′ĭ-nī′sēz) grew up, they both wanted to rule Thebes and killed each other in battle. Their uncle Creon (krē′ŏn′) then became king of Thebes. He set out to show the people how strong a leader he would be.

---

1. *Antigone* (ăn-tĭg′ə-nē)
2. Sophocles (sŏf′ə-klēz′)

## CAST OF CHARACTERS

**Antigone** } daughters of Oedipus,
**Ismene** } former king of Thebes

**Creon**, king of Thebes, uncle of Antigone and
Ismene

**Haemon** (hē′mŏn′), Creon's son, engaged to
Antigone

**Eurydice** (yŏŏ-rĭd′ĭ-sē), wife of Creon

**Teiresias** (tī-rē′sē-əs), a blind prophet

**Chorus,** made up of about 15 elders of Thebes

**Choragus** (kō-rā′gəs), leader of the Chorus

**a Sentry**

**a Messenger**

*Scene:* *Before the palace of Creon, king of
Thebes. A central double door, and two
doors at the side. A platform extends the
length of the stage, and from this platform
three steps lead down into the orchestra, or
chorus ground.*

*Time:* *Dawn of the day after the repulse³ of
the Argive army from the assault on Thebes*

**READ ALOUD**

Read aloud the names of the characters in this play. Note that several characters are members of the same royal family.

**MARK IT UP** **KEEP TRACK**

As you read, you can use these marks to keep track of your understanding.

✔ ..... I understand.

? ..... I don't understand this.

! ..... Interesting or surprising idea

---

3. **repulse** (rĭ-puls′): the act of turning away or beating back.

Antigone and Ismene are alone on stage. Antigone
tells her sister what their uncle Creon, the new king
of Thebes, has sworn to do. He wants to dishonor
the body of Polyneices, their slain brother. Read
to find out how the two sisters react to Creon's
decision.

**MARK IT UP** As you read, circle details that help you
get to know Antigone. An example is highlighted.

## PROLOGUE

(Antigone *and* Ismene *enter from the central door of the palace.*)

**Antigone.** Ismene, dear sister,
    You would think that we had already suffered enough
    For the curse on Oedipus:
    I cannot imagine any grief
5    That you and I have not gone through. And now—
    Have they told you the new decree of our king Creon?

**Ismene.** I have heard nothing: I know
    That two sisters lost two brothers, a double death
    In a single hour; and I know that the Argive army
10    Fled in the night; but beyond this, nothing.

**Antigone.** I thought so. And that is why I wanted you
    To come out here with me. There is something we
    must do.

**Ismene.** Why do you speak so strangely?

**Antigone.** Listen, Ismene:

15    Creon buried our brother Eteocles
    With military honors, gave him a soldier's funeral,
    And it was right that he should; but Polyneices,
    Who fought as bravely and died as miserably—
    They say that Creon has sworn
20    No one shall bury him, no one mourn for him,
    But his body must lie in the fields, a sweet treasure
    For carrion birds to find as they search for food.

    That is what they say, and our good Creon is coming here
    To announce it publicly; and the penalty—
25    Stoning to death in the public square!
                         There it is,
    And now you can prove what you are:
    A true sister, or a traitor to your family.

## GUIDE FOR READING

Use this guide for help with unfamiliar words
and difficult passages.

**Prologue:** In Greek drama, the Prologue is
the first scene. It introduces important
characters and the main conflict.

**6 decree:** an order having the force of law.

**8 That two sisters . . . two brothers:**
Ismene and Antigone are the two sisters.
Their two brothers, Eteocles and Polyneices,
have died in battle.

**9 the Argive army:** The Argives were long-
standing enemies of Thebes. Eteocles and
Polyneices had agreed to share the kingship
of Thebes, ruling in alternate years. When
Eteocles took control, however, he banished
his brother. Polyneices then went to a
neighboring city-state, Argos. He commanded
an Argive army in an attack on Thebes.

**20–22** The obligation to bury the dead with
appropriate burial rites was considered a
sacred law among the ancient Greeks. They
believed that the soul of someone left
unburied would never find peace.

**22 carrion birds:** birds of prey that eat dead
bodies.

**25 Stoning to death in the public square:**
In ancient times, citizens carried out this
sentence by throwing rocks at a convicted
person until he or she was killed.

**◤ JOT IT DOWN | Reread Lines 15–22**

How does Creon plan to dishonor Polyneices'
corpse? **(Clarify)**

_____

_____

_____

_____

**Ismene.** Antigone, you are mad! What could I
possibly do?

**Antigone.** You must decide whether you will help me
or not.

30 **Ismene.** I do not understand you. Help you in what?

**Antigone.** Ismene, I am going to bury him. Will
you come?

**Ismene.** Bury him! You have just said the new law
forbids it.

**Antigone.** He is my brother. And he is your brother, too.

**Ismene.** But think of the danger! Think what Creon
will do!

35 **Antigone.** Creon is not strong enough to stand in my way.

**Ismene.** Ah sister!
Oedipus died, everyone hating him
For what his own search brought to light, his eyes
Ripped out by his own hand; and Jocasta died,
40 His mother and wife at once: she twisted the cords
That strangled her life; and our two brothers died,
Each killed by the other's sword. And we are left:
But oh, Antigone,
Think how much more terrible than these
45 Our own death would be if we should go against Creon
And do what he has forbidden! We are only women;
We cannot fight with men, Antigone!
The law is strong, we must give in to the law
In this thing, and in worse. I beg the dead
50 To forgive me, but I am helpless: I must yield
To those in authority. And I think it is dangerous business
To be always meddling.

**Antigone.** If that is what you think,
I should not want you, even if you asked to come.
You have made your choice; you can be what you want to be.

**READ ALOUD** Lines 26–35

Complete the following sentence by inserting the words *brave* and *fearful* in the correct slots:

Ismene is _____

and refuses to break the law; Antigone, however, is _____

and is determined to bury her brother at any cost. **(Compare and Contrast)**

**39 Jocasta** (jō-kăs′tə), the mother of Antigone and Ismene, hanged herself when she realized the truth about her relationship with Oedipus. He was not only her husband but also her son.

**44–45 Think how much more terrible . . . against Creon:** Ismene reminds Antigone of the death by stoning that awaits anyone who disobeys Creon's order.

**52 meddling:** interfering.

> But I will bury him; and if I must die,
> I say that this crime is holy: I shall lie down
> With him in death, and I shall be as dear
> To him as he to me.
>                          It is the dead,
> Not the living, who make the longest demands:
> We die forever. . . .

55

60

                                              You may do as you like,
Since apparently the laws of the gods mean nothing to you.

**Ismene.** They mean a great deal to me; but I have no strength
To break laws that were made for the public good.

**Antigone.** That must be your excuse, I suppose. But as for me,
65  I will bury the brother I love.

**Ismene.**                            Antigone,
I am so afraid for you!

**Antigone.**                   You need not be:
You have yourself to consider, after all.

**Ismene.** But no one must hear of this; you must tell no one!
I will keep it a secret, I promise!

**Antigone.**                          Oh tell it! Tell everyone!
70  Think how they'll hate you when it all comes out
If they learn that you knew about it all the time!

**Ismene.** So fiery! You should be cold with fear.

**Antigone.** Perhaps. But I am doing only what I must.

**Ismene.** But can you do it? I say that you cannot.

75  **Antigone.** Very well: when my strength gives out, I shall do no more.

**Ismene.** Impossible things should not be tried at all.

**Antigone.** Go away, Ismene:
I shall be hating you soon, and the dead will too,
For your words are hateful. Leave me my foolish plan:
80  I am not afraid of the danger; if it means death,
It will not be the worst of deaths—death without honor.

**58–60 It is the dead . . . forever:** Antigone is referring to her duty to her brother. She must give his corpse the proper burial.

**76–79** Ismene has a strong sense of her human limitations. Antigone, on the other hand, will try to do the impossible if she feels it is right to do so.

---

✏️ **JOT IT DOWN**    **Reread Lines 55–60**

Why is Antigone willing to risk so much to give Polyneices a proper burial? **(Infer)**

_____

_____

_____

_____

**Ismene.** Go then, if you feel that you must.

    You are unwise,

    But a loyal friend indeed to those who love you.

(*Exit into the palace.* Antigone *goes off, left. Enters the* Chorus, *with* Choragus.)

**Pause & Reflect**

**FOCUS**

The Chorus and its leader, the Choragus, come on stage to give the audience important background information. They describe the attack on Thebes in which Polyneices, brother to Antigone and Ismene, was killed. Read to find out about this battle.

## PARODOS

**Chorus.** Now the long blade of the sun, lying

    Level east to west, touches with glory

    Thebes of the Seven Gates. Open, unlidded

    Eye of golden day! O marching light

5    Across the eddy and rush of Dirce's stream,

    Striking the white shields of the enemy

    Thrown headlong backward from the blaze of morning!

**Choragus.** Polyneices their commander

    Roused them with windy phrases,

10    He the wild eagle screaming

    Insults above our land,

    His wings their shields of snow,

    His crest their marshaled helms.

**Chorus.** Against our seven gates in a yawning ring

15    The famished spears came onward in the night;

    But before his jaws were <u>sated</u> with our blood,

    Or pine fire took the garland of our towers,

    He was thrown back; and as he turned, great Thebes—

    No tender victim for his noisy power—

20    Rose like a dragon behind him, shouting war.

WORDS
TO
KNOW    **sated** (sā′tĭd) *adj.* satisfied fully **sate** *v.*

1. Review the details you circled as you read. What values are important to Antigone? Cross out the phrase below that does *not* apply. (**Infer**)

   respect for the laws of the state

   reverence toward the gods

   love for her dead brother

   death with honor

2. How would you **summarize** the conflict between Antigone and her sister, Ismene?

   _____

   _____

   _____

   _____

3. Who do you think is being more sensible, Antigone or Ismene? Give your reasons. (**Connect**)

   _____

   _____

   _____

   _____

**Parodos** (păr′ə-dŏs′): The parodos is a song that marks the entry of the Chorus, which represents the leading citizens of Thebes.

**1–7 Now the long blade . . . the blaze of morning:** These lines describe Thebes at dawn on the day Polyneices' forces attacked the city. A brilliant ray from the rising sun **(long blade of the sun)** lights up the seven gates of the city of Thebes. The sun is pictured as an open eye and as a force marching to meet the enemy.

**5 Dirce's** (dûr′sēz) **stream:** a stream flowing past Thebes. The stream is named after a murdered queen who was thrown into it.

**10–13** Polyneices is pictured as a huge wild eagle coming to attack Thebes. His wings are the white shields of his soldiers, and his headpiece **(crest)** is made up of their helmets **(helms)**.

**14–15** Thebes had seven gates, which the Argives attacked at the same time.

**16–17 But before . . . towers:** before Polyneices and his men killed any Thebans or set fire to the city. The towers of Thebes are compared to a decoration of branches and flowers woven together **(garland of our towers)**.

---

✏️ **CHALLENGE**

One way that Sophocles reveals Antigone's character is through the use of a **foil.** A foil is a character who provides a striking contrast to another character. How does Ismene serve as a foil for Antigone? Mark details in the Prologue to support your views. (**Reading Classical Drama**)

**Choragus.** For God hates utterly
    The bray of bragging tongues;
    And when he beheld their smiling,
    Their swagger of golden helms,
25    The frown of his thunder blasted
    Their first man from our walls.

**Chorus.** We heard his shout of triumph high in the air
    Turn to a scream; far out in a flaming arc
    He fell with his windy torch, and the earth struck him.
30    And others storming in fury no less than his
    Found shock of death in the dusty joy of battle.

**Choragus.** Seven captains at seven gates
    Yielded their clanging arms to the god
    That bends the battle line and breaks it.
35    These two only, brothers in blood,
    Face to face in matchless rage,
    Mirroring each the other's death,
    Clashed in long combat.

**Chorus.** But now in the beautiful morning of victory
40    Let Thebes of the many chariots sing for joy!
    With hearts for dancing we'll take leave of war:
    Our temples shall be sweet with hymns of praise,
    And the long night shall echo with our chorus.

*Pause* **&** *Reflect*

**FOCUS**

Creon is the uncle of Antigone and Ismene. He speaks to the people for the first time as their new ruler. He states the principles that will guide him as their leader.

**MARK IT UP** As you read, circle details that tell you about his principles.

## SCENE ONE

**Choragus.** But now at last our new king is coming:
    Creon of Thebes, Menoeceus' son.
    In this <u>auspicious</u> dawn of his reign

**21–26** These lines describe the death of the first warrior who tried to scale the walls of Thebes. Zeus (zoōs), the king of the gods, threw a thunderbolt, which killed the first Argive attacker.

**32–34** When the seven captains were killed, their armor was offered as a sacrifice to Ares (âr′ēz), the god of war.

**35 These two only:** The battle is left to Antigone's two brothers, Eteocles and Polyneices, to decide. They fight and kill each other.

**2 Menoeceus** (mə-nē′syoōs).

## Pause & Reflect

**READ ALOUD** **1.** Read aloud the boxed passage on page 286 and the accompanying note in the Guide for Reading. What type of conduct does the king of the gods punish? **(Infer)**

_____

_____

_____

_____

**MARK IT UP** **2.** Reread lines 32–38. Circle the phrase that shows how Antigone's brothers felt about each other as they fought to the death. **(Clarify)**

**3.** In lines 39–43, the Chorus looks forward to a time of peace and joy. Do you think this time will come? *Yes / No,* because _____

_____

_____.

**(Predict)**

What are the new complexities

5 That shifting Fate has woven for him?

What is his counsel? Why has he summoned

The old men to hear him?

(*Enter* Creon *from the palace. He addresses the* Chorus *from the top step.*)

**Creon.** Gentlemen: I have the honor to inform you that our ship of state, which recent storms have threatened to destroy, has come

10 safely to harbor at last, guided by the merciful wisdom of heaven. I have summoned you here this morning because I know that I can depend upon you: your devotion to King Laius was absolute; you never hesitated in your duty to our late ruler Oedipus; and when Oedipus died, your loyalty was transferred to his children.

15 Unfortunately, as you know, his two sons, the princes Eteocles and Polyneices, have killed each other in battle; and I, as the next in blood, have succeeded to the full power of the throne.

I am aware, of course, that no ruler can expect complete loyalty from his subjects until he has been tested in office. Never-

20 theless, I say to you at the very outset that I have nothing but contempt for the kind of governor who is afraid, for whatever reason, to follow the course that he knows is best for the state; and as for the man who sets private friendship above the public welfare—I have no use for him, either. I call God to witness

25 that if I saw my country headed for ruin, I should not be afraid to speak out plainly; and I need hardly remind you that I would never have any dealings with an enemy of the people. No one values friendship more highly than I; but we must remember that friends made at the risk of wrecking our ship are not real

30 friends at all.

These are my principles, at any rate, and that is why I have made the following decision concerning the sons of Oedipus: Eteocles, who died as a man should die, fighting for his country, is to be buried with full military honors, with all the cere-

35 mony that is usual when the greatest heroes die; but his brother Polyneices, who broke his exile to come back with fire and sword against his native city and the shrines of his fathers' gods, whose one idea was to spill the blood of his blood and sell his own people into slavery—Polyneices, I say, is to have no

40 burial: no man is to touch him or say the least prayer for him; he shall lie on the plain, unburied; and the birds and the scavenging dogs can do with him whatever they like.

**5** The Greeks believed that human destiny was controlled by three sisters called the Fates: Clotho (klō'thō), who spun the thread of human life; Lachesis (lăk'ĭ-sĭs), who determined its length; and Atropos (ăt'rə-pŏs'), who cut the thread.

**7 old men:** the members of the Chorus.

**8–9 our ship of state . . . safely to harbor:** The city of Thebes has survived the attack by Polyneices and his army.

**12 Laius** (lā'əs)**:** father of Oedipus.

**21 contempt:** scorn; utter lack of respect.

**26–27 I would never . . . an enemy of the people:** Creon is referring to Polyneices here. According to Creon, Polyneices is a traitor because he made a deal with an enemy of Thebes—the city-state of Argos.

**36 exile:** forced removal from his own country.

**37 shrines . . . gods:** places where religious worship is paid to the gods of Thebes.

**41–42 scavenging dogs:** wild dogs, looking for something to eat.

---

**✎ MARK IT UP  KEEP TRACK**

Remember to use these marks to keep track of your understanding.

✔ ..... I understand.

? ..... I don't understand this.

! ..... Interesting or surprising idea

---

**📖 READ ALOUD  Lines 35–42**

In these lines Creon describes how Polyneices' corpse is to be treated. Do you think Creon is doing the right thing in trying to punish a dead man? *Yes / No,* because

_____

_____

_____

_____

(Evaluate)

This is my command, and you can see the wisdom behind it.
As long as I am king, no traitor is going to be honored with the
45 loyal man. But whoever shows by word and deed that he is on
the side of the state—he shall have my respect while he is living,
and my reverence when he is dead.

**Choragus.** If that is your will, Creon son of Menoeceus,
You have the right to enforce it: we are yours.

50 **Creon.** That is my will. Take care that you do your part.

**Choragus.** We are old men: let the younger ones carry it out.

**Creon.** I do not mean that: the sentries have been appointed.

**Choragus.** Then what is it that you would have us do?

**Creon.** You will give no support to whoever breaks this law.

55 **Choragus.** Only a crazy man is in love with death!

**Creon.** And death it is; yet money talks, and the wisest
Have sometimes been known to count a few coins too many.

*Pause* **&** *Reflect*

**FOCUS**

A sentry enters to tell Creon important news about
Polyneices' corpse. Read to find out about this news
and Creon's reaction to it.

(*Enter* Sentry.)

**Sentry.** I'll not say that I'm out of breath from running, King, because
every time I stopped to think about what I have to tell you, I felt
60 like going back. And all the time a voice kept saying, "You fool, don't
you know you're walking straight into trouble?"; and then another
voice: "Yes, but if you let somebody else get the news to Creon first,
it will be even worse than that for you!" But good sense won out, at
least I hope it was good sense, and here I am with a
65 story that makes no sense at all; but I'll tell it anyhow, because, as
they say, what's going to happen's going to happen, and—

**Creon.** Come to the point. What have you to say?

**Sentry.** I did not do it. I did not see who did it. You must not punish
me for what someone else has done.

70 **Creon.** A comprehensive defense! More effective, perhaps,
If I knew its purpose. Come: what is it?

**48–49** Like Ismene, the Choragus admits that Creon has the right to enforce his own law.

**51 it:** the job of guarding Polyneices' corpse to make sure that no one tries to bury it.

**70–71 A comprehensive defense . . . its purpose:** Creon is using legal language in a sarcastic way. He says that the sentry has offered a complete explanation of his innocence—but Creon has no idea what he is talking about.

## Pause & Reflect

**1.** Review the details you circled as you read. What principle is most important to Creon? Circle the phrase below that tells the answer. **(Evaluate)**

family ties

loyalty to the state

reverence for the gods

**MARK IT UP** **2.** Imagine you are in the position of the Choragus, the leader of the Chorus. What is your impression of Creon as a new king? Write your answer below. Then underline any details on pages 288 and 290 that support it. **(Draw Conclusions)**

_____

_____

_____

_____

**Sentry.** A dreadful thing . . . I don't know how to put it—

**Creon.** Out with it!

**Sentry.**              Well, then;

The dead man—

            Polyneices—

(*Pause. The* Sentry *is overcome, fumbles for words.*
Creon *waits impassively.*)

                  out there—

                        someone—

75  New dust on the slimy flesh!

(*Pause. No sign from* Creon.)

Someone has given it burial that way, and
Gone. . . .

(*Long pause.* Creon *finally speaks with deadly control.*)

**Creon.** And the man who dared do this?

**Sentry.**                        I swear I

Do not know! You must believe me!

                  Listen:

80  The ground was dry, not a sign of digging, no,
Not a wheel track in the dust, no trace of anyone.
It was when they relieved us this morning: and one of them,
The corporal, pointed to it.

                  There it was,

The strangest—

            Look:

85  The body, just mounded over with light dust: you see?
Not buried really, but as if they'd covered it
Just enough for the ghost's peace. And no sign
Of dogs or any wild animal that had been there.

And then what a scene there was! Every man of us

90  Accusing the other: we all proved the other man did it;
We all had proof that we could not have done it.
We were ready to take hot iron in our hands,
Walk through fire, swear by all the gods,
*It was not I!*

95  *I do not know who it was, but it was not I!*

(Creon's *rage has been mounting steadily, but the* Sentry *is
too intent upon his story to notice it.*)

**JOT IT DOWN** **Reread Lines 75–77**

The sentry can barely tell Creon that someone has honored the corpse of Polyneices. What do you think Creon might be thinking and feeling as he hears the news? **(Infer)**

_____

_____

_____

_____

**78** Creon assumes it is a man who has tried to bury the body.

**85–88** The burial of Polyneices is symbolic and ritualistic rather than actual.

And then, when this came to nothing, someone said
A thing that silenced us and made us stare
Down at the ground: you had to be told the news,
And one of us had to do it! We threw the dice,
100 And the bad luck fell to me. So here I am,
No happier to be here than you are to have me:
Nobody likes the man who brings bad news.

**Choragus.** I have been wondering, King: can it be that
     the gods have done this?

**Creon** (*furiously*). Stop!
105 Must you doddering wrecks
Go out of your heads entirely? "The gods!"
Intolerable!
The gods favor this corpse? Why? How had he
     served them?
Tried to loot their temples, burn their images,
110 Yes, and the whole state, and its laws with it!
Is it your senile opinion that the gods love to honor
     bad men?

A pious thought!—
                              No, from the very beginning
There have been those who have whispered together,
Stiff-necked anarchists, putting their heads together,
115 Scheming against me in alleys. These are the men,
And they have bribed my own guard to do this thing.
(*sententiously*) Money!
There's nothing in the world so demoralizing
     as money.
Down go your cities,
120 Homes gone, men gone, honest hearts corrupted,
Crookedness of all kinds, and all for money!
                         (*to* Sentry) But you—!
I swear by God and by the throne of God,
The man who has done this thing shall pay for it!
Find that man; bring him here to me, or your death
125 Will be the least of your problems: I'll string you up
Alive, and there will be certain ways to make you
Discover your employer before you die;
And the process may teach you a lesson you seem to
     have missed:
The dearest profit is sometimes all too dear.

**104–109** Creon is upset by the suggestion that the gods might have been responsible for honoring Polyneices' corpse. In Creon's opinion, the gods could never honor someone who attacked Thebes.

**105 doddering wrecks:** Creon insults the Chorus by calling them weak-minded old men.

**111 senile:** mentally weak because of old age.

**112** Creon is speaking sarcastically. He means it is ridiculous to suggest that the gods might have spread the dust on the body of Polyneices; **pious:** showing religious devotion.

**114 anarchists** (ăn′ər-kĭsts): persons working to overthrow the government. For the Greeks, anarchy, or lack of order, was a great evil.

**117 *sententiously*** (sĕn-tĕn′shəs-lē): in a know-it-all, preachy way.

**118 demoralizing:** corrupting.

**126–127 there will be . . . die:** Creon means that if the sentry keeps insisting that he doesn't know who buried Polyneices, he will be tortured until he suddenly "discovers" who it was.

---

**READ ALOUD** Lines 103–111

What can you conclude about Creon from his response to the Choragus' question? Check two phrases below. **(Draw Conclusions)**

is hot-tempered

respects the opinions of others

assumes he knows how the gods think

questions his own judgment

---

**MARK IT UP** WORD POWER

Remember to mark words that you'd like to add to your **Personal Word List**. Later, you can record the words and their meanings beginning on page 316.

130     That depends on the source. Do you understand me?
        A fortune won is often misfortune.

**Sentry.** King, may I speak?

**Creon.**                          Your very voice distresses me.

**Sentry.** Are you sure that it is my voice, and not your
        conscience?

**Creon.** By God, he wants to analyze me now!

135 **Sentry.** It is not what I say, but what has been done, that
        hurts you.

**Creon.** You talk too much.

**Sentry.**                          Maybe; but I've done nothing.

**Creon.** Sold your soul for some silver: that's all you've
        done.

**Sentry.** How dreadful it is when the right judge judges
        wrong!

**Creon.** Your figures of speech
140     May entertain you now; but unless you bring me
                the man,

        You will get little profit from them in the end.

(*Exit* Creon *into the palace.*)

**Sentry.** "Bring me the man"—!
        I'd like nothing better than bringing him the man!
        But bring him or not, you have seen the last of
                me here.
145     At any rate, I am safe!

(*Exit* Sentry.)

*Pause* & **Reflect**

**131** In other words, what appears to be good may turn out to be evil. Creon directs those words at the sentry. Creon does not realize, however, that his words may apply to himself. He has just received his "fortune"—the kingship of Thebes. It may turn out to be a misfortune.

### Pause & Reflect

1. What does Creon assume the sentry is guilty of doing? Write the answer below. Then circle details on pages 294 and 296 that led you to the answer. **(Infer)**

_____

_____

_____

_____

2. What do you think will happen when Creon discovers that Antigone is the one who has buried Polyneices? **(Predict)**

_____

_____

_____

_____

**145** Like Ismene, the sentry is concerned about saving himself and not confronting Creon.

### CHALLENGE

When you read or view a play by Sophocles, it is important to appreciate his use of **dramatic irony**. This type of irony occurs when the reader or audience knows something that a character does not know. For example, the audience knows that Antigone has disobeyed Creon before Creon learns about her actions. Mark lines in this scene that are ironic. How do these ironies influence your opinion of Creon? **(Reading Classical Drama)**

**FOCUS**

Again the Chorus is alone on the stage. In this poem,
or ode, the Chorus praises human achievements.
**MARK IT UP** As you read, circle details that tell you
about these achievements.

## ODE 1

**Chorus.** Numberless are the world's wonders, but none
More wonderful than man; the storm-grey sea
Yields to his prows; the huge crests bear him high;
Earth, holy and inexhaustible, is graven
5  With shining furrows where his plows have gone
Year after year, the timeless labor of stallions.

The light-boned birds and beasts that cling to cover,
The <u>lithe</u> fish lighting their reaches of dim water,
All are taken, tamed in the net of his mind;
10  The lion on the hill, the wild horse windy-maned,
Resign to him; and his blunt yoke has broken
The sultry shoulders of the mountain bull.

Words also, and thought as rapid as air,
He fashions to his good use; statecraft is his,
15  And his the skill that deflects the arrows of snow,
The spears of winter rain: from every wind
He has made himself secure—from all but one:
In the late wind of death he cannot stand.

O clear intelligence, force beyond all measure!
20  O fate of man, working both good and evil!
When the laws are kept, how proudly his city stands!
When the laws are broken, what of his city then?
Never may the anarchic man find rest at my hearth,
Never be it said that my thoughts are his thoughts.

*Pause* **&** *Reflect*

WORDS
TO        **lithe** (līth) *adj.* limber; physically flexible
KNOW

**Ode:** An ode is a song chanted by the Chorus.

**3 prows:** the front section of ships; **crests:** waves.

**4–6 Earth . . . stallions:** The earth is sacred and yields endless riches. For countless years, strong horses, driven by men, have pulled plows that have carved **(graven)** rows in the soil for planting seed.

**9 net of his mind:** Human intelligence is pictured as a fishing net. It can understand or take in the other creatures **(All are taken)** of the earth.

**10–12 The lion . . . mountain bull:** The animals of the earth, from lions to horses, must submit to human beings. The crossbar and harness **(yoke)** put across the shoulders of a massive bull put it under human control.

**15–17 the skill that deflects . . . made himself secure:** Humans construct buildings to protect them from severe weather.

**23 hearth** (härth)**:** fireside.

## Pause & Reflect

1. Review the details you circled as you read. Based on these details, how would you describe the Chorus's view of human beings? **(Infer)**

_____

_____

_____

2. Reread lines 13–18. In these lines, the Chorus mentions a limitation of human beings. What is that limitation? **(Clarify)**

_____

_____

_____

**READ ALOUD**  3. Read aloud lines 21–24. How do you think the Chorus feels about Creon at this point in the play? **(Draw Conclusions)**

_____

_____

_____

### CHALLENGE

**External conflict** occurs when a character is pitted against an outside force. **Internal conflict** occurs when the struggle takes place within a character. Identify the conflicts in the opening sections of *Antigone,* and classify each one as external or internal. What conflict might develop between Antigone and Creon? How might this conflict be resolved? **(Reading Classical Drama)**

## Moving On

If you are using *The Language of Literature,* go to page 1031 of that book to continue reading *Antigone.* As you do so, continue to be an active reader. Ask yourself the kinds of questions you found in this lesson.

# Active Reading SkillBuilder

## Strategies for Reading Classical Drama

Use the following strategies to understand a classical drama such as *Antigone*.

- Imagine the play as it might be staged, visualizing as you read.

- Try to understand the hero—the motivations and qualities that make him or her a noble figure, the causes of the conflict the hero faces, and the circumstances or flaws that lead to the hero's downfall.

- Consider how the words and actions of minor characters help you understand the main characters. Notice how the comments of the Chorus interpret the action and point to universal themes.

- Monitor your own reading strategies and modify them as needed.

As you read this excerpt from *Antigone,* apply the strategies listed above. On the chart below, jot down questions that come to mind. When you finish reading, answer the questions you listed. An example is shown.

| Questions | Answers |
|---|---|
| Why does Antigone want to bury her brother's corpse? | She wants his soul to be at peace. |
|  |  |
|  |  |
|  |  |
|  |  |
|  |  |
|  |  |

# Literary Analysis SkillBuilder

## Classical Drama

The Chorus plays an important role in **classical drama.** Through its
leader the **Choragus,** the Chorus sometimes takes part in the dialogue.
Between scenes, the Chorus sings and dances, giving insights into the
message of the play. As you read this excerpt from *Antigone,* pay attention to
the role of the Chorus. On the chart below, record key lines sung by the Chorus
or spoken by its leader. Then write down your response, telling why you
think the lines are important to the play. An example is shown.

| Lines | Responses |
|---|---|
| "I have been wondering, King: can it be that the gods have done this?" (Scene I, line 103) | The Choragus suggests that the gods would want Polyneices' corpse to be honored. Perhaps Antigone did the right thing. |
| | |
| | |

# Words to Know SkillBuilder

## Words to Know

| | | | | |
|---|---|---|---|---|
| auspicious | defile* | edict* | lithe | sated |
| compulsive* | dirge* | lamentation* | perverse* | transgress* |

**A.** Each of the following sentences suggests a word in the word list. The word itself is hidden in the sentence. Underline the hidden word and then write it on the line. An example, using another word from the play, has been done for you.

*Example:* I see for myself a terrible destiny, and there is nothing I can do to change it.

*fate*

Almost anybody can manage a few of the positions, but to do yoga well, it helps if you are relaxed and have some flexibility in your joints.

_____ (1)

No one is going to eat those! They may be top-grade filets, but dropping them in the mud has made them considerably less than appetizing.

_____ (2)

She was starving when they started filming the commercial, but after the actress ate dozens of Barney's Big Burgers, she couldn't imagine ever being hungry again.

_____ (3)

Hey, if you think people vote in this country, you've got another thing coming. What the dictator says, goes. There are no ifs, ands, or buts about it.

_____ (4)

Henry likes making trouble, but he's creative, so we figured he could write some super verses for the school song. He did, but he wrote them in pig Latin just to drive the principal crazy.

_____ (5)

**B.** For each phrase in the first column, find the phrase in the second column that is closest in meaning. Write the letter of that phrase in the blank.

_____ 1. solitary sobbing

_____ 2. deliberately disobey

_____ 3. uncontrollable uncertainty

_____ 4. melancholy, mournful music

_____ 5. a favorable fall for farming

A. intentionally transgress

B. a depressing dirge

C. lonely lamentation

D. an auspicious autumn for agriculture

E. compulsive questioning

*These words appear later in *Antigone*. You can use a dictionary to check the definitions. These words are also defined in the lesson for *Antigone,* found in **The Language of Literature.**

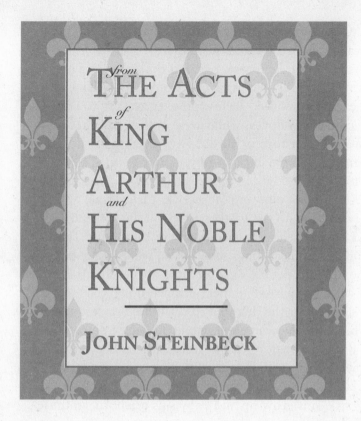

*from*
# THE ACTS
*of*
# KING
# ARTHUR
*and*
# HIS NOBLE
# KNIGHTS

## JOHN STEINBECK

**PREVIEW** Stories of King Arthur and his noble knights have been told and retold for hundreds of years. This excerpt from John Steinbeck's retelling of this classic **romance** focuses on King Arthur's most valued knight—Sir Lancelot (lăn′sə-lŏt). It tells about Lancelot's relationship with King Arthur and his wife, Queen Guinevere (gwĭn′ə-vîr′). How well does Lancelot live up to your definition of a brave and loyal knight?

**FOCUS**
A joyous celebration is taking place in the city of Winchester. In the castle, King Arthur is joined by his knights and ladies and other important members of his kingdom. As you read, try to picture the event in your mind.

**King Arthur held Whitsun[1] court** at Winchester, that ancient royal town favored by God and His clergy as well as the seat and tomb of many kings.[2] The roads were clogged with eager people, knights returning to stamp in court the record of their deeds, of bishops, clergy, monks, of the defeated

---

1. **Whitsun:** another name for Pentecost, a Christian festival celebrated on the seventh Sunday after Easter.

2. **Winchester . . . seat and tomb of many kings:** Winchester was an important center of learning, religion, and government. Many kings were buried there.

fettered to their paroles,[3] the prisoners of honor. And on

[10] Itchen water, pathway from Solent and the sea, the little ships brought succulents, lampreys, eels and oysters, plaice and sea trout, while barges loaded with casks of whale oil and casks of wine came tide borne.[4] Bellowing oxen walked to the spits on their own four hooves, while geese and swans, sheep and swine, waited their turn in hurdle pens. Every householder with a strip of colored cloth, a ribbon, any textile gaiety,[5] hung it from a window to flap its small festival, and those in lack tied boughs of pine and laurel over their doors.

In the great hall of the castle on the hill the king sat high,

[20] and next below the fair elite company of the Round Table, noble and <u>decorous</u> as kings themselves, while at the long trestle boards[6] the people were as fitted as toes in a tight shoe.

Then while the glistening meat dripped down the tables, it was the custom for the defeated to celebrate the deeds of those who had overcome them, while the victor dipped his head in <u>disparagement</u> of his greatness and fended off the compliments with small defensive gestures of his hands. And as at public <u>penitence</u> sins are given stature they do not deserve, little sins grow up and baby sins are born, so those

[30] knights who lately claimed mercy perchance might raise the exploits of the brave and merciful beyond reasonable gratitude for their lives and in anticipation of some small notice of value.[7]

### Pause & Reflect

---

3. **fettered to their paroles:** bound by their word of honor to lay down arms.

4. **And on Itchen water, pathway from Solent . . . came tide borne:** Itchen and Solent are waterways in southern England. Many ships and barges traveled up these waterways to Winchester, bringing a variety of fish, wine, and other products to be used for the feasts.

5. **textile gaiety:** any bit of brightly-colored cloth.

6. **trestle boards:** tables made from large planks of wood held up by two pairs of legs.

7. **And as at public penitence . . . notice of value:** Sinners exaggerate their faults or misdeeds (**baby sins become big sins**) when they talk about them publicly. In a similar way, knights exaggerate the skills and strengths of those who defeated them in battle. By doing so, both sinners and knights call attention to themselves (**some small notice of value**).

| WORDS TO KNOW | **decorous** (dĕk′ər-əs) *adj.* behaving in a manner appropriate to the occasion; proper |
| --- | --- |
| | **disparagement** (dĭ-spăr′ĭj-mənt) *n.* belittlement |
| | **penitence** (pĕn′ĭ-təns) *n.* expression of regret for sins or wrongdoing |

### Pause & Reflect

**1.** Cross out the phrase below that does *not* describe the celebration in the great hall. **(Clarify)**

a huge crowd

a great variety of food

serious, dignified atmosphere

sinners waiting for punishment

✎ MARK IT UP **2.** What kinds of stories are told in the great hall? Underline passages in the story that support your answer. **(Summarize)**

_____

_____

_____

_____

**3.** Would you enjoy attending such a feast? *Yes/No,* because_____

_____

_____

_____ .

**(Connect)**

**FOCUS**

Now it is Lancelot's turn to be honored by those he has defeated.

**▶MARK IT UP** As you read, underline details that help you understand how Lancelot feels about the stories of his greatness. An example is highlighted.

40

**This no one said of Lancelot,** sitting with bowed head in his golden-lettered seat at the Round Table. Some said he nodded and perhaps dozed, for the testimony to his greatness was long and the monotony[8] of his victories continued for many hours. Lancelot's immaculate fame had grown so great that men took pride in being unhorsed by him—even this notice was an honor.[9] And since he had won many victories, it is possible that knights he had never seen claimed to have been overthrown by him. It was a way to claim attention for a moment. And as he dozed and wished to be otherwise, he heard his deeds <u>exalted</u> beyond his recognition, and some mighty exploits once attributed to other men were brought bright-painted out and laid on the shining pile of his achievements. There is a seat of worth beyond the reach of envy whose occupant ceases to be a man and becomes the receptacle of the wishful longings of the world, a seat most often reserved for the dead, from whom neither <u>reprisal</u> nor reward may be expected, but at this time Sir Lancelot was its unchallenged tenant.[10] And he vaguely heard his strength favorably compared with elephants, his ferocity with lions, his agility with deer, his cleverness with foxes, his beauty with the stars, his justice with Solon,[11] his stern probity[12] with St. Michael, his humility with newborn lambs; his military niche would have caused the Archangel Gabriel[13] to raise his head. Sometimes the guests paused in

50

60

---

8. **monotony:** a boring sameness.

9. **Lancelot's immaculate fame . . . was an honor:** Lancelot's reputation as a knight was faultless. Because he was considered to be so perfect, even to be thrown from your horse by him was considered an honor.

10. **There is a seat . . . its unchallenged tenant:** A person may become so honored that he represents the wishes of the world. Usually, this respect is given only to the dead. Lancelot has achieved this honored position (**seat of worth**) in his own lifetime.

11. **Solon:** Athenian statesman and lawgiver who lived in the sixth century B.C.

12. **probity:** uprightness; honesty.

13. **St. Michael . . . Archangel Gabriel:** In several religious traditions, Michael and Gabriel are archangels, the chief messengers of God. Both are celebrated as warriors against evil.

**▶MARK IT UP** WORD POWER

Mark words that you'd like to add to your **Personal Word List.** After reading, you can record the words and their meanings beginning on page 316.

WORDS TO KNOW

**exalt** (ĭg-zôlt') v. to glorify, praise, or honor

**reprisal** (rĭ-prī'zəl) n. retaliation in the form of harm or injury similar to that received; revenge

their chewing the better to hear, and a man who slopped his
metheglin[14] drew frowns.

Arthur on his dais[15] sat very still and did not fiddle with his
bread, and beside him sat lovely Guinevere, still as a painted
statue of herself. Only her inward eyes confessed her <u>vagrant</u>
thoughts. And Lancelot studied the open pages of his hands—
not large hands, but delicate where they were not knobby and
scarred with old wounds. His hands were fine-textured—soft
**70** of skin and very white, protected by the pliant leather lining
of his gauntlets.[16]

The great hall was not still, not all upturned listening.
Everywhere was movement as people came and went, some
serving huge planks of meat and baskets of bread, round and
flat like a plate. And there were restless ones who could not
sit still, while everyone under burden of half-chewed meat and
the floods and freshets of mead[17] and beer found necessity for
repeated departures and returns.

Lancelot exhausted the theme of his hands and squinted
**80** down the long hall and watched the movement with eyes so
nearly closed that he could not see faces. And he thought how
he knew everyone by <u>carriage</u>. The knights in long full floor-
brushing robes walked lightly or thought their feet barely
touched the ground because their bodies were released from
their crushing boxes of iron. Their feet were long and slender
because, being horsemen, they had never widened and
flattened their feet with walking. The ladies, full-skirted,
moved like water, but this was schooled and designed, taught
to little girls with the help of whips on raw ankles, while their
**90** shoulders were bound back with nail-studded harnesses and
their heads held high and rigid by painful collars of woven
willow or, for the forgetful, by supports of painted wire, for to
learn the high proud head on a swan's neck, to learn to flow
like water, is not easy for a little girl as she becomes a gentle-
woman. But knights and ladies both matched their movements

14. **metheglin** (mə-thĕgʹlĭn): a liquor made from honey.
15. **dais** (dāʹĭs): a raised platform used for a seat of honor.
16. **pliant leather lining of his gauntlets:** soft leather of the gloves worn with armor.
17. **floods and freshets of mead:** great quantities of mead, an alcoholic drink made from honey and water.

WORDS TO KNOW
**vagrant** (vāʹgrənt) *adj.* wandering
**carriage** (kărʹĭj) *n.* manner of moving one's body

to their garments; the sweep and rhythm of a long gown informs the manner of its moving. It is not necessary to inspect a serf or a slave, his shoulder wide and sloping from burdens, legs short and thick and crooked, feet splayed[18] and widespread, the whole frame slowly crushed by weights. In the great hall the serving people walked under burdens with the slow weight of oxen and scuttled[19] like crabs, crooked and nervous when the weight was gone.

A pause in the recital of his virtues drew Lancelot's attention. The knight who had tried to kill him in a tree had finished, and among the benches Sir Kay was rising to his feet. Lancelot could hear his voice before he spoke, reciting deeds like leaves and bags and barrels. Before his friend could reach the center of the hall, Sir Lancelot wriggled to his feet and approached the dais. "My lord king," he said, "forgive me if I ask leave to go. An old wound has broken open."

Arthur smiled down on him. "I have the same old wound," he said. "We'll go together. Perhaps you will come to the tower room when we have attended to our wounds." And he signed the trumpets to end the gathering, and the bodyguards to clear the hall.

## Pause & Reflect

FOCUS

The three friends meet in Arthur's room. Guinevere questions Lancelot about the ladies he met during his adventures.

MARK IT UP As you read, circle details that tell you whether or not Lancelot answers the queen truthfully.

**The stone stairway** to the king's room was in the thickness of the wall of the round tower of the keep.[20] At short intervals a deep embrasure[21] and a long, beveled[22] arrow slit commanded some aspect of the town below.

No armed men guarded this stairway. They were below and had passed Sir Lancelot in. The king's room was round, a horizontal slice of the tower, windowless save for the arrow slits, entered by a narrow arched door. It was a sparsely furnished room, carpeted with rushes. A wide bed, and at its foot a carved oaken chest, a

---

18. **splayed:** spead out or apart.

19. **scuttle:** to run or move with short, hurried movements.

20. **keep:** the stronghold, or the fortified area, of a castle.

21. **embrasure** (ĕm-brā′zhər): opening in a wall, through which cannons are fired.

22. **beveled:** having a sloping edge.

---

## Pause & Reflect

1. Review the details that you underlined as you read. How does Lancelot feel about the stories of his greatness? **(Infer)**

   _____

   _____

   _____

   _____

2. Why do you think the knights go to such extremes in their praise of Lancelot? **(Analyze)**

   _____

   _____

   _____

   _____

3. Lancelot can tell the rank of people by the way they move. Why is he able to do this? Circle the answer below. **(Draw Conclusions)**

   He knew every person in the hall.

   People were trained to move and act in certain ways, based on their position in society.

4. Why do you think Lancelot and Arthur suddenly leave the hall? **(Infer)**

   _____

   _____

   _____

   _____

130 bench before the fireplace, and several stools completed the furnishing. But the raw stone of the tower was plastered over and painted with solemn figures of men and angels walking hand in hand. Two candles and the reeky[23] fire gave the only light.

When Lancelot entered, the queen stood up from the bench before the fire, saying, "I will retire, my lords."

"No, stay," said Arthur.

"Stay," said Lancelot.

The king was stretched comfortably in the bed. His bare 140 feet projecting from his long saffron[24] robe caressed each other, the toes curled downward.

The queen was lovely in the firelight, all lean, down-flowing lines of green samite.[25] She wore her little mouth-corner smile of concealed amusement, and her bold golden eyes were the same color as her hair, and odd it was that her lashes and slender brows were dark, an oddity contrived with kohl[26] brought in a small enameled pot from an outland by a far-wandering knight.

"How are you holding up?" Arthur asked.

150 "Not well, my lord. It's harder than the quest."

"Did you really do all the things they said you did?"

Lancelot chuckled. "Truthfully, I don't know. It sounds different when they tell about it. And most of them feel it necessary to add a little. When I remember leaping eight feet, they tell it at fifty, and frankly I don't recall several of those giants at all."

The queen made room for him on the fire bench, and he took his seat, back to the fire.

Guinevere said, "The damsel—what's her name—talked 160 about fair queen enchantresses,[27] but she was so excited that her words tumbled over each other. I couldn't make out what happened."

Lancelot looked nervously away. "You know how excitable young girls are," he said. "A little back-country necromancy[28]

---

23. **reeky:** smelly.

24. **saffron:** golden yellow, named for the spice that has that color.

25. **samite:** a heavy silk fabric.

26. **kohl:** a cosmetic preparation used as eye makeup.

27. **fair queen enchantresses:** Morgan le Fay and three other queens, the four of whom imprisoned Lancelot, demanding that he take one of them as his lover.

28. **necromancy:** magic.

in a pasture."

"But she spoke particularly of queens."

"My lady, I think everyone is a queen to her. It's like the giants—makes the story richer."

"Then they were not queens?"

170 "Well, for that matter, when you get into the field of enchantment, everyone is a queen, or thinks she is. Next time she tells it, the little damsel will be a queen. I do think, my lord, there's too much of that kind of thing going on. It's a bad sign, a kind of restlessness, when people go in for fortunetelling and all such things. Maybe there should be a law about it."

"There is," said Arthur. "But it's not in secular[29] hands. The Church is supposed to take care of that."

"Yes, but some of the nunneries are going in for it."

180 "Well, I'll put a bug in the archbishop's ear."

The queen observed, "I gather you rescued damsels by the dozen." She put her fingers on his arm and a searing[30] shock ran through his body, and his mouth opened in amazement at a hollow ache that pressed upward against his ribs and shortened his breath.

After a moment she said, "How many damsels did you rescue?"

His mouth was dry. "Of course there were a few, madame. There always are."

190 "And all of them made love to you?"

"That they did not, madame. There you protect me."

"I?"

"Yes. Since with my lord's permission I swore to serve you all my life and gave my knightly courtly love to you, I am sheltered from damsels by your name."

"And do you want to be sheltered?"

"Yes, my lady. I am a fighting man. I have neither time nor inclination for any other kind of love. I hope this pleases you, my lady. I sent many prisoners to ask your mercy."

200 "I never saw such a crop of them," Arthur said. "You must have swept some counties clean."

Guinevere touched him on the arm again and with side-glancing golden eyes saw the spasm that shook him. "While we are on this subject, I want to mention one lady you did not save. When I saw her, she was a headless corpse and not in

---

29. **secular**: worldly, rather than religious.
30. **searing**: burning.

MARK IT UP WORD POWER

Remember to mark words that you'd like to add to your **Personal Word List**. Later, you can record the words and their meanings beginning on page 316.

1. Review the details you circled
as you read. Does Lancelot
answer Guinevere's questions
truthfully? **(Draw Conclusions)**
*Yes/No, because*_____

_____

_____.

✎ MARK IT UP   2. How does
Lancelot feel about Guinevere?
Mark passages that support
your opinion. **(Infer)**

_____

_____

_____

_____

3. Which two statements below
tell how Guinevere feels about
Lancelot? Circle them. **(Infer)**

She is jealous of his attentions
to other women.

She is angry at him.

She is in love with him.

She does not like him.

good condition, and the man who brought her in was half crazed."[31]

"I am ashamed of that," said Lancelot. "She was under my protection, and I failed her. I suppose it was my shame that made me force the man to do it. I'm sorry. I hope you released him from the burden."

"Not at all," she said. "I wanted him away before the feast reeked up the heavens. I sent him with his burden to the Pope. His friend will not improve on the way. And if his loss of interest in ladies continues, he may turn out to be a very holy man, a hermit or something of that nature, if he isn't a maniac first."

The king rose on his elbow. "We will have to work out some system," he said. "The rules of errantry[32] are too loose, and the quests overlap. Besides, I wonder how long we can leave justice in the hands of men who are themselves unstable. I don't mean you, my friend. But there may come a time when order and organization from the crown will be necessary."

The queen stood up. "My lords, will you grant me permission to leave you now? I know you will wish to speak of great things foreign and perhaps tiresome to a lady's ears."

The king said, "Surely, my lady. Go to your rest."

"No, sire—not rest. If I do not lay out the designs for the needlepoint, my ladies will have no work tomorrow."

"But these are feast days, my dear."

"I like to give them something every day, my lord. They're lazy things and some of them so woolly in the mind that they forget how to thread a needle from day to day. Forgive me, my lords."

### Pause & Reflect

FOCUS

As Guinevere leaves, Lancelot experiences something strange and magical. Read to find out what effect his experience has on him.

**She swept from the room** with proud and powerful steps, and the little breeze she made in the still air carried a strange scent to Lancelot, a perfume which sent a shivering excitement coursing through his body. It was an odor he did not, could not, know, for it was the smell of

---

31. **When I saw her . . . half crazed:** Guinevere is referring to a woman Lancelot was unable to save—a woman who was beheaded by her jealous husband. As punishment, Lancelot commanded the husband to take the woman's body to Guinevere and to throw himself on her mercy.

32. **errantry** (ĕr´ən-trē): the knightly pursuit of adventure.

Guinevere distilled by her own skin. And as she passed through the door and descended the steps, he saw himself leap up and follow her, although he did not move. And when she was gone, the room was bleak, and the glory was gone from it, and Sir Lancelot was dog-weary, tired almost to weeping.

"What a queen she is," said King Arthur softly. "And what a woman equally. Merlin was with me when I chose her. He tried to dissuade me with his usual doomful prophecies. That was one 250 of the few times I differed with him. Well, my choice has proved him <u>fallible</u>. She has shown the world what a queen should be. All other women lose their sheen when she is present."

Lancelot said, "Yes, my lord," and for no reason he knew, except perhaps the <u>intemperate</u> dullness of the feast, he felt lost, and a cold knife of loneliness pressed against his heart.

The king was chuckling. "It is the device of ladies that their lords have great matters to discuss, when if the truth were told, we bore them. And I hope the truth is never told. Why, you look <u>haggard</u>, my friend. Are you feverish? Did you mean 260 that about an old wound opening?"

"No. The wound was what you thought it was, my lord. But it is true that I can fight, travel, live on berries, fight again, go without sleeping, and come out fresh and fierce, but sitting still at Whitsun feast has wearied me to death."

Arthur said, "I can see it. We'll discuss the realm's health another time. Go to your bed now. Have you your old quarters?"

"No—better ones. Sir Kay has cleared five knights from the lovely lordly rooms over the north gate. He did it in memory 270 of an adventure which we, God help us, will have to listen to tomorrow. I accept your dismissal, my lord."

And Lancelot knelt down and took the king's beloved hand in both of his and kissed it. "Good night, my liege[34] lord, my liege friend," he said and then stumbled blindly from the room and felt his way down the curving stone steps past the arrow slits.

*Pause* **&** Reflect

---

33. **dissuade:** to discourage or advise against.

34. **liege** (lēj): under feudal law, entitled to the service or allegiance of subjects.

WORDS
TO
KNOW

**fallible** (făl′ə-bəl) *adj.* capable of being wrong or mistaken
**intemperate** (ĭn-tĕm′pər-ĭt) *adj.* extreme
**haggard** (hăg′ərd) *adj.* appearing worn and exhausted

---

*Pause* **&** Reflect

1. In your own words, describe what Lancelot experiences as Guinevere leaves the room. (Summarize)

_____

_____

_____

_____

✎ MARK IT UP   2. What effect does this experience have on Lancelot? Underline details on this page that support your answer. (Cause and Effect)

_____

_____

_____

_____

## Pause & Reflect

1. Were you surprised by the turn of events involving Lancelot and Guinevere? Explain. **(Connect)**

_____

_____

_____

_____

2. Reread the last paragraph of the story. Why do you think Lancelot weeps? **(Infer)**

_____

_____

_____

_____

✎ CHALLENGE

How does Steinbeck prepare the reader for the passionate kiss between Lancelot and Guinevere? Review the selection, looking for hints about their relationship. Mark passages that help to **foreshadow** the ending.

## Wrapping Up

If you are using **The Language of Literature,** you can now move to the questions and activities on pages 1099–1101 of that book.

**FOCUS**

After leaving the king, Lancelot sees Guinevere a second time. Read to find out why this meeting brings tears to his eyes.

**As he came to** the level of the next landing, Guinevere issued silently from a darkened entrance. He could see her in the thin light from the arrow slit. She took his arm and led him to her dark chamber and closed the oaken door.

"A strange thing happened," she said softly. "When I left you, I thought you followed me. I was so sure of it I did not even look around to verify it. You were there behind me. And when I came to my own door, I said good night to you, so certain I was that you were there."

He could see her outline in the dark and smell the scent which was herself. "My lady," he said, "when you left the room, I saw myself follow you as though I were another person looking on."

Their bodies locked together as though a trap had sprung. Their mouths met, and each devoured the other. Each frantic heartbeat at the walls of ribs trying to get to the other until their held breaths burst out and Lancelot, dizzied, found the door and blundered down the stairs. And he was weeping bitterly.

### Pause & Reflect

# Active Reading SkillBuilder

## Making Inferences

**Inferences** are logical guesses based on information in the text, common sense, and the reader's own experience. To best appreciate this selection, readers need to make inferences about Lancelot's feelings and behavior. For example, when Queen Guinevere asks Lancelot whether he has really encountered fair queen enchantresses, he looks away nervously and does not answer her directly. The reader can infer that he did meet such women and does not want to tell Guinevere about his encounters. As you read, look for other clues to help you understand Lancelot. On the chart that follows, keep track of your inferences about Lancelot. Remember to consider both the evidence in the text and your own experience when making your inferences. An example is given.

| Inferences About Lancelot | | |
|---|---|---|
| | **Clues** | **Inferences** |
| **His Attitude Toward His Fame** | *"dozed and wished to be otherwhere"* (lines 46-47) | *He's bored by stories of his great deeds.* |
| **His Feelings About Guinevere** | | |
| **Other Aspects of His Life** | | |

# Literary Analysis SkillBuilder

## Style

**Style** is the particular way in which a piece of literature is written. Style refers not so much to what is said but to how it is said. Use of descriptive detail, dialogue, depth of characterization, diction (word choice), and tone all contribute to a writer's style. On the chart below, note key aspects of Steinbeck's style. Use the questions as guides. One example is given.

| Aspect of Style | Analysis |
| --- | --- |
| **Descriptive Detail**<br>Does the author use many details, or are the details kept to a minimum? | *uses vivid, elaborate descriptions* |
| **Dialogue**<br>Is there a lot of dialogue?<br>Is it realistic? | |
| **Characterization**<br>How does the author make the characters come alive for the reader? | |
| **Diction**<br>Does the author use long, complex words or use simple and common words? | |
| **Tone**<br>How would you describe the author's attitude toward the subject? | |

# Words to Know SkillBuilder

## Words to Know

| | | | | |
|---|---|---|---|---|
| carriage | disparagement | fallible | intemperate | reprisal |
| decorous | exalt | haggard | penitence | vagrant |

**A.** Decide which word from the word list belongs in each numbered blank in the story below. Then write the word on corresponding the blank line on the right.

Ever since I was a pup, I've been taking care of my master, Prince Herbert L. Charming. I call him Herb. That may not seem respectful, but don't take it as any (1) of him. I wouldn't ridicule the guy for all the bones in Bavaria. No way! I have a lot of respect for him. Who wouldn't? Everything about him is princely—from his behavior, which is always (2), to his (3), which is proud and graceful. I call him Herb due to how fond I am of the fellow.

Herb's main interest in life is Doing Knightly Things. As a result, we live a (4) life, traveling all over in search of adventure. One day, we hear about a spell that has put a whole kingdom to sleep. The way the story goes, there was this unpleasant woman who got ticked off when she wasn't invited to some royal bash. The king and queen refused to show the slightest (5) for failing to invite her, because they didn't regret it. So she thought she'd make them regret it by getting even. She wasn't satisfied with a (6) like not inviting them to her parties. Oh, no. She monkeyed around with a spinning wheel and magic and now everybody in the kingdom is sawing logs. Seems like a pretty (7) response to me, but I guess she isn't known for being reasonable. Rumor has it there's a lovely princess, a real snoozing beauty, and waking her up will break the spell. So Herb and I set off in search of this Land of Nod.

Herb keeps barging into the wrong castles and so on, and I can tell he needs my help. I've got your animal kingdom's superior nose and ears, so I'm nowhere near as (8) as he is. I don't waste time barking up the wrong tree, so to speak. In no time at all, I pick up the sound of snores from behind a wall of thorns and Herb grabs his sword and starts whacking. After about 12 hours of this, he's looking a bit (9), but he sticks with it.

Finally, we get through and find the castle and the princess. Herb shakes her and tickles her feet, but no dice. Again, it's up to me. Sure enough, one big, doggie-type lick and she opens her baby blues. The rest is history. Everybody in town is eager to (10) Herb's efforts. Yak, yak, yak about how wonderful he is. I'm pretty much ignored, but, hey, like all pooches, I live to serve. And now that Herb's settled down, I haven't had to fight a dragon in years.

_____ (1)

_____ (2)

_____ (3)

_____ (4)

_____ (5)

_____ (6)

_____ (7)

_____ (8)

_____ (9)

_____ (10)

**B.** Write a diary entry that Arthur, Lancelot, or Guinevere might have written following the events described in the excerpt from *The Acts of King Arthur and His Noble Knights.* Use at least **four** of the Words to Know.

# Personal Word List

Use these pages to build your personal vocabulary. As you read the selections take time to mark unfamiliar words. These should be words that seem interesting or important enough to add to your permanent vocabulary. After reading, look up the meanings of these words and record the information below. For each word, write a sentence that shows its correct use.

Review your list from time to time. Try to put these words into use in your writing and conversation.

Word: _____

Selection: _____

Page/Line: _____ / _____

Part of Speech: _____

Definition: _____
_____
_____

Sentence: _____
_____

Word: _____

Selection: _____

Page/Line: _____ / _____

Part of Speech: _____

Definition: _____
_____
_____

Sentence: _____
_____

Word: _____

Selection: _____

Page/Line: _____ / _____

Part of Speech: _____

Definition: _____
_____
_____

Sentence: _____
_____

Word: _____

Selection: _____

Page/Line: _____ / _____

Part of Speech: _____

Definition: _____
_____
_____

Sentence: _____
_____

Word: _____

Selection: _____

Page/Line: _____ / _____

Part of Speech: _____

Definition: _____
_____
_____

Sentence: _____
_____

Word: _____

Selection: _____

Page/Line: _____ / _____

Part of Speech: _____

Definition: _____
_____
_____

Sentence: _____
_____

Word:_____

Selection: _____

Page/Line: _____ / _____

Part of Speech: _____

Definition: _____

_____

_____

Sentence: _____

_____

Word:_____

Selection: _____

Page/Line: _____ / _____

Part of Speech: _____

Definition: _____

_____

_____

Sentence: _____

_____

Word:_____

Selection: _____

Page/Line: _____ / _____

Part of Speech: _____

Definition: _____

_____

_____

Sentence: _____

_____

Word:_____

Selection: _____

Page/Line: _____ / _____

Part of Speech: _____

Definition: _____

_____

_____

Sentence: _____

_____

Word:_____

Selection: _____

Page/Line: _____ / _____

Part of Speech: _____

Definition: _____

_____

_____

Sentence: _____

_____

Word:_____

Selection: _____

Page/Line: _____ / _____

Part of Speech: _____

Definition: _____

_____

_____

Sentence: _____

_____

Word:_____

Selection: _____

Page/Line: _____ / _____

Part of Speech: _____

Definition: _____

_____

_____

Sentence: _____

_____

Word:_____

Selection: _____

Page/Line: _____ / _____

Part of Speech: _____

Definition: _____

_____

_____

Sentence: _____

_____

# Personal Word List (continued)

Word:_____
Selection: _____
Page/Line: _____ / _____
Part of Speech: _____
Definition: _____
_____
_____
Sentence: _____
_____

Word:_____
Selection: _____
Page/Line: _____ / _____
Part of Speech: _____
Definition: _____
_____
_____
Sentence: _____
_____

Word:_____
Selection: _____
Page/Line: _____ / _____
Part of Speech: _____
Definition: _____
_____
_____
Sentence: _____
_____

Word:_____
Selection: _____
Page/Line: _____ / _____
Part of Speech: _____
Definition: _____
_____
_____
Sentence: _____
_____

Word:_____
Selection: _____
Page/Line: _____ / _____
Part of Speech: _____
Definition: _____
_____
_____
Sentence: _____
_____

Word:_____
Selection: _____
Page/Line: _____ / _____
Part of Speech: _____
Definition: _____
_____
_____
Sentence: _____
_____

Word:_____
Selection: _____
Page/Line: _____ / _____
Part of Speech: _____
Definition: _____
_____
_____
Sentence: _____
_____

Word:_____
Selection: _____
Page/Line: _____ / _____
Part of Speech: _____
Definition: _____
_____
_____
Sentence: _____
_____

Word:_____

Selection: _____

Page/Line: _____ / _____

Part of Speech: _____

Definition: _____
_____
_____

Sentence: _____
_____

Word:_____

Selection: _____

Page/Line: _____ / _____

Part of Speech: _____

Definition: _____
_____
_____

Sentence: _____
_____

Word:_____

Selection: _____

Page/Line: _____ / _____

Part of Speech: _____

Definition: _____
_____
_____

Sentence: _____
_____

Word:_____

Selection: _____

Page/Line: _____ / _____

Part of Speech: _____

Definition: _____
_____
_____

Sentence: _____
_____

Word:_____

Selection: _____

Page/Line: _____ / _____

Part of Speech: _____

Definition: _____
_____
_____

Sentence: _____
_____

Word:_____

Selection: _____

Page/Line: _____ / _____

Part of Speech: _____

Definition: _____
_____
_____

Sentence: _____
_____

Word:_____

Selection: _____

Page/Line: _____ / _____

Part of Speech: _____

Definition: _____
_____
_____

Sentence: _____
_____

Word:_____

Selection: _____

Page/Line: _____ / _____

Part of Speech: _____

Definition: _____
_____
_____

Sentence: _____
_____

# Personal Word List (continued)

Word:_____

Selection: _____

Page/Line: _____ / _____

Part of Speech: _____

Definition: _____

_____

_____

Sentence: _____

_____

Word:_____

Selection: _____

Page/Line: _____ / _____

Part of Speech: _____

Definition: _____

_____

_____

Sentence: _____

_____

Word:_____

Selection: _____

Page/Line: _____ / _____

Part of Speech: _____

Definition: _____

_____

_____

Sentence: _____

_____

Word:_____

Selection: _____

Page/Line: _____ / _____

Part of Speech: _____

Definition: _____

_____

_____

Sentence: _____

_____

Word:_____

Selection: _____

Page/Line: _____ / _____

Part of Speech: _____

Definition: _____

_____

_____

Sentence: _____

_____

Word:_____

Selection: _____

Page/Line: _____ / _____

Part of Speech: _____

Definition: _____

_____

_____

Sentence: _____

_____

Word:_____

Selection: _____

Page/Line: _____ / _____

Part of Speech: _____

Definition: _____

_____

_____

Sentence: _____

_____

Word:_____

Selection: _____

Page/Line: _____ / _____

Part of Speech: _____

Definition: _____

_____

_____

Sentence: _____

_____

Word:_____

Selection: _____

Page/Line: _____ / _____

Part of Speech: _____

Definition: _____

_____

_____

Sentence: _____

_____

Word:_____

Selection: _____

Page/Line: _____ / _____

Part of Speech: _____

Definition: _____

_____

_____

Sentence: _____

_____

Word:_____

Selection: _____

Page/Line: _____ / _____

Part of Speech: _____

Definition: _____

_____

_____

Sentence: _____

_____

Word:_____

Selection: _____

Page/Line: _____ / _____

Part of Speech: _____

Definition: _____

_____

_____

Sentence: _____

_____

Word:_____

Selection: _____

Page/Line: _____ / _____

Part of Speech: _____

Definition: _____

_____

_____

Sentence: _____

_____

Word:_____

Selection: _____

Page/Line: _____ / _____

Part of Speech: _____

Definition: _____

_____

_____

Sentence: _____

_____

Word:_____

Selection: _____

Page/Line: _____ / _____

Part of Speech: _____

Definition: _____

_____

_____

Sentence: _____

_____

Word:_____

Selection: _____

Page/Line: _____ / _____

Part of Speech: _____

Definition: _____

_____

_____

Sentence: _____

_____

# Personal Word List (continued)

Word: _____

Selection: _____

Page/Line: _____ / _____

Part of Speech: _____

Definition: _____

_____

Sentence: _____

_____

Word: _____

Selection: _____

Page/Line: _____ / _____

Part of Speech: _____

Definition: _____

_____

Sentence: _____

_____

Word: _____

Selection: _____

Page/Line: _____ / _____

Part of Speech: _____

Definition: _____

_____

Sentence: _____

_____

Word: _____

Selection: _____

Page/Line: _____ / _____

Part of Speech: _____

Definition: _____

_____

Sentence: _____

Word: _____

Selection: _____

Page/Line: _____ / _____

Part of Speech: _____

Definition: _____

_____

Sentence: _____

_____

Word: _____

Selection: _____

Page/Line: _____ / _____

Part of Speech: _____

Definition: _____

_____

Sentence: _____

_____

Word: _____

Selection: _____

Page/Line: _____ / _____

Part of Speech: _____

Definition: _____

_____

Sentence: _____

_____

Word: _____

Selection: _____

Page/Line: _____ / _____

Part of Speech: _____

Definition: _____

_____

Sentence: _____

Word:_____

Selection: _____

Page/Line: _____ / _____

Part of Speech: _____

Definition: _____

_____

_____

Sentence: _____

_____


Word:_____

Selection: _____

Page/Line: _____ / _____

Part of Speech: _____

Definition: _____

_____

_____

Sentence: _____

_____


Word:_____

Selection: _____

Page/Line: _____ / _____

Part of Speech: _____

Definition: _____

_____

_____

Sentence: _____

_____


Word:_____

Selection: _____

Page/Line: _____ / _____

Part of Speech: _____

Definition: _____

_____

_____

Sentence: _____

_____


Word:_____

Selection: _____

Page/Line: _____ / _____

Part of Speech: _____

Definition: _____

_____

_____

Sentence: _____

_____


Word:_____

Selection: _____

Page/Line: _____ / _____

Part of Speech: _____

Definition: _____

_____

_____

Sentence: _____

_____


Word:_____

Selection: _____

Page/Line: _____ / _____

Part of Speech: _____

Definition: _____

_____

_____

Sentence: _____

_____


Word:_____

Selection: _____

Page/Line: _____ / _____

Part of Speech: _____

Definition: _____

_____

_____

Sentence: _____

_____

# Personal Word List (continued)

Word: _____
Selection: _____
Page/Line: _____ / _____
Part of Speech: _____
Definition: _____
_____
_____
Sentence: _____
_____

Word: _____
Selection: _____
Page/Line: _____ / _____
Part of Speech: _____
Definition: _____
_____
_____
Sentence: _____
_____

Word: _____
Selection: _____
Page/Line: _____ / _____
Part of Speech: _____
Definition: _____
_____
_____
Sentence: _____
_____

Word: _____
Selection: _____
Page/Line: _____ / _____
Part of Speech: _____
Definition: _____
_____
_____
Sentence: _____

Word: _____
Selection: _____
Page/Line: _____ / _____
Part of Speech: _____
Definition: _____
_____
_____
Sentence: _____
_____

Word: _____
Selection: _____
Page/Line: _____ / _____
Part of Speech: _____
Definition: _____
_____
_____
Sentence: _____
_____

Word: _____
Selection: _____
Page/Line: _____ / _____
Part of Speech: _____
Definition: _____
_____
_____
Sentence: _____
_____

Word: _____
Selection: _____
Page/Line: _____ / _____
Part of Speech: _____
Definition: _____
_____
_____
Sentence: _____

**Word:** _____

**Selection:** _____

**Page/Line:** _____ / _____

**Part of Speech:** _____

**Definition:** _____

_____

_____

**Sentence:** _____

_____


**Word:** _____

**Selection:** _____

**Page/Line:** _____ / _____

**Part of Speech:** _____

**Definition:** _____

_____

_____

**Sentence:** _____

_____


**Word:** _____

**Selection:** _____

**Page/Line:** _____ / _____

**Part of Speech:** _____

**Definition:** _____

_____

_____

**Sentence:** _____

_____


**Word:** _____

**Selection:** _____

**Page/Line:** _____ / _____

**Part of Speech:** _____

**Definition:** _____

_____

_____

**Sentence:** _____

_____


**Word:** _____

**Selection:** _____

**Page/Line:** _____ / _____

**Part of Speech:** _____

**Definition:** _____

_____

_____

**Sentence:** _____

_____


**Word:** _____

**Selection:** _____

**Page/Line:** _____ / _____

**Part of Speech:** _____

**Definition:** _____

_____

_____

**Sentence:** _____

_____


**Word:** _____

**Selection:** _____

**Page/Line:** _____ / _____

**Part of Speech:** _____

**Definition:** _____

_____

_____

**Sentence:** _____

_____


**Word:** _____

**Selection:** _____

**Page/Line:** _____ / _____

**Part of Speech:** _____

**Definition:** _____

_____

_____

**Sentence:** _____

_____

# Personal Word List (continued)

Word: _____
Selection: _____
Page/Line: _____ / _____
Part of Speech: _____
Definition: _____
_____
_____
Sentence: _____
_____

Word: _____
Selection: _____
Page/Line: _____ / _____
Part of Speech: _____
Definition: _____
_____
_____
Sentence: _____
_____

Word: _____
Selection: _____
Page/Line: _____ / _____
Part of Speech: _____
Definition: _____
_____
_____
Sentence: _____
_____

Word: _____
Selection: _____
Page/Line: _____ / _____
Part of Speech: _____
Definition: _____
_____
_____
Sentence: _____
_____

Word: _____
Selection: _____
Page/Line: _____ / _____
Part of Speech: _____
Definition: _____
_____
_____
Sentence: _____
_____

Word: _____
Selection: _____
Page/Line: _____ / _____
Part of Speech: _____
Definition: _____
_____
_____
Sentence: _____
_____

Word: _____
Selection: _____
Page/Line: _____ / _____
Part of Speech: _____
Definition: _____
_____
_____
Sentence: _____
_____

Word: _____
Selection: _____
Page/Line: _____ / _____
Part of Speech: _____
Definition: _____
_____
_____
Sentence: _____
_____

**Word:** _____

**Selection:** _____

**Page/Line:** _____ / _____

**Part of Speech:** _____

**Definition:** _____

_____

_____

**Sentence:** _____

_____

**Word:** _____

**Selection:** _____

**Page/Line:** _____ / _____

**Part of Speech:** _____

**Definition:** _____

_____

_____

**Sentence:** _____

_____

**Word:** _____

**Selection:** _____

**Page/Line:** _____ / _____

**Part of Speech:** _____

**Definition:** _____

_____

_____

**Sentence:** _____

_____

**Word:** _____

**Selection:** _____

**Page/Line:** _____ / _____

**Part of Speech:** _____

**Definition:** _____

_____

_____

**Sentence:** _____

**Word:** _____

**Selection:** _____

**Page/Line:** _____ / _____

**Part of Speech:** _____

**Definition:** _____

_____

_____

**Sentence:** _____

_____

**Word:** _____

**Selection:** _____

**Page/Line:** _____ / _____

**Part of Speech:** _____

**Definition:** _____

_____

_____

**Sentence:** _____

_____

**Word:** _____

**Selection:** _____

**Page/Line:** _____ / _____

**Part of Speech:** _____

**Definition:** _____

_____

_____

**Sentence:** _____

_____

**Word:** _____

**Selection:** _____

**Page/Line:** _____ / _____

**Part of Speech:** _____

**Definition:** _____

_____

_____

**Sentence:** _____

_____

# Personal Word List (continued)

Word:_____

Selection: _____

Page/Line: _____ / _____

Part of Speech: _____

Definition: _____
_____
_____

Sentence: _____
_____

Word:_____

Selection: _____

Page/Line: _____ / _____

Part of Speech: _____

Definition: _____
_____
_____

Sentence: _____
_____

Word:_____

Selection: _____

Page/Line: _____ / _____

Part of Speech: _____

Definition: _____
_____
_____

Sentence: _____
_____

Word:_____

Selection: _____

Page/Line: _____ / _____

Part of Speech: _____

Definition: _____
_____
_____

Sentence: _____
_____

Word:_____

Selection: _____

Page/Line: _____ / _____

Part of Speech: _____

Definition: _____
_____
_____

Sentence: _____
_____

Word:_____

Selection: _____

Page/Line: _____ / _____

Part of Speech: _____

Definition: _____
_____
_____

Sentence: _____
_____

Word:_____

Selection: _____

Page/Line: _____ / _____

Part of Speech: _____

Definition: _____
_____
_____

Sentence: _____
_____

Word:_____

Selection: _____

Page/Line: _____ / _____

Part of Speech: _____

Definition: _____
_____
_____

Sentence: _____
_____

Word:_____

Selection: _____

Page/Line: _____ / _____

Part of Speech: _____

Definition: _____

_____

_____

Sentence: _____

_____


Word:_____

Selection: _____

Page/Line: _____ / _____

Part of Speech: _____

Definition: _____

_____

_____

Sentence: _____

_____


Word:_____

Selection: _____

Page/Line: _____ / _____

Part of Speech: _____

Definition: _____

_____

_____

Sentence: _____

_____


Word:_____

Selection: _____

Page/Line: _____ / _____

Part of Speech: _____

Definition: _____

_____

_____

Sentence: _____

_____


Word:_____

Selection: _____

Page/Line: _____ / _____

Part of Speech: _____

Definition: _____

_____

_____

Sentence: _____

_____


Word:_____

Selection: _____

Page/Line: _____ / _____

Part of Speech: _____

Definition: _____

_____

_____

Sentence: _____

_____


Word:_____

Selection: _____

Page/Line: _____ / _____

Part of Speech: _____

Definition: _____

_____

_____

Sentence: _____

_____


Word:_____

Selection: _____

Page/Line: _____ / _____

Part of Speech: _____

Definition: _____

_____

_____

Sentence: _____

_____

# Personal Word List (continued)

Word:_____

Selection: _____

Page/Line: _____ / _____

Part of Speech: _____

Definition: _____

_____

_____

Sentence: _____

_____

Word:_____

Selection: _____

Page/Line: _____ / _____

Part of Speech: _____

Definition: _____

_____

_____

Sentence: _____

_____

Word:_____

Selection: _____

Page/Line: _____ / _____

Part of Speech: _____

Definition: _____

_____

_____

Sentence: _____

_____

Word:_____

Selection: _____

Page/Line: _____ / _____

Part of Speech: _____

Definition: _____

_____

_____

Sentence: _____

Word:_____

Selection: _____

Page/Line: _____ / _____

Part of Speech: _____

Definition: _____

_____

_____

Sentence: _____

_____

Word:_____

Selection: _____

Page/Line: _____ / _____

Part of Speech: _____

Definition: _____

_____

_____

Sentence: _____

_____

Word:_____

Selection: _____

Page/Line: _____ / _____

Part of Speech: _____

Definition: _____

_____

_____

Sentence: _____

_____

Word:_____

Selection: _____

Page/Line: _____ / _____

Part of Speech: _____

Definition: _____

_____

_____

Sentence: _____

Word:_____

Selection: _____

Page/Line: _____ / _____

Part of Speech: _____

Definition: _____

_____

_____

Sentence: _____

_____

Word:_____

Selection: _____

Page/Line: _____ / _____

Part of Speech: _____

Definition: _____

_____

_____

Sentence: _____

_____

Word:_____

Selection: _____

Page/Line: _____ / _____

Part of Speech: _____

Definition: _____

_____

_____

Sentence: _____

_____

Word:_____

Selection: _____

Page/Line: _____ / _____

Part of Speech: _____

Definition: _____

_____

_____

Sentence: _____

_____

Word:_____

Selection: _____

Page/Line: _____ / _____

Part of Speech: _____

Definition: _____

_____

_____

Sentence: _____

_____

Word:_____

Selection: _____

Page/Line: _____ / _____

Part of Speech: _____

Definition: _____

_____

_____

Sentence: _____

_____

Word:_____

Selection: _____

Page/Line: _____ / _____

Part of Speech: _____

Definition: _____

_____

_____

Sentence: _____

_____

Word:_____

Selection: _____

Page/Line: _____ / _____

Part of Speech: _____

Definition: _____

_____

_____

Sentence: _____

_____

# Personal Word List (continued)

Word:_____
Selection: _____
Page/Line: _____ / _____
Part of Speech: _____
Definition: _____
_____
_____

Sentence: _____
_____

Word:_____
Selection: _____
Page/Line: _____ / _____
Part of Speech: _____
Definition: _____
_____
_____

Sentence: _____
_____

Word:_____
Selection: _____
Page/Line: _____ / _____
Part of Speech: _____
Definition: _____
_____
_____

Sentence: _____
_____

Word:_____
Selection: _____
Page/Line: _____ / _____
Part of Speech: _____
Definition: _____
_____
_____

Sentence: _____
_____

Word:_____
Selection: _____
Page/Line: _____ / _____
Part of Speech: _____
Definition: _____
_____
_____

Sentence: _____
_____

Word:_____
Selection: _____
Page/Line: _____ / _____
Part of Speech: _____
Definition: _____
_____
_____

Sentence: _____
_____

Word:_____
Selection: _____
Page/Line: _____ / _____
Part of Speech: _____
Definition: _____
_____
_____

Sentence: _____
_____

Word:_____
Selection: _____
Page/Line: _____ / _____
Part of Speech: _____
Definition: _____
_____
_____

Sentence: _____
_____

Word:_____

Selection: _____

Page/Line: _____ / _____

Part of Speech: _____

Definition: _____

_____

_____

Sentence: _____

_____


Word:_____

Selection: _____

Page/Line: _____ / _____

Part of Speech: _____

Definition: _____

_____

_____

Sentence: _____

_____


Word:_____

Selection: _____

Page/Line: _____ / _____

Part of Speech: _____

Definition: _____

_____

_____

Sentence: _____

_____


Word:_____

Selection: _____

Page/Line: _____ / _____

Part of Speech: _____

Definition: _____

_____

_____

Sentence: _____


Word:_____

Selection: _____

Page/Line: _____ / _____

Part of Speech: _____

Definition: _____

_____

_____

Sentence: _____

_____


Word:_____

Selection: _____

Page/Line: _____ / _____

Part of Speech: _____

Definition: _____

_____

_____

Sentence: _____

_____


Word:_____

Selection: _____

Page/Line: _____ / _____

Part of Speech: _____

Definition: _____

_____

_____

Sentence: _____

_____


Word:_____

Selection: _____

Page/Line: _____ / _____

Part of Speech: _____

Definition: _____

_____

_____

Sentence: _____

_____

## Acknowledgments *(Continued from page ii)*

**Don Congdon Associates:** "A Sound of Thunder" by Ray Bradbury. First published in *Collier's,* 28 June 1952. Copyright © 1952 by Crowell-Collier Publishing, renewed 1980 by Ray Bradbury. Reprinted by permission of Don Congdon Associates, Inc.

**Delacorte Press/Seymour Lawrence:** "Harrison Bergeron," from *Welcome to the Monkey House* by Kurt Vonnegut, Jr. Copyright © 1961 by Kurt Vonnegut, Jr. Used by permission of Delacorte Press/Seymour Lawrence, a division of Bantam Doubleday Dell Publishing Group, Inc.

**Farrar, Straus & Giroux:** Excerpt from *The Acts of King Arthur and His Noble Knights* by John Steinbeck. Copyright © 1976 by Elaine Steinbeck. Reprinted by permission of Farrar, Straus & Giroux, Inc.

**Harcourt Brace & Company:** "Everyday Use," from *In Love & Trouble: Stories of Black Women* by Alice Walker. Copyright © 1973 by Alice Walker. / *Antigone,* from *Sophocles: The Oedipus Cycle, An English Version* by Dudley Fitts and Robert Fitzgerald. Copyright 1939 by Harcourt Brace & Company and renewed © 1967 by Dudley Fitts and Robert Fitzgerald. CAUTION: All rights, including professional, amateur, motion picture, recitation, lecturing, performance, public reading, radio broadcasting, and television are strictly reserved. Inquiries on all rights should be addressed to Harcourt Brace & Company, Permissions Department, Orlando, FL 32887-6777. / Reprinted by permission of Harcourt Brace & Company.

**Hill and Wang:** Excerpt from *Night* by Elie Wiesel, translated by Stella Rodway. Copyright © 1960 by MacGibbon & Kee. Copyright renewed © 1988 by The Collins Publishing Group. Reprinted by permission of Hill and Wang, a division of Farrar, Straus & Giroux, Inc.

**Henry Holt & Company:** "Birches" by Robert Frost, from *The Poetry of Robert Frost,* edited by Edward Connery Lathem. Copyright © 1944 by Robert Frost. Copyright 1916, © 1969 by Henry Holt & Company. Reprinted by permission of Henry Holt and Company, Inc.

**Liveright Publishing Corporation:** "Those Winter Sundays" by Robert Hayden, from *Collected Poems of Robert Hayden,* edited by Frederick Glaysher. Copyright © 1966 by Robert Hayden. / "look at this)," from *Complete Poems, 1904–1962* by E. E. Cummings, edited by George J. Firmage. Copyright 1926, 1954, © 1991 by the Trustees for the E. E. Cummings Trust. Copyright © 1985 by George J. Firmage. / Reprinted by permission of Liveright Publishing Corporation.

**Random House:** Excerpt from *I Know Why the Caged Bird Sings* by Maya Angelou. Copyright © 1969 and renewed 1997 by Maya Angelou. Reprinted by permission of Random House, Inc.

**Random House UK:** "Puedo Escribir Los Versos . . ."/"Tonight I Can Write . . . ," from *Selected Poems* by Pablo Neruda, translated by W. S. Merwin. Originally published by Jonathan Cape Ltd. Reprinted by permission of Random House UK Ltd.

**Tilbury House:** "Once More to the Lake," from *One Man's Meat* by E. B. White. Text copyright © 1941 by E. B. White. Reprinted by permission of Tilbury House, Publishers, Gardiner, Maine.

**O. W. Toad Ltd.:** "Through the One-Way Mirror" by Margaret Atwood, *The Nation,* 22 March 1986. Reprinted by permission of O. W. Toad Ltd. on behalf of the author.

**University of New Mexico Press:** "The Border: A Glare of Truth," from *Nepantla: Essays from the Land in the Middle* by Pat Mora. Copyright © 1993 by University of New Mexico Press. Reprinted by permission of the University of New Mexico Press.

**Ralph M. Vicinanza, Ltd.:** "Dial Versus Digital," from *The Dangers of Intelligence and Other Scientific Essays* by Isaac Asimov. Copyright © 1986 by Isaac Asimov. Published by permission of the Estate of Isaac Asimov, c/o Ralph M. Vicinanza, Ltd.

**Viking Penguin:** "Piano" by D. H. Lawrence, from *The Complete Poems of D. H. Lawrence,* edited by V. de Sola Pinto and F. W. Roberts. Copyright © 1964, 1971 by Angelo Ravagli and C. M. Weekley, Executors of the Estate of Frieda Lawrence Ravagli. Used by permission of Viking Penguin, a division of Penguin Putnam Inc.

## Cover

Illustration copyright © 1998 Michael Steirnagle.